AFFLICTION

AFFLICTION

Edith Schaeffer

Fleming H. Revell Company
Old Tappan, New Jersey

Scripture references not otherwise identified are based on the King James Version of the Bible.

Scripture references identified NIV are from the NEW INTERNATIONAL VERSION. Copyright © 1973 by New York International Bible Society. Used by permission.

Excerpt from "Great Is Thy Faithfulness" by Thomas Chisholm is © by Hope Publishing Company, Carol Stream, Illinois 60187. Used by permission.

The poem "Afraid? Of What?" is from *The Triumph of John and Betty Stam* by Geraldine Howard Taylor. Reprinted by permission of the publisher, Overseas Missionary Fellowship.

Library of Congress Cataloging in Publication Data

Schaeffer, Edith.
  Affliction.

  1. Suffering. 2. Consolation. I. Title.
BV4909.S33   242'.4   78-7993
ISBN 0-8007-0926-8

This book is dedicated to the people who have so willingly shared some of the deep and most private and precious portions of their lives, in order to make available help that will be relevant to others in another geographic location or in another moment of history. Sharing in each other's sufferings is a very delicate thing—and that which brings "togetherness" into focus.

Contents

Preface

Everyone has struggled with the question *Why?* in the midst of his own or someone else's misery or difficulty. Affliction is a universal problem. Rich, poor, educated, uneducated, cultured, barbaric, city dwellers, farmers, bank presidents, street sweepers, musicians, coal miners, old, young, Eastern, Western—all people of every tribe, nation, and language group have experienced and are experiencing and will experience some form of suffering, troubles, disappointments, or tragedy, and will continue to do so in their daily lives. Whether you know a person very well—or have just struck up a conversation on a plane or bus, or in a doctor's waiting room—some portion of an exchange of communication is very often taken up with discussing each other's "woes" or the troubles of the world at large.

Who has the answers to the often-heard questions: "How could a good God exist in the light of all the misery in the world?" or "If God created the world, then where did all the ugliness come from?"

This book is an attempt to look at the biblical explanations for the existence of affliction, as well as an attempt to deal with the great variety of purposes to be found in the blending of faith, long-suffering, love, and patience with persecution and affliction, as we go through examples from the real lives of modern and ancient people.

There is an inner excitement in the midst of stringency and hardship as a gymnast is preparing for the Olympics. Similarly, affliction—with the goal ahead, understood, and vividly in sight—is a different thing from the blind, dogged suffering of prisoners in a chain gang, being whipped, with no hope of anything beyond the present ugliness. The understanding comfort unfolded in these pages is a setting forth of the balance of some measure of the completeness of what God has given in His Word. Is a child of God meant to know pure joy, because of a life of ease and the removal of all that might hinder a painless existence? When people try to live on the basis of erroneous ideas they have picked up about what happens (or is supposed to happen) concerning affliction when one becomes a Christian, it is apt to be like riding with a flat tire, trying to carry all the weight in one bag, reading by the light of one candle, or "seeing through dirty glasses."

This book is not meant to be just theoretical. Its purpose is to give practical help for men and women, young and old, bedridden or active, in the daily problems of living in the midst of unexpected or expected, sudden or long awaited troubles and afflictions. An affliction can be physical, psychological, material, emotional, intellectual, or cultural. An affliction can be having too much or too little, having too many demands upon one or no feeling of being needed. An affliction can be a sudden shock—or a daily, constant dragging on with no change. An affliction can be planned by some human being who wants to do us harm, or can apparently come with no explanation at all. An affliction can be that which turns our whole lives upside down and changes the course of our lives so completely that we find ourselves in another location, another house, even another country; or it can be seemingly so small and insignificant that we might feel that no one else would define it as "trouble" at all.

This book is not only to give some measure of fresh understanding, but some measure of comfort and some help in the practical area of how to go on in the next step of life. It is my prayer that the result will not only be something positive in the life of the reader, but that there will also be many results in the lives of people the reader will be helping with greater incentive and understanding and love. We need to constantly remember that we cannot wait until we have attained a place of sufficiency before we turn from our own needs to help another.

AFFLICTION

1
Why? Why? Why?

Philip had often had his glass of apple juice and a muffin, along with his sister and the other children, as Claire-Lise, his mother, and the other ladies had tea or coffee before my Thursday-morning Bible class. Bright blue eyes full of response and sparkle, a shock of thick blond hair, and pink cheeks spoke of a robust, healthy little three-year-old with a zest for life. His five-year-old sister had been playing by his bedside during his seemingly minor illness—croup—when he choked, and within seconds his breathing stopped. "Mother, Mother. Philip has *gone* . . . ." Gwen understood instinctively that her brother was no longer in the room with her. His body was there, but Philip was out of her reach. How could it be? Impossible! Why?

The Lausanne Conservatoire of Music conjures up the picture of musicians of all ages—coming, going, practicing on a diversity of instruments, having lessons, concentrating on corrections. There is such a variety of intensity, interest, pleasure, and earnestness in this atmosphere of music and culture. Anne-Françoise, the dear nine-year-old daughter of José Flores and his wife, Anne-Lise, was in the hall of the conservatoire one April afternoon in 1972, waiting downstairs for her mother to finish talking to the teacher. Suddenly a young madman (who had become violent after leaving a psychiatric hospital to spend a day at home) surged down the street, slashing people with a kitchen carving knife. Six adults were injured in the frightening seven minutes, and his last deed before being stopped was to push into the hall of the music building and devastatingly murder the little girl. A flash, a crash of a murderous knife, and she was suddenly absent from her body, separated from her family. How could it be? Impossible? Why?

Twenty-year-old David Koop, on a springtime climb in the mountains of New Hampshire, was hit by a huge falling rock, slipped from the steep mountainside, and in brief moments was no longer there—as his body hung suspended from his companion seven hundred feet above the valley floor. A mere statistic for the summer? No. As each of the others, this boy of twenty was a beloved child of his parents, in this case, Dr. and Mrs. C. Everett Koop. This great surgeon has saved the lives of countless children, operating on babies in great need, giving them years of life in place of the imminent deaths they were facing. David was also a son of the Living God, in active service for the Lord, and seemed to have so very much to do in the needed area of making truth known to his contemporaries who were searching in the dark. The Bible he left behind—when he so suddenly was absent from his body, his family, and the others who needed him—was marked in a way so that his family knew which was the last verse he had read before going on that climb. His Bible was open to verse 24 of the Book of Jude: "Now unto him that is able to keep you from falling, and to present you faultless before the presence of his glory with exceeding joy." God was able to keep him from physically falling. How could he fall? Impossible! Why?

I have just finished writing to the mother and father of a nineteen-year-old boy who is dying of a cancer which was arrested for a time and has now returned. Why didn't the disease stay in remission? Why?

Why? The letter before that was to a young woman who had jumped from a window, trying to kill herself. Why did she only break her back and ankles? Why didn't she die? Why?

John and Betty Stam had finished years of preparation in college and Bible school. God had brought them together to complement each other in a work which seemed to lie before them for years in China, where they had learned the language and were prepared for an unusual service for the Lord. Their first baby was in their arms as they were captured by a band of teenage Communists in the mid-thirties. How could it happen that Betty—who wrote this poem:

Afraid? Of What?
To feel the spirit's glad release?
To pass from pain to perfect peace,
The strife and strain of life to cease?
Afraid—of that?

Afraid? Of What?
Afraid to see the Saviour's face,

To hear His welcome, and to trace
The glory gleam from wounds of grace
    Afraid—of that?

Afraid? Of What?
A flash, a crash, a pierced heart;
Darkness, light, O Heaven's art!
A wound of His a counterpart!
    Afraid—of that?

Afraid? Of What?
To do by death what life could not—
Baptize with blood a stony plot,
Till souls shall blossom from the spot?
    Afraid—of that?

with such deep understanding—could be experiencing the reality of being led through the streets in her underwear, along with her young husband, hands tied behind their backs? Their baby was left behind in her "snuggle bunny" on the bed in the room where they had been imprisoned for the night. How could it be that this well-prepared missionary couple, with so many praying for them, could have their heads placed on a chopping block with a sharp knife at the back of their necks? So suddenly they were absent from their bodies, their heads severed and rolling in the dust! How could it be that the old Chinese Christian so willingly offered to take the baby's place and placed his own head where the baby's head would otherwise have been? A life for a life—and two others snapped off. Martyrdom. How could it be possible? Why?

Baroness Christa Von Mirbach hummed a little tune as she prepared to go out for the day. She would be meeting her husband for lunch, and there were errands to do before that moment. It wasn't a foolishly careless kind of humming, as Christa well knew the dangers of life in an embassy at this moment of history, when violence and hatred spring forth with little warning all over the world. So she prayed for her husband's safety with a carefulness that was natural to her. Her husband, Baron Von Mirbach was the military attaché in the German Embassy in Stockholm, Sweden. As a Christian he had asked God to show him and his wife whether there was another place of service for them; and there had been a long period of waiting to see what the Lord's direction would be. In the embassy that morning, a political takeover was in progress, as Baader-Meinhof terrorists forced their way in—and at gunpoint herded secretaries and other workers upstairs as hostages.

The terrorists' demand was: "Let our imprisoned members out of prison, and we will let these people go free. Otherwise we will shoot one person every fifteen minutes." Why was the baron to be chosen as the first to die? Perhaps because of his military and noble bearing, his heritage and quiet air of authority coupled with strong convictions which would have been sufficiently observed and blended together to pose a threat. Whatever the reason, seven bullets were soon to plow into his body, and he was thrown down the stairs.

At this very moment, Baroness Von Mirbach was perhaps the only person not watching television in Stockholm; she was waiting at the appointed place for her husband to meet her for lunch. He had said, "If I am not there within twenty minutes, it will be because I have another appointment." So, when he did not come, she was not alarmed and went about her other errands. How God gave Christa and her twelve-year-old twins, a boy and a girl, His strength in their weakness to receive this news later that day—to keep on loving and trusting the Lord—is a story that has been repeated throughout the history of God's own people. Such grace is given for a crisis moment, and it does not mean that anyone—these three, Jeremiah or Paul, Mrs. Rookmaaker, or the parents of the murdered child in Lausanne—is free from low periods of depression and recurrent agony from time to time. We must not expect each other to float above the reality of loneliness and wondering, "What if. . . ?"

Yet again one can cry, "Why? What a waste!" What senseless violence does terrorist war continue to use! A shocking time of peace—that is no peace—both terrorizes and removes any sense of security from a supposedly protected place. It is a frustrating situation when pacifism uses violence to propagate its projected state of "warlessness." What's wrong with the world? Why do people kill others so easily? Where does it all come from?

We had been called to Philadelphia because Grandmother Schaeffer had had a stroke, and the doctor did not expect her to live. Careful hours, days, and weeks of personal nursing and special attention to nutrition changed that expectation—and Grandmother was well enough seven weeks later to come to Switzerland, to be cared for at Chalet les Mélèzes for seven years. When she was eighty-nine, she fell in the chalet and broke her upper leg and hip, and a long operation in the little Aigle hospital was successful. She even came back to using a walker for a time. When the next stroke came, it cut off communication, and gradually, as we cared for her in a hospital bed set up near us in the chalet's third-floor bedroom, she needed twenty-four-hour, round-the-clock attention. Months of feeding her with a spoon—flavors and textures she liked and could swallow—were followed by weeks of her not being able to swallow at all. Yet breathing and heartbeat were strong. Then the breathing became gasps, but the heart kept on just as strongly. No communication, fighting for breath, and a struggle to stay in the body were a vivid demonstration of something necessary for people to know about. The separation of spirit from body is *not* always quick, and "natural death" cannot be viewed as natural. How can that be? Why?

My own father lived to be a hundred and one. His hundredth birthday was a time when the portion of the family who could be present—children, grandchildren, and great-grandchildren—were astonished at his puns and witty remarks, which showed a "keeping-up with the times" in world affairs, sports, and other news events, as well as with the family affairs. At one hundred, his mind was encased in a body which was a hindrance. One knew this as he looked disgustedly at his finger joints getting stiff, and his need of a cane to walk, and his falling off to sleep when he wanted to keep on talking.

His "I always wanted to live to be a hundred, but now I think I have made a mistake!" seemed an amusing remark for him to make, but it was actually profound. An understanding of "living death" had come. Increasing hindrances in the smooth functioning of creative acts directed by a creative brain became such a contrast to former life that the reality of death as a gradual event became painfully sharp to both mind and emotions. Fear of diminishing life was beginning to replace fear of death. Is the word *natural* to be used? How can it be? Impossible! What is *natural* death?

When is death "convenient"? When is death "timely" for the individual, for the family, for friends, for the one closest to the dying person? When is death not a shock? When is death "normal"? What is death?

History moves in only one direction. Effect follows cause. When one of us regrets what we have done during a period of time, there is no way of going back and reliving that period, whether it is a

matter of minutes or day or weeks or years. The words "If only I had
. . ." or "If they only had not . . ." can be nothing but wishful
imagination or fanciful dreaming. The entrance of death into the
world was the result of an act based on a decision. There was a
cause-and-effect happening in the history of the human race,
through which death was and will be experienced by every individual until that marvelous moment arrives in future history when
the promised Second Coming of Christ becomes reality and then
passes into history, bringing about permanent and fantastic results.

The first death of a human being took place as an "effect." The
"cause" was not a chance happening. It was a deliberate decision
on the part of a significant human being who had been carefully
warned that in the familiar garden there was one tree, the fruit of
which must not be touched or eaten—because if it were, death
would be the result. Death was not what God made man and
woman to experience. Body and spirit were made to be one, not to
be torn apart. The body is a marvelous creation more intricate than
any other individual part of the created universe. The body is precious, not only to each total personality of which each body is a part,
but to God who created the body to fulfill the capacities of the whole
person—to taste, smell, feel, hear, see, think, love, communicate,
choose, and be creative. The body is involved along with the spirit
in the oneness of the whole person to fulfill the possibility of expressing in art and music, science and literature, agriculture and forestry,
food preparation and architecture, and so many other areas something of the tremendous scope which Man—male or female—has
been given to enjoy. Eyes can express love or scorn, response or
revulsion. The vocal cords can communicate a fantastic range of
things which seem to be intangible. The tongue and lips are important but cannot replace hands or feet. Yet, as we stand beside a
body which has been separated from the spirit in death, although
perhaps the physical parts are intact, one knows the person has
gone, as even the little five-year-old knew so immediately. The
body is there, but the person is not there to use it.

Although Cain had never before seen a dead body, as he looked
at Abel whom he had just killed and saw the first dead body, he
knew that Abel had gone. He could say nothing more to Abel, and
Abel could no longer reply. Cain saw the first effect of his mother's
and father's choice to eat of the fruit which God had clearly told
them would bring death as a result. He saw the result of his own sin

of murder, but he also saw the first death which was the first fulfillment of the effect of human death, resulting from his parents' choice
to *not believe* and *not act* upon the verbalized, audible words of
God to them. Cain saw the vivid reality of separation of spirit from
body. Adam and Eve had experienced both the awful separation
from God Himself and exile from the dwelling where they had
walked and talked with God in the cool of the evening. Adam and
Eve had experienced the transition from living in a perfect world to
living in a spoiled world. Adam and Eve had known what it was to
be "normal human beings" living in the "normal world," but they
were the only ones who were able to compare by personal experience what "normal" and "abnormal" were like! Their choice to act
upon the lie of Satan, as if it were truth, brought about the result that
God had predicted. The world became abnormal. We have lived
in—and do live in—an *abnormal* world. Things have been spoiled,
vandalized by Satan, by a whole period of cause-and-effect history,
spanning however many thousands of years there have been from
Adam and Eve's time until now. Death has been thought of as
"normal" only because it has taken place throughout all history.
When we come to Genesis 5, the flow of accounts, no matter
whether it is of Adam's 930 years or Methuselah's 969 years, ends
always with "and he died." That is the end of every life story except
Enoch's and Elijah's.

Satan, when he lied so blatantly to Eve and wheedled her with
"You won't die . . ." (flatly contradicting God), was attacking—
with intent to destroy the perfect Creation of God. A battle was
going on which had started sometime before (we have no idea how
long), when Satan was called Lucifer, the highest of the angels. He
was the most beautiful of them all (we know from Isaiah 14) and,
along with all the other created angels, he had choice. The period of
testing was not over when Satan became desirous of being equal
with God and started a revolt, a coup against God—gathering other
angels as terrorists in heaven to attempt a "surprise attack" in rebellion against his Creator. The battle was real and there were cause-
and-effect results. Lucifer and the angels who banded with him in
the attack were put out of heaven, no longer angels, but became
Satan and the demons.

The desire to be equal with God did not seem to stop in any
degree, and the fury of the battle continues. Although Lucifer had
said to Eve, "You won't die," he knew not only that she would, but

that her sons and her sons' sons and her daughters and her daughters' daughters would die. Satan's false promises, based on destructive motives, end in destruction. Eve was to see her own son's dead body as her first sight of what "Ye shall surely die" meant in practical experience. She was to find out what being separated from a person through the separation of spirit and body was like. She probably cried out, "Abel has gone!" and felt the utterly desperate feeling of the finality of the results of choice. Separation of her spirit from her body was yet ahead of her, but the painful reality was now her experience. She knew what the spoiled Creation meant in the area of human relationships. No longer had she a perfect relationship with Adam. And it is also clear that she would have been aware that Cain and Abel had never had a perfect relationship—and that this violence was very likely a result of smaller violences and disputes in their relationship as brothers.

It is a fact that Abel was the first martyr for worshiping God in the God-given manner of bringing the Lamb, pointing forward to all which is told us throughout the rest of Scripture. Abel was killed—for worshiping correctly—by Cain, who was furious at the nonacceptance of his false manner of worship based on his own works (the bringing of the fruits of his own labors as a means of entrance into God's presence). Whether or not Eve understood this is a matter of speculation, but she must have thought of her own disregard and disbelief of God's command and warning to her. She must have realized that here before her in the inert body of her son was the death which was now to be a part of human experience, but was not normal. God had created the body and spirit to be one. Spirit and body are woven together, and death is an ugly ripping apart of what is meant to be together. Satan won a victory in his temptation of Adam and Eve and their falling into his trap. Satan's victory was the introduction of the "abnormal" reality of death, and of all the smaller "deaths" which take place in the destruction of parts of the body by germs and viruses, accidents, or deliberate violence.

We are told in 1 Corinthians 15:26: "The last enemy that shall be destroyed is death." And in Isaiah 25:8, the promise comes strongly: "He will swallow up death in victory; and the Lord God will wipe away tears from off all faces; and the rebuke of his people shall he take away from off all the earth: for the Lord God hath spoken it." The first and important thing for each of us to understand in our minds and throughout the warp and woof of our very beings is that death is an enemy, and it is something which God hates, too. Death is a part of the battle between Satan and God—and the final victory will be God's. Death will be swallowed up in the victory—the victory of God over Satan and of God's solution to Satan's destructive attack.

Jesus stood at the tomb of Lazarus and wept. He was angry at death in that moment, but He wept also, as Martha and Mary wept, with sorrow at the separation. Weeping is *not* something which Christians are not supposed to do or to feel. Hot tears sliding down our cheeks, salty in the corner of our lips, is not a wrong thing to feel as part of our experience of life. It is only when the final enemy is destroyed and the last victory is won that all tears are to be wiped away. Until then we are meant to weep with those who weep, as well as to rejoice with those who rejoice. We are to rejoice over the joys and special happinesses of other people, rather than be jealous or covetous of their successes and possessions.

However, it is just as wrong to be hard and cold about people's deep sorrows, especially the separation from a loved one by death. Smiling and saying, "It is all so lovely and peaceful . . ." is a type of hardness and coldness to the enemy death. Christians are blending into the truth of what exists in this fallen, abnormal world when they experience the emptiness of a room which a person has just left as Philip left his room by death. Christians are behaving as God describes in His Word as "natural" when they weep as a result of death. It is God who will wipe away all tears—not another human being. There is something totally different ahead—different from what anyone has ever experienced—when the final results of the victory which Christ purchased on the cross will be part of the then "present history." There is a difference between the "before and after," a difference between the belief in prophecy and the moment of its fulfillment. There is a difference between the waiting and the moment of fulfillment of what is the object of our expectation.

"And it shall be said in that day, Lo, this is our God; we have waited for him, and he will save us: this is the Lord; we have waited for him, we will be glad and rejoice in his salvation" (Isaiah 25:9). Moment after moment, hour after hour, day after day, week after week, and year after year, the waiting period continues. History is going by, significant events are taking place, time is being used in certain ways which negate that same time being used in other ways, whether by nations or individuals. This waiting is not like waiting in the dentist's office for him to send his nurse to tell you it is your turn. Waiting for the realization of God's promises is to be a conscious waiting, such as the music which ballet dancers have as a part of their movements. This "waiting" is not just background music, but a vital part of what is going on—in a very woven-together way, as the melody and the movement to that music are intertwined. We are meant to be affected in the steps we take, *by* the waiting, the conscious waiting for the fulfillment of the final promises of the Living God. People were meant to act differently, to be influenced in their actions, to make choices *differently,* based on the background of their conscious waiting and expectancy of the Messiah's First Coming. People in the family of God *now* are also meant to act differently, to be influenced in actions and choices on the background of waiting with expectancy and reality for the Second Coming of Christ—expecting to have this day arrive in history, in the geography of the physical world, when the great final victory will affect us as a *present experience,* rather than a hope.

True hope changes sorrow, but does not obliterate it. Death is not to be taken as a "normal, beautiful release" but as an enemy which separates body from spirit and human beings from each other. It spoils the beautiful Creation of God. It is so basically an enemy that God says that He will pay a great price, a ransom, to deliver us from death's power: "I will ransom them from the power of the grave: I will redeem them from death: O death, I will be thy plagues; O grave, I will be thy destruction . . ." (Hosea 13:14). A solution begins to unfold in the verses of Genesis where God speaks to Eve and Adam of His promise to send someone who will bruise the head of Satan. It is not that there is no solution, but that—since the solution to death involves the great price of death for the Second Person of the Trinity—death's existence is basically an ugly enemy. We, as believers, do not need to pretend that it is "lovely" to feel the harshness of suddenly being out of communication, of having our hand suddenly without a responsive squeeze from a loved one, or another's eyes no longer speaking to our eyes. We can be angry at Satan, who tempted Eve to fall into his trap and therefore succeeded in spoiling so much for each of us. We can be angry at sin and Satan without being angry at God. We can weep, and God can comfort us in our weeping, but we do not need to try to pretend that it is all an ennobling experience. Satan would try to fool people, as they decide to swallow poison or jump from a bridge, that death is better than life. It is also his lie.

Forasmuch then as the children are partakers of flesh and blood, he also himself likewise took part of the same; that through death he might destroy him that had the power of death, that is, the devil; And deliver them who through fear of death were all their lifetime subject to bondage. For verily he took not on him the nature of angels; but he took on him the seed of Abraham.

Hebrews 2:14–16

It is conclusive that death is a terrible enemy, since it could not be put out of the way, except by the coming of the Second Person of the Trinity as truly man—so that He could "taste death" in our place. John 1:14 says: "And the Word was made flesh, and dwelt among us . . . ." Philippians 2:7, 8 tells of Jesus' taking the form of a servant and being made in the likeness of men, so that He could humble Himself and be obedient even to the death of the cross. Death is something which cost Jesus Christ Himself the awful separation from the rest of the Trinity. When He took our sins upon Himself, so that He could give us His righteousness in exchange, He experienced death in order to abolish its sting. "But is now made manifest by the appearing of our Saviour Jesus Christ, who hath abolished death, and hath brought life and immortality to light through the gospel" (2 Timothy 1:10).

The devil is the one who brought about death, and is referred to as the one who has the "power of death," as well as the one who can hold people in the bondage of a great diversity of fears. But God's power is made clear not only in His having a solution to Satan's bondage, but in providing the solution at such a great cost to the Trinity. To ignore the reality of death as an enemy is also to diminish the wonder of the available victory over sin and the permanent results of death. One day, death and Satan will be permanently cast out, along with those who have rejected God and followed Satan. This is referred to in the end of the Book of Revelation as "the second death." This is the death which will have nothing to do with those who have been born into the family of God through the wonder of what Christ did in His substitutionary death. The second death will have no power on those who have had a *second birth.* The victory will be complete and everlasting.

When the whispered cry comes at death: "He's gone," the reality to the child of the Living God is that the departure is not only a real going *from* but also a going *to.* The spirit has left the body to go somewhere else. Second Corinthians 5:8 tells us so clearly that the absence is also an entrance into the presence of the Lord. When a child, or an old father, leaves his body, he is "somewhere," and that "somewhere" is marvelous; it is in the presence of the Lord. "We are confident [of good courage], I say, and willing rather to be absent from the body, and to be present [at home] with the Lord" (2 Corinthians 5:8). In Philippians, Paul tells of his own longing to be out of his body of suffering and into the next step: "For I am in a strait betwixt two, having a desire to depart, and be with Christ; which is far better: Nevertheless to abide in the flesh is more needful for you [your sake] (1:23, 24). Notice that it is a departure from the body, as contrasted to a staying in the body. But the departure takes the person into the presence of the Lord, if he or she is a child of God. This is our comfort—with which we are to comfort each other when we feel the sorrow of separation. But the comfort carries with it a reality of waiting, not only waiting to "go" also—to depart for the same place someday—but a waiting for the return of Jesus which will finish the whole abnormality of the body's being someplace other than with the spirit.

What we are waiting for is a complete restoration, a togetherness of the body and spirit, a resurrection which has been promised and of which Christ's Resurrection was the example, the "first fruits." What we are waiting for is gloriously described to us:

> For the Lord himself shall descend from heaven with a shout, with the voice of an archangel, and with the trump [trumpet] of God: and the dead in Christ shall rise first: Then we which are alive and remain shall be caught up together with them in the clouds, to meet the Lord in the air: and so shall we ever be with the Lord. Wherefore comfort one another with these words.
>
> 1 Thessalonians 4:16–18

The comfort is in the *truth* of the Bible, the trustworthiness of the accuracy of not only history but the prophecy and promises yet to be fulfilled. In the midst of our weeping at the grave, we have the certain hope that the grave will not forever be a prison to that body. It will burst open, and if we are in our bodies at that moment, we will never know death ourselves, but only the transformation of our bodies into ones changed as Christ's resurrected body was changed. Think of 1 Corinthians 15:51–55. While you are reading and thinking of this passage, perhaps you'd like to put on the third part of the Messiah by Handel and listen to the bass solo: "Behold, I tell you a mystery . . ." and the next one: "The trumpet shall sound . . . ." It may help the reality to become more vivid and the comfort to be more enveloping.

Behold, I shew you a mystery; We shall not all sleep, but we shall all be changed, In a moment, in the twinkling of an eye, at the last trump: for the trumpet shall sound, and the dead shall be raised incorruptible, and we shall be changed. For this corruptible must put on incorruption, and this mortal must put on immortality. So when this corruptible shall have put on incorruption, and this mortal shall have put on immortality, then shall be brought to pass the saying that is written, Death is swallowed up in victory. O death, where is thy sting? O grave [death] where is thy victory?

"Believest thou this?" We are asked this question along with Martha as Jesus speaks to her before He raises Lazarus from the dead. Jesus has just told Martha that Lazarus shall rise again, and then He goes on to say very definitely: "I am the resurrection, and the life: he that believeth in me, though he were dead, yet shall he live: And whosoever liveth and believeth in me shall never die. Believest thou this?" (John 11:25, 26). He is asking Martha and all of us whether we really believe that He is able to give a sure and certain expectation to each of us, that we may know in our thinking and in our emotions, in our "bones," so to speak, that His death and Resurrection will give us future changed bodies over which death can have no power. The victory which Christ died to give us has a future aspect that we know will one day take place and then be history. That victory is the one that will destroy death. Bodies, those same bodies, are to be raised from the dead in exact likeness to Christ's body after His Resurrection. He, who made us in His image, came in a body like ours—which died for us and rose for us. That resurrected form shows us what we are to be like through all eternity, in the image of the resurrected Christ.

To say that we sorrow not as those who have no hope is to say all this. Yet we are not to cancel out the reality of living on this side of the resurrection of our bodies. We are now in the "before." It is important to comfort each other, but not with false platitudes. To say, "It doesn't hurt . . ." further frustrates a child who is having a dentist drill near a nerve. To say, "You shouldn't cry . . ." to a Christian, whose husband has just been killed by a terrorist gang, puts a burden upon that person which adds an unbearable weight. God gave us the possibility of tears to help express sorrow at the reality of battle wounds in the midst of life. The comfort is found in recognizing that this is an abnormal universe since the Fall, and that *there is coming a time of restoration.* "Hang on—until He comes. Hang on!"—but *how?* There will be more unfolding of this concept as we continue our study of affliction and persecution, trouble and sorrow.

To return to the series of examples of death and its tearing separation—we need to say firmly that the question *Why?* is without an answer for our finite minds, except in the concept of the total picture of what history has been since the Fall. We cannot ask God to give us a detailed answer to the *Why?* We likewise learn that He gave no such explanation to Job. A portion of God's answer to Job consisted of pointing out to him that if he could not understand how Creation took place—where the fantastic design of snowflakes originated—he could not understand the intricacies of the total battle between God and Satan, in which he had become the battlefield, so to speak. We are meant to find in the Word of God a balance in our understanding of affliction, but we will never end up (at least not in this life) with a precise, mathematical explanation of why the child Philip choked at that moment, why the demented fellow attacked Anne-Françoise with his knife, why David's fingers clung to that specific loose rock on the mountain climb, why the virus or cancer hit that individual at that particular time, or why death is fast for one and long drawn out for another. But, as children having a Father who does understand, we can find an amazing amount of help in His message to us, His unfolding of truth to us in His Word. Therefore, we need not be confronted with accusing people who are like Job's "comforters," demanding that we not only act in a certain mechanical fashion, but that we repeat certain words, parrotlike, when we are torn apart with shock or suffering.

We do not live in a Moslem, fatalistic universe. The infinite, personal Living God has done what our minds cannot grasp. If we could understand all that God understands, we would no longer be finite and human. To demand this is rebellion against remaining in our own place as His creatures, akin to Lucifer's demanding equality with God. We are enticed by the same kind of temptation to be equal with God, in being able to say, "Oh, yes, I understand how God created angels and human beings with choice, without putting chance behind His own sovereignty." But we are to bow to the *truth* which God has given us, with the amount of explanation He has given us. We need to be willing to let God be God, and to stay in our own place as human beings. It is not necessary for us to say something like: "God led the terrorists into that building and chose my husband to be the first one shot, riddled with seven bullets, and thrown down the stairs." God does not ask us to place any such explanation upon a situation in which Satan's emissaries are striking out against the work of the Lord or His servants. The death of martyrs must not be placed anywhere but where it belongs: in the battle by which Satan is trying to stamp out the spread of true truth. This applies in China in 1935 or in Chad in 1975, in Uganda or Cambodia or anyplace else in the world. There is a battle going on that is real. History is taking place. This is not a puppet show, but a cause-and-effect history. Yet God is sovereign and all-powerful—and the victory is His.

What does this mean practically, as we sit talking or weeping with the mother of the little boy, the wife of the assassinated diplomat, the parents of the lad who fell from the mountain, the loved ones of the dear little girl who was brutally murdered, or the family of the dying young man? It means that we must acknowledge that we can't understand everything, but that we do have much to help and comfort us in the Bible. As we go to the Word of God, we ask for a measure of balance (a *measure,* since none of us can ever have perfect balance—any more than we can be perfect in any other area of life, until Jesus returns). We must look at the whole problem of affliction and suffering which includes *death*—death of a precious body, death of cells which govern parts of the body, death of personal energy, death of a relationship, death of a state or country. We must talk not in trite phrases, but try to search sufficiently in the blend of facts and examples which the Lord has given to help us. It is important never to feel as if we were only talking about someone else's problem of sorrow or affliction without facing the reality ourselves. We must let the Word of God speak not only *through* us but *to* us. That attitude is of basic importance in seeking answers. We are seeking answers which we need moment by moment and in constantly changing and shifting kinds of situations. One can think of affliction as made up of many aspects. Thus, concentrating on only one aspect is apt to be out of balance—in the same way that listening to only one instrument in the midst of a symphony, which needs the blend of many instruments, would make the music seem out of balance.

God's Word picks up first one note, then another, but we are meant to consider it over a lifetime, with a growing understanding that never comes to a point of completion. No one individual at any one point of history can say, "This is it, the final word of explanation of all affliction." However, we can help each other to trust God and to wake up one more day, willing to go on to do whatever is His plan for us in the midst of what Satan is trying to use to devastate us. We need to help each other to "overcome." We are pointed to the need of "overcoming" in the Book of Revelation where the Spirit is speaking to the churches. We are told: "And they overcame him by the blood of the Lamb, and by the word of their testimony; and they loved not their lives unto the death" (Revelation 12:11). Satan is the one spoken of here as "him," and we will examine this passage later. But, as a beginning point, we need to say that the purpose in studying affliction is to help point each other to the need of *overcoming by the blood of the Lamb*. This is accomplished by a conscious recognition of a portion of what is going on—and of our need for calling out for help from the One who has promised us His strength in our weakness.

Affliction must be recognized as something we all need to deal with. There is no place to go for a vacation from the abnormality of the universe, from the effects of the Fall upon every area of life, and from the conflict of the ages. Persecution and affliction are a *normal* part of the Christian life. We need not be surprised or ashamed when our work, our family, our church, or our individual person is hit by some form of affliction. Satan does not fight against himself. So when those in the midst of false religions seem to be having an easier time than Christians, it should not be surprising. The criterion of living a growing, fruitful Christian life in a close walk with the Lord is neither to be "abased" nor to "abound." Both situations present temptations, but both can be places of victory.

We cannot compare our own pattern to someone else's to discover whether or not we are in the Lord's will. God has individual and very diverse plans for the lives of His children, and Satan's attempts to turn us aside are also diverse. Poverty can be an attack, but so can affluence. Hardship can be an attack, but so can ease. And when we face the death of a loved one, the attempt to twist us into bitterness can be an attack, but so can be a false covering up of sorrow.

Tremendous victory is only possible in the face of a tremendous battle. As we consider affliction, our desire should be to help each other find victory in hidden places and "overcome him by the blood of the Lamb" in very practical moment-by-moment happenings in our day-to-day lives. Between our own birth and death, that is our second birth and our death or the Second Coming of Christ, we are in danger of losing what we are meant to be experiencing, as well as knowing in our heads, because we are not recognizing something of what is taking place. We are also in danger of not caring enough about showing God our love and trust of Him in the all-too-short period of time that we are given to take part in the "battle of the heavenlies." We are too easily turned toward thinking of what we can "get" in the way of happiness by being a Christian. We fail to remember the seriousness of total history and of our own particular moment of history. ". . . and they loved not their lives unto death." This speaks of a conviction and willingness to be used by God at tremendous cost . . . .

Give me strength, Lord, for living this hard moment to Your glory. May I honestly be willing to pay the price that is my part of the whole, because Christ died to make it possible to go on after this particular devastation.

Why? We don't know why each individual accident and death has taken place, but we know that though there is a fierce battle with heavy casualties, the victory is sure and absolute! Death *will* be swallowed up in victory.

David Koop's death did not cancel out the promise of that verse he read on the morning of his leaving his body. "Now unto him that is able to keep you from falling, and to present you faultless before the presence of his glory with exceeding joy." Yes, there was a literal fulfillment of that verse on *that* day, and David was presented faultless before the throne of the Living God, on the basis of the blood of Christ which has been shed to make this a reality.

Whether a tiny baby, a toddler, a nine-year-old, a teenager, a person in the prime of life, or a very old person, the entrance into "the presence of his glory with exceeding joy" is a reality. Jesus—who wept over Jerusalem and at the death of Lazarus—and God the Father—who tells us so vividly that He takes no pleasure in the death of even the wicked (Ezekiel 33:11)—tell us of exceeding joy here. Whose joy? It is *His* joy to be able to present us as "faultless" on the basis of His own shed blood as the Second Person of the Trinity. What a victory! At this point we should sing with Martin Luther, "The body they may kill: God's truth abideth still; His Kingdom is forever."

The enemy—death—has an end. Satan's long history of attempts to separate every living being from God (and to separate every person from his or her own body in some sort of agonizing tearing apart) is not going to succeed. Death does not kill the spirit, nor does it spoil the truth. These remain unscratched. And one day death itself will be finished, and we will be in our new bodies to see and experience that day.

2
The Message From Stephen and Paul

Do people swarm around you when you have gone through a tragedy of some sort and nearly destroy you with the kind of "comfort" which Job's comforters threw at him? "There must be something wrong with your prayer life." Or "God must be pointing to a terrible sin in your life. You'd better search your heart." Or "I am sure that if you had more faith, your child would be healed." Or "I know it will all turn out right. If you let Jesus lead you, you won't have difficulties like this anymore." Or "What you need is a real 'experience.' Then you won't have any more problems; every day will be filled with perfect joy." Every sentence of such "comfort" comes out as a criticism and a comparison.

We have had individuals come to us who have been crushed and discouraged to an extreme because of being mistakenly taught that the criterion of being in the Lord's will, and in contact with Him through prayer, is to have everything go well—with no shocks and disappointments. The Word of God is very fair in giving us realistic examples of God's servants throughout history. The Bible not only tells us that affliction is an expected part of the lives of God's people, but helps us to relate to others who have faced the same things we face, or much worse.

When Kato, a brilliant young black theologian and defender of the truth of the Word of God in Nigeria, was drowned last summer, one felt a rush of dismay and wanted to cry out, "What a waste!" He was not murdered, as far as we know, but his death—as a husband and father, as well as a church leader—was a death which Satan would have been glad to see take place. Where do we look in the Word of God for a similar happening? We live in a world where we badly need strong Christians who can speak with conviction and certainty. When irreplaceable leaders are suddenly taken out of the

31

land of the living, like Kato, Professor Rookmaaker, or Dr. Little, is it necessary to flay ourselves with an agonized "Oh, we didn't pray enough or with enough faith—or it would not have happened"?

Find the story of Stephen in chapters 6 and 7 of the Book of Acts. This was in the midst of the time of the early church, and those who were preaching and teaching were all too few. The twelve apostles were able to do real miracles and to teach and preach with great power, but accounts of how they were beaten do not indicate that the lashes of the whips did not cut into their flesh and draw blood, or that they were not in pain or limping. As they rejoiced in "suffering shame for His name," it was a real suffering they were experiencing, not a series of occasions of having pain miraculously removed. They had seen Jesus suffer. They knew it was for them and for the ones to whom they were preaching—and they felt a kinship with the cost involved in preparing the Good News or the Gospel which they were now able to give freely. It did not seem strange to them that affliction had visible as well as feelable results in their physical bodies.

We are told that there was a murmuring or complaining among the believers because the numbers were growing so rapidly that the Greek-speaking believers felt that their widows and people needing special care were not receiving the same attention as the Hebrew-speaking needy. So the twelve apostles called a "multitude" of believers to meet with them and asked them to search out seven men who could be appointed to do these things well. The apostles already had more than they could do in preaching and praying for the people. Among those selected was Stephen, described as a man "full of faith and of the Holy Ghost." This would certainly mean that he was an outstanding Christian among those young men in the early church, one very close to the Lord, full of the Holy Spirit, and exhibiting in his prayer life and other ways that he was a man of faith. The apostles prayed for these seven men, among them Stephen, and laid hands on them to set them aside for this special task.

Because Stephen was a man who spoke and preached with such power, a group of men began to discuss and argue and dispute with him, trying to put him down. "And they were not able to resist the wisdom and the spirit by which he spake" (Acts 6:10). In other words, they didn't get anywhere in trying to push his arguments aside. The next thing they tried was lying about him, finally getting him brought before a council to try him for blaspheming. As all of the eyes of the council were on him, waiting for him to defend himself, they "saw his face as it had been the face of an angel" (v. 15). In other words, it was the very opposite of a dejected, frightened look. Stephen was showing forth an inner strength in the face of terrible opposition and false accusations, which was visible in the glow and certainty in his eyes and face. It was the reality of the fulfillment of God's strength in his weakness.

Now Stephen went on to give a marvelous bird's-eye view of history, telling of Abraham, Joseph, and then Moses, and the things that happened in Egypt before the Israelites were led out of the wilderness. Stephen then related the stories of the golden calf, the tabernacle, and Solomon's temple, and of how through the centuries the Israelites had persecuted and afflicted the prophets and servants of God. We are told that the men who heard him were "cut to the heart," not with a result of believing, but with anger. When Stephen told them that, as he looked up into heaven, he could see the glory of God—and Jesus standing on the right hand of God—their reaction was to grab him and drag him to the outside of the city, where they stoned him.

Now, was Stephen's faith not sufficient to have those stones turn into pebbles which would have no effect? Were the prayers of all the multitudes of believers inefficient for some reason? From the account, we know the stones hit Stephen and that they hit vital parts of his body. He felt pain and had the same injuries to his body as anyone else would have, as stones gradually bruised him and finally snuffed out heartbeat and breathing. Stephen died. Stephen's spirit was separated from his body and went to be with the Lord, but Stephen's body lay dead in the street, inert and bleeding. Was this a total victory for Satan, for the unbelieving enemies who had organized the attack? As Stephen called out for help, did God not answer him? What really happened?

First, let me quickly say that, of course, we don't know the total combinations in any event in history. However, we have been given a glimpse here of a fantastic victory for the glory of God. "How can you say that?" someone may ask. "What a defeat for a servant of God!"—"Why did he not stand up again and preach?"—"What a waste of a brilliant, young, earnest missionary in the early church!"—"What was wrong with the faith of Stephen, or of the other Christians around him?" What was wrong?

There are several very basic and exciting things to notice before going any further. In the midst of the stoning, Stephen *did* have several victories which were more important and more startling than would have been a healing from the bruises and injuries or even being raised from the dead. Stephen very clearly loved God and trusted Him in the midst of this terrible affliction, and thus was not turned into a bitter complainer at the time of his stoning. Do you know what Stephen did as the stones crashed against his body, pelting him at every angle? *Stephen prayed.* And his prayer was not for himself or for the Christians he was leaving behind, but for the people who were involved in stoning him. Stephen prayed with a loud voice, "Lord, lay not this sin to their charge." Now we know, and Stephen of course knew, that there is only one way that the sin would be not laid to their charge, and that would be if, one by one, these men (or even some of them) completely changed and—instead of resisting the Gospel and persecuting the people who believed it—would themselves become believers. This was the miracle Stephen was praying for, a miracle more "impossible" than the miracle of being healed or being raised from the dead as Lazarus had been raised. Remember Jesus saying—when He was being taunted by the Pharisees, as He stood before the man lame from birth—"Which is it harder to say: 'Thy sins be forgiven thee,' or 'Take up thy bed and walk'?" Jesus taught that the miracle of which He spoke to Nicodemus, when he told him: "Ye must be born again," was the greatest miracle of all.

Now here was Stephen with his last breath, praying for the men who were stoning him, praying for their salvation and forgiveness, which could only take place by a titanic change of heart. This very last "act" of Stephen was a prayer which was answered in such a way as to affect the whole of Christianity from that time on.

Standing in that crowd, among those who were glad to see Stephen die, was a man who was guarding the coats of those who had removed them, the better to swing their arms and heave the stones. The guardian of the coats was Saul, who not only "was consenting unto his death" (as we are told in Acts 8:1), but who went right on persecuting the church people. There was no distinction between the importance of men and women as objects of Saul's persecution. He entered homes, "haling men and women," and dragged them off to prison. Others were scattered abroad and went everywhere to tell people the truth of Christianity. So the truth spread like a fire scattered through dry fields! Stephen's prayer, which I believe was one of the most important acts of his life, was to be answered, not immediately but after a short period of time. Saul continued persecuting the Christians with a fervor described in Acts 9:1, 2: "And Saul, yet breathing out threatenings and slaughter against the disciples of the Lord, went unto the high priest, And desired of him letters to Damascus to the synagogues, that if he found any of this way [being believers in Jesus as Saviour and Messiah], whether they were men or women, he might bring them bound unto Jerusalem."

It was at this point that the miracle of answered prayer took place. God answered Stephen—and as Saul journeyed on his trip of destruction and slaughter to do his next piece of terrorist violence, he suddenly was stopped in his tracks.

And as he journeyed, he came near Damascus: and suddenly there shined round about him a light from heaven: And he fell to the earth, and heard a voice saying unto him, Saul, Saul, why persecutest thou me? And he said, Who art thou, Lord? And the Lord said, I am Jesus whom thou persecutest . . . And he trembling and astonished said, Lord, what wilt thou have me to do? . . . .

Acts 9:3–6

This is a marvelous story of conversion that thrills us to the depths. Saul, who was one of the most learned and brilliant opponents of the early Christians among leading Jews, became convinced that Jesus was God indeed: the Messiah and his Saviour. After three days of blindness and refraining from food and drink, this same Saul—later Paul—went to be among the disciples to be prepared for what was ahead of him: a long work of preaching and writing, but also a time of being persecuted and experiencing affliction.

An earthshaking miracle had taken place:

But all that heard him were amazed [this was because he preached in the synagogues that Christ was the Son of God], and said; Is not this he that destroyed them which called on this name in Jerusalem, and came hither for that intent, that he might bring them bound unto the chief priests? But Saul increased the more in strength, and confounded the Jews which dwelt at Damascus, proving that this is very Christ.

Acts 9:21, 22

A double event happened soon after that. The Jews plotted to kill
Saul—but until Barnabas vouched for Saul's sincerity, the believers
in Jerusalem were afraid to let him come into their midst, because
they couldn't believe that he had been genuinely changed. What a
victory of answered prayer! Saul converted to Paul: great preacher
and writer of the Epistles. A greater victory than Stephen's own
healing would have been! What is the balanced truth in God's plan
for the early church and in His Word to us in this moment of
history—and the part Stephen had in it by achieving victory when
Satan was trying to make him cry out against God? It is a balance
we cannot see, but we are meant to realize that Stephen's victory
did make a difference. That day, there was victory in the heavenly
battle which made a difference to the glory of God. The victory
which sprang forth from that prayer in the midst of the *unchanging
circumstance* (there was an increase rather than decrease of stones
raining upon him) brought forth something which changed history.
The work which Stephen did in his death had greater effect upon
history than simply a longer life. The victory in the midst of an
unchanging circumstance so often is a victory of tremendous faith,
as we will later discover in the Book of Hebrews. Stephen knew this
victory. Satan had lost.

We are told something that makes this battle clearer to us. The
words are directly from Jesus, as He spoke to Saul on the Damascus
road: "I am Jesus whom thou persecutest." Jesus is saying that
Saul's persecution of Christians is actually a direct persecution of
Him, Jesus. It is the counterpart of "Inasmuch as ye have done it
unto the least of these my brethren, ye have done it unto me."

It is possible to persecute and afflict the Lord through the persecution and affliction of His people. The battle is fought in this way, as
Satan tries to fight against God and to destroy the love of His people
for Him. Satan is not only trying to make Christians bitter and
complaining against God; he is trying to hurt God directly. We have
a piece of information from Isaiah that God means us to have, to
help our understanding. It fits in with "Why persecutest thou
me? . . . . I am Jesus whom thou persecutest." Isaiah speaks of
the loving-kindness of the Lord:

For he said, Surely they are my people, children that will not
lie: so he was their Saviour. In all their affliction he was afflicted,
and the angel of his presence saved them: in his love and in his

pity he redeemed them; and he bare them, and carried them all the days of old.

Isaiah 63:8, 9

This is not simply a statement of the fact that the Lord feels our sorrows and afflictions in loving concern, but it tells us also that the thrusts of Satan which come against us hit Him in some very real way. What is going on is beyond our complete comprehension, but we are meant to have a real measure of understanding to give us courage to go on. Our personal afflictions involve the Living God; the only way in which Satan can persecute or afflict God is through attacking the people of God. The only way we can have personal victory in the midst of these flying arrows raining down on us is to call upon the Lord for help. It is His strength, supplied to us in our weakness, which makes victory after victory possible.

There *is* something to say when people ask, "Why?" or feel, in the midst of their struggles with an affliction, as if no one else had ever had this particular combination of things before. There is no pat answer or suitable trite phrase—but there is the reality of history to consider, as well as the absolute fairness of the Word of God in the examples He lets us look into. We have the reassurance, time after time, that our particular combination of characteristics is really unique, because we are individual personalities, not puppets or parts of a machine. It helps us to hear about other Christians in pain, difficulty, persecution, and affliction, because we then can recognize that in our own struggles we are not alone in history. We are surrounded by those who are a veritable "cloud of witnesses" who can encourage us. They can help, not because they had perfect lives with shining successes and joys following one another like a bubbling stream through flower-filled fields—but because they, too, have discovered something about the diversity of meaning to be found in affliction and the bittersweet possibilities of victory.

A red-haired girl with a lovely freckled face and burning blue eyes sat on the low stool, hugging her knees as we nibbled raisins and nuts and had tea together. She had poured out her story to me, a story that in its very content screamed out, "How could it have happened? Why?" without needing to use those words at all. It was the story of a sudden change of personality and way of life on the part of her Christian husband who had been told he had only a short time to live. It was like hearing of a nightmare to listen to her tell about his change from a seemingly growing Christian, who had a warm and close relationship with his wife, to a bitter blasphemer who used his last period of life to have a wild fling, walking away completely from his marriage in every sense of that word. As the story of sorrow and agony tumbled out, the flow of words told of many hours of prayer and the willingness to forgive and try to understand. There was a thread throughout the story which hinted at a "last straw" kind of situation.

That "last straw" for this girl was the reaction of a stream of well-meaning but misinformed Christian friends who were "Job's comforters" indeed! "Why don't you pray?" is a question that can be an insult to someone who is already spending sleepless hours in prayer. "If you only had enough faith, everything would change!" is a judgment which only God can make. No one can ever know what reality of faith there is present within the person whose prayer does not seem to be answered. "There must be something wrong with your life. This is a judgment." This is another cruel sentence on the part of a human being who is in no position to make such bald statements. "If you had the Holy Spirit . . ." is another judgmental statement, akin to saying that someone has not been born again.

The criterion of being born again is a personal relationship between an individual and the Lord. When a person has truly bowed before God, acknowledging his or her sin and need of forgiveness and cleansing—and when that person has accepted that Jesus Christ, Second Person of the Trinity, came to die in his place—it is God Himself who accepts the individual into His family. It is someone in heaven who writes that name in the Lamb's Book of Life, the roll call which counts. It is God who sends the Third Person of the Trinity, the Holy Spirit, to dwell in that person as a sign, or "an earnest" of our salvation. "Now he which stablisheth us with you in Christ, and hath anointed us, is God; Who hath also sealed us, and given the earnest of the Spirit in our hearts" (2 Corinthians 1:21, 22).

The word *earnest* is used again in Ephesians 1:13, 14:

> In whom [that is, in Christ] ye also so trusted, after that ye heard the word of truth, the gospel of your salvation: in whom also after that ye believed, ye were sealed with that holy Spirit of promise, which is the earnest of our inheritance until the redemption of the purchased [God's own] possession, unto the praise of his glory.

An *earnest* was a kind of seal which made the purchase of a field a fixed agreement. A bit of earth was scooped up and given to the person who had arranged to buy a piece of land. That earth was called the *earnest,* a proof or certainty that the transaction was completed. The Holy Spirit is given by God the Father to each one who has believed upon His Son and accepted Him as Saviour and Lord. The Holy Spirit is God's *earnest* to us. Whether we are actually showing forth the fruits of the Spirit, for other people to notice, is another thing. It is possible to hinder the work of the Spirit in us or through us. But the criterion of His presence in us is not an unbroken flow of answered requests. That is what some people try to suggest will be the results which Christians are meant to expect— but it can be a measuring rod of discouragement.

As the troubled young woman and I spent the afternoon together, we watched from the window as the sun went down behind the Alps and the room became dark. Much of what I will write in this book was unfolded to her then. After prayer together, her reaction was to give me a quick hug and to sigh with relief: *"Please* put this all in a book. I want to go over it all again and again."

A letter arrived from Germany, relating something of the same onslaught of discouragement from Christian friends. The circumstances of affliction in this case were quite different, but the obvious lack of understanding on the part of "comforters" was the same:

My husband became a Christian at a university in England and we married and emigrated to Canada. There we "progressed" socially. My husband is now a professor of chemistry and we have a ten-year-old daughter and twin seven-year-old sons. We are in Germany for a sabbatical year . . . . God forced us also to progress spiritually. We discovered soon after birth that our sons were brain damaged. John is grossly retarded—a human vegetable, the doctors say. David is severely retarded, with a potential mental ability of a four- or five-year-old child . . . . Needless to say, these children have confronted us, our families, and friends with many deep questions concerning the nature of God, evil, predestination, God's supreme omnipotence, His will, the powers and timing for healing, and so on. We often find ourselves counseling well-meaning friends who feel that *now* is God's time to heal our sons and are deeply shocked when obvious healing does not take place. We find ourselves recoiling when we are told that brain damage is the punishment for our sins, or symbols of our lack of faith. I can say now with Job that earlier I had heard of God, but now I know Him personally as the only Rock on whom one can depend in such crises. My husband finds problems at work with colleagues who cannot see that the truths of science and the truths of God are not incompatible, but rather that they gloriously illustrate each other. He experiences much criticism and rejection for Christ's sake.

Here in the midst of the ongoing results of a birth accident (so similar to any other accident as far as cause-and-effect history goes) and the daily affliction of a certain amount of isolation from the academic world, the way is made more difficult by Christian friends who have no understanding of the basic battle going on between God and Satan in the whole of history—and no understanding of the diversity of victories there can be. The most flaming victories so apparent in this letter go unnoticed! The common attitude is that the only victory that demonstrates a closeness to God is the healing of physically spoiled or ill bodies, or the smoothing out of all circumstances so as to give ease and peace in day-by-day living. Such false expectations have plunged many people into despair and forced others to ignore what is really taking place.

After his transformation, dear Paul, who had experienced being on "the other side" (fighting against the truth, persecuting Christians and Christ Himself) went through a titanic variety of persecutions and afflictions. For any one of us in the midst of difficulties who needs reassurance, the life of Paul will be a help to us. When questions are thrown against us which add to our suffering, when what we need is comfort, it is time to read First and Second Corinthians again. As we read, we need to use our imaginations to place ourselves in Paul's circumstances. We must not read as if we were simply observing something afar off and irrelevant to our moment of personal history. Rather, we must "feel with Paul" and recognize that the same Holy Spirit who indwelt Paul also indwells us; the same Heavenly Father who heard his prayer and cries for help also hears us; and the same Lord Jesus Christ who was his Lord and Saviour is also ours. Paul's constant intercessor was Jesus, and He is also *our* intercessor, praying for us at the right hand of the Father.

In the fourth chapter of First Corinthians, Paul pleads for faithful stewards among all of us who are "stewards of the mysteries of God." This is to be a stewardship of that which we know and which opens up to us as we continually read the Word of God throughout our lifetime. Paul goes on to ask that none of the Corinthian church people be "puffed up for one against another. For who maketh thee to differ from another? and what hast thou that thou didst not receive? now if thou didst receive it, why dost thou glory, as if thou hadst not received it?" (vv. 6, 7). We are being asked to remember that if we have health, energy, food, shelter, and an abundance of things in the midst of peace to enjoy them, then the need is to recognize that they have been given to us. We have received these gifts for the purpose of being "good stewards" in the context of whatever we have surrounding us at the moment. However, Paul goes on to point out that he and the other apostles during that period of history are experiencing great hardship:

> For I think that God hath set forth us the apostles last, as it were appointed to death [as men doomed unto death]: for we are made a spectacle unto the world, and to angels, and to men. We are fools for Christ's sake, but ye are wise in Christ; we are weak, but ye are strong; ye are honourable, but we are despised. Even unto this present hour we both hunger, and thirst, and are naked, and are buffeted, and have no certain dwellingplace; And labour, working with our own hands: being reviled, we bless; being persecuted, we suffer [endure] it. Being defamed, we intreat: we are made as the filth of the world, and are the offscouring of all things unto this day. I write not these things to shame you, but as my beloved sons I warn you.
> 1 Corinthians 4:9–14

Paul is saying to us, as well as to them, "Do you think you have more faith, live closer to the Lord, know more of the power of the Holy Spirit, and have greater answers to prayer because you live a life that has more comfort, less illness or hardship, less persecution, less slashing criticism, less attacks of Satan in one form or another? If the apostles are fools for Christ's sake, do you think you are more spiritual because you are counted as wise? If the apostles are weak and acknowledge it, do you feel comfortable in counting yourself as strong? If the apostles are despised on every side, do you feel pride in being honored in so many ways? As you are well filled with food and drink and have wonderful homes to dwell in, can you look down upon the apostles' reality of closeness to the Lord while they are hungry and thirsty and without a fixed place to live in?''

As people were reviling and persecuting Paul and the other apostles, could the Corinthians be complacent in their freedom from these things? Can we? What is the criterion for faithful stewardship and a growing Christian life? Is it a stream of deliverances from hardships, troubles, afflictions, and persecutions? Or is it more diverse and deeper than that? Listen to Paul's own experiences of victory in the midst of *unchanging* circumstances. Paul is one who can warn *us*—as well as the Corinthians. Let us *be* warned in our practical attitudes and daily actions, as well as in the basic understanding of our heads and hearts.

In Second Corinthians, Paul warns the Corinthians about the subtlety of false apostles:

". . . deceitful *workers,* transforming themselves into the apostles of Christ. And no marvel; for Satan himself is transformed into an angel of light. Therefore it is no great thing if his ministers also be transformed as the ministers of righteousness; whose end shall be according to their works.

2 Corinthians 11:13–15

Although it is early in the history of the church, already there are false ministers, clearly tied in with Satan's attacks against God in the ongoing battle. These deceitful teachers are called Satan's ministers, who can be transformed into seemingly righteous teachers—in the same way that Satan can come as an "angel of light." Here we are shown that the affliction and persecution which has been thrown at Christians from the early days of the church can take an even more dangerous form because of the subtlety of the attack. It can come from within, dressed up as a wolf in sheep's clothing, "transformed" outwardly into something which is not inwardly true. So, while we are to be aware of the direct attacks against Christian truth from outside—and all the various forms of persecution this entails—we are also warned that Satan can be "inside," giving warped versions of truth, insidiously changing seemingly small things, and thus undermining the full Word of God. The bending of truth into heresy comes at times through a seemingly innocent and gentle breeze.

Paul follows this warning with an account of his own ministry up to that point:

Are they Hebrews? so am I. Are they Israelites? so am I. Are they the seed of Abraham? so am I. Are they ministers of

Christ? (I speak as a fool [as one beside himself]) I am more; in labours more abundant, in stripes above measure, in prisons more frequent, in deaths oft. Of the Jews five times received I forty stripes save one. Thrice was I beaten with rods, once was I stoned, thrice I suffered shipwreck, a night and a day I have been in the deep; In journeyings often, in perils of waters, in perils of robbers, in perils by mine own countrymen, in perils by the heathen [Gentiles], in perils in the city, in perils in the wilderness, in perils in the sea, in perils among false brethren; In weariness and painfulness, in watchings often, in hunger and thirst, in fastings often, in cold and nakedness. Beside those things that are without, that which cometh upon me daily, the care of [anxiety for] all the churches. Who is weak, and I am not weak? who is offended [made to stumble] and I burn not? If I must needs glory, I will glory of the things which concern mine infirmities. The God and Father of our Lord Jesus Christ, which is blessed for evermore, knoweth that I lie not.

2 Corinthians 11:22–31

As proof of his real ministry for the Lord, as one who is being mightily used by God to spread His truth in that part of that century, Paul points not to miracles he has been instrumental in bringing forth through God's hand as an apostle among the Twelve, nor to powerful sermons he has preached, nor to great answers to prayer he has had (and, of course, he has had many), but he reminds them of the stream of persecution and afflictions which he has suffered. Paul is saying with great emphasis that he is in the midst of a battle and that he has experienced scars that were very vivid and real. His body has been a battlefield, and this is what he wants us to consider as proof of the reality of the power which he has been given. It is not his own natural strength which has allowed him to carry on his work in the midst of the "impossibilities" of tribulations and afflictions.

Let us rethink what Paul had been through up to that point. He had worked extremely hard, through long sleepless hours. He had had "stripes," that is, marks of the whip's lashes had cut into the flesh of his back and buttocks as thoroughly as the flesh of anyone whipped had ever been cut anywhere in history. He felt the pain of bleeding, raw flesh as it healed into tight scar tissue; and he knew about fever and sweating, with no clean hospital sheets and gentle nursing with sips of cool drinks through straws to ease his suffering.

He was in prison "more frequent," according to his description— more frequently than the men and women to whom he is talking. He knew what it was like to be in cold filthy prisons which had not been touched by any "reform movements." Lice and germs were known to him, and the agony of his bed of stones cut into already bruised and torn flesh. He also knew "death's oft." How? He knew what it was to be left for dead, to be so beaten and injured that people thought he could not recover and left him for dead. He tells of five times being beaten forty lashes, save one—in other words, thirty-nine lashes—with all the strength that the man administering the lashes could give by the cruelty standards of that day. That can only be matched by today's cruelty of man to man in all the places where torture is now being administered. Paul knew by his own experience what people are suffering today as the results of the Fall and the abnormal world. The cruelty of person to person continues in all its excruciating forms. Paul was *not* lifted out of these situations supernaturally; but he lived through them to continue to serve the Lord in the land of the living.

Three times he was beaten with rods, evidently worse beatings than the whiplashes and probably thoroughly injuring his very bones. He was once stoned. Go back to Acts 14:19 and read the account: "And there came thither certain Jews from Antioch and Inconium, who persuaded the people, and, *having stoned Paul,* drew him out of the city, supposing he had been dead." Paul experienced what it felt like to be stoned, as did Stephen. I wonder if he thought of Stephen as the stones hit him in one place after another and injured various parts of his body. Here is the man Stephen prayed for, now so thoroughly the Lord's man that he is willing to be faithful to the Lord right up to actually bleeding for what he declares to be truth. When he was knocked unconscious and left for someone to bury, dragged to the outside of the city, he would have been truly "out" for at least a period of time, and he would not have been conscious of the fact that this was not going to be the end of his life. He had been as thoroughly willing for martyrdom in those minutes of stoning as Stephen had been. Our prayer at this point can only be: "God help us to be faithful in the area in which we are meant to show forth a practical aspect of faithfulness. May we not give in to whatever subtle or more blatant kinds of persecution and affliction we face now, or will face in the future. Help us to know some measure of the honest reality of showing You our love and trust, even as Paul did so thoroughly."

Three times Paul went through a shipwreck. He was not saved from the ordeals of fear and stormy waves, of fingers wrinkling up from hours in the water, nor of the feelings of imminent drowning. He went through it all—not as a dream, but as a part of the day-by-day history of his life as a missionary, minister, apostle, and writer. Return to Acts 27 to refresh our minds as to some of the details of one of those shipwrecks. As we read this chapter we see that Paul was certain of being saved this time, but, nevertheless, fourteen days of fasting could not have been comfortable! The confrontation with the sailors was real, as they endangered the safety of everyone by starting to "run away" secretly in a small boat. When the ship ran on the rocks and broke up, the water and waves were not part of a theatrical production; the danger was real. Paul was certain that he and the others would be saved that time, but the effect of floating around on a bobbing piece of broken wood from the ship was not the same as being in a comfortably appointed rescue lifeboat. Therefore, as he speaks in Corinthians of three shipwrecks, and of once being in the water for thirty-six hours, it is with memory of what it felt like to his eyes, arms, legs, and lungs, as well as to his emotions.

Paul had all the intricacies of personality and psychological makeup that any one of us has. Although he was given special inspiration to write what God wanted us to know (as God's Word to us in our moment of time), he did not live his life in a "bubble" protected from the agonies of the battle and the struggle, the ups and downs of feeling in the midst of such hardships. God means us to be encouraged by Paul's experience and also to understand that our mélange of difficulties—our mix of troubles, our flow of blows from left and right, our sorrows and disappointments, our dark surprises and crushing telegrams—is not some strange thing that has nothing to do with a Christian life. God is warning us to not "go under the waves," to not "give up the fight." We are in a war, but we are also to understand that the "good race" gives an explanation of what we are to understand as a natural clarification of the deluge of difficulties we find surrounding us. The race is hindered by weather conditions and by planned hindrances which tend to cause us to drop out through utter exhaustion and a feeling that it is impossible and hopeless to make it to the finish line.

Paul goes on to say that he was often in "journeyings," which in those days usually meant walking many tedious miles. The Roman roads made it possible, but horses and chariots were for the affluent, and Paul undoubtedly often walked. He walked long, hot, tedious miles to teach the churches and lead people to an understanding of the truth of the Gospel. He was in perils of water and of robbers, in peril from the heathen, in perils in the city, in the wilderness, in the sea—and, as a final peril, he mentions "false brethren."

We read in J. Gresham Machen's *The New Testament: An Introduction to Its Literature and History:*

> Under the Roman Empire a remarkable system of roads rendered land travel probably easier than it has been up to modern times. Brigands on land and pirates on the sea were held in check. Travel became a common thing. A merchant of Hierapolis in Phrygia is declared to have made the voyage to Italy no less than 72 times.
>
> Of course the ease of travel must not be exaggerated. It did not compare with modern conditions. Perils of rivers, perils of robbers, perils in the wilderness, perils in the sea, were not lacking (II Cor. 11:26). It is difficult for us to form any adequate conception of the hardships of a missionary life like that of Paul—especially since, except for men of means, the land journeys would have to be made on foot. Nevertheless, the value of the Roman system of communication remains. Even with it, the early Christian mission was difficult; without it, it would have been impossible . . . .
>
> These things did not come by chance. It was not by chance that Jesus was born in the golden age of the Roman Empire, when the whole of the civilized world—the world which was to determine the whole subsequent course of history—was for the first time unified, so that a movement started in an obscure corner could spread like wildfire to the centre and from the centre to all the extremities. God is the ruler of history. His times are well chosen. The Roman Empire was an instrument in his hand. And so are the nations of the modern world.

The author of these words did not live to see the increase of violence, hardships, imprisonment, and martyrdom that missionaries today are living and dying through. But it is a marvelous recognition that Dr. Machen has passed on: the fact that God works in the midst of history—not by chance but by choice. However, human beings' choices also affect history. The parallel lines flow on, and God continually brings us up short in His Word by telling us of the effect which people have on history.

Paul began 2 Corinthians 11 by warning of the danger of Satan's beguiling their minds, even as Satan had beguiled Eve's mind with his subtle lies. And now, in the list of "perils" counted as real as Paul's physical perils, he lists the "perils among false brethren" as equally dangerous. Paul says that he himself has experienced danger—not to the body, but to the continuation of preserving the clarity of true truth, without being "muddied up." He says that he has been in danger among those who are teaching a twisted, false doctrine in the guise of truth. He tells us to beware. Paul couples exhaustion, tiredness, fatigue, and weariness with pain. He must have had a variety of pain: the more common ailments of stomachache, headache, stiff joints, head cold, sore throat, fever, and vomiting, as well as the pain of injuries inflicted by whips and stones. He speaks of being "in watchings often." (In Acts 20:28–31 we learn that this refers at least in part to his careful fasting and praying that his little flocks of believers would not be devoured by false teachers described as "grievous wolves [who] enter in among you.")

In other words, Paul cared enough about the people he had led to the Lord to take time away from food and sleep to pray for their continued growth and understanding and their protection from the false teaching prevalent in that day. His continuing list includes hunger and thirst (which were forced upon him in various situations) and then, separately, fasting (which he himself did voluntarily as he prayed and pleaded for the needs of the people—and probably his own needs, too). Added to the list is a particularly strong kind of suffering and affliction: "Besides those things that are without, that which cometh upon me daily, the care of [anxiety for] all the churches." This is an especially painful kind of anxiety, and *not* something that God points out as wrong. It was something Paul rightfully suffered—to be anxious about the safety of the babes in Christ, that they would have the spiritual food and drink (without added "poison") necessary for proper growth. He finishes by admitting his own weakness and his own ability to stumble. The apostle makes it clear that no one suddenly arrives at a pinnacle of faith where all difficulties—every weakness, pain, and stumbling—are at an end. No one arrives at such a peak of Christian faith and complete life of prayer that there is nothing to be seen but perfection within and without.

Before we continue, come back to where you and I are right now. What about *our* string of present difficulties: our weariness or exhaustion, our flu or headache, the continued infirmities from torn cartilage, polio, broken limbs, or arthritis? Are our ears becoming hard of hearing, our eyes losing their vision, our teeth needing constant dental care? Perhaps cancer has necessitated a breast removal or has recurred—with a prediction of a short life-span. What about birth defects and sudden accidents? What about deterioration from virus attacks or from the years' effects upon physical appearance or energy span? What about the unfair criticism of business associates—false reports which cost us our job or our standing in a university? What about direct attacks by members of our blood relations, or by those who are with us in the family of the Living Lord? What about depressions or nervous breakdowns, the exchange of a bright dream for a crushing disappointment? What about death that seems to separate us at the most "untimely" moment of life from a loved one? What about the difference between my life as a child of God's, and the life of someone who is walking in darkness with Satan's directions to follow as a road map and no light to find the true path? Is my life meant to be a collection of *visible* benefits that would make every non-Christian immediately conscious of the need to make a change? Is affliction something that can be designated as an area having only one kind of explanation? Or is there a balance to be studied?

Paul's life, even up to this point, can give us comfort. Surely he had faith, if anyone has ever had. Surely he knew what communication with the Lord in prayer could bring forth, if anyone ever did. Surely Paul was a "spiritual Christian" who was filled with the Holy Spirit. Yet, we can relate to him in all our variety of sufferings and know that he experienced far more loneliness, misunderstanding, and violence than most of us will ever experience. We know that his words and his life negate the tendency to feel and say: "There must be something wrong with my Christian life because I don't have a more exciting flow of answered prayer, or an easier, more fulfilling time." Do you ever wonder whether Paul agonized over being "fulfilled"? Did he have time to be frustrated about whether he was having either fulfillment or a "big experience" that was always increasing in magnitude?

If we were making a chart of "ups and downs," it seems to me that the "up" of Paul's hearing the voice of the Lord and seeing the blinding light was soon followed by the "down" of blindness and going without food. In his hour-by-hour living, the "blood, sweat, and tears" of his years were more frequent than the moments of coming close to being "too exalted."

3
A Crack in the Curtain

At this point there are important lessons to be learned by reviewing something of Job's lifework. Job held a key piece of work in the overall discovery of the meanings of the total picture of history. If we view history as a tapestry, Job's life would be one of the key threads in bringing out the true perspective of the rest. Job did not realize what an important thing he was doing as he sat in the ashes covered with boils. (And he had no Book of Job to help him, any more than he had Paul's life to encourage him.) Pioneers always have a harder time in their uncharted experiences, as they push through jungles or wilderness without marked roads or maps. Job was a pioneer in a certain area of the battles between God and Satan, as far as we know from the Bible. He had no one to offer any comfort, except men who stood around and criticized him. From then on, everyone has known what is referred to as "Job's comforters." The very use of the phrase can help diminish some of the sting from the things people often say which hurt the one being chided, rather than ease his pain. Job, however, couldn't say of those men, "They are like Job's comforters"! We have a lot to thank Job for—he sailed an uncharted sea and stayed on course!

We are told that Job was the greatest man in his part of the world. He had tremendous property, thousands of sheep and camels and every evidence of prosperity, as well as seven sons and three daughters. It is clear that he worshiped God sincerely and in the right manner, that he truly "feared" God in the proper sense of the word, and lived in accordance with this in his daily life.

In the first chapter of Job, the curtain is pulled back for us, to reveal what was going on in the heavenlies. We are told that Satan appeared before God. This enemy—the adversary—stood there as a challenge before God, saying that he had been "going to and fro in the earth." (In 1 Peter 5:8, we are warned that this is the devil's *constant* occupation [that is, walking up and down throughout the earth to see what harm he can do]: "Be sober, be vigilant; because your adversary the devil, as a roaring lion, walketh about, seeking whom he may devour.") God spoke to Satan and asked whether he had noticed Job and that there was nobody else like him who feared God and hated evil. "Job is truly an upright man," God told Satan. Here was someone who evidently brought joy to the Lord, a man after His own heart, dear to Him, someone who loved Him and expressed that love, who believed in Him and lived in the light of the reality of His existence. Job's life and the inner reality of his love and worship obviously mattered to God. This is an exciting portion of the glimpse we are given of this conversation. Job was a *person* to the infinite, personal Living God, and he meant enough to God to be made a part of His challenge to Satan. The fact that there existed a man who really put God first in his life was a victory for God in the continual challenge by Satan. The adversary obviously came to point out what a mess men and women were making throughout the earth. What an exciting revelation this is to us! We matter, as individuals, to the Living God. However—here is a sober warning—we also matter to Satan!

Conversation like this also goes on about us. Satan's answer was that Job didn't really love God, but only the things which God had given him. "You have protected him from difficulties," was Satan's accusation, "so that he has a hedge of protection around him." Satan went on to point out that Job had had great success in all of his projects. He really had everything: material affluence, health, a family that surrounded him, and the peace in which to go on accumulating these good things. "It's not for nothing that Job fears God!" was Satan's nasty interpretation of the whole relationship between Job and God. His next challenge was this: "Just spoil everything he has, and he will curse You to Your face." A dare to God! God's answer in this portion of the battle of the heavenlies was: "The hedge is removed, Satan, and you can put forth your hand and touch the things Job has. But you can't touch Job himself." So Satan left the presence of God and went to do the worst he could imagine to everything Job had.

The deluge of calamity that fell upon Job was pretty complete. One shock followed another in quick succession (*see* Job 1:13–19). Job's sons and daughters were gathered together at a family dinner party when the Sabeans came and took away all the oxen and asses, killing all the servants except the one who escaped to bring the news to Job. This fits in with our own moment of history—as many have known what it means to have terrorists take whatever they want by force, leaving behind a pile of dead bodies. It is important to remember that Satan is able to use human beings to do his work for him.

While this servant was bringing his tragic piece of news to Job, another one arrived before the first had finished speaking and told of fire (probably lightning) which had struck all his sheep and killed the servants caring for them, except this one who had escaped to tell Job. Before this second bearer of shocking news had finished his story, a third man appeared—one of Job's workmen who cared for his camels—and told of the sudden appearance of a band of brigands, the Chaldeans, who came in three groups and attacked them, taking away all the camels and killing Job's workmen, leaving only the one who was bringing the news. A fourth man came, before the third one had stopped speaking, and brought more news from the dinner party. He said that while they were eating, a terrific wind came (possibly a cyclone or tornado) and whipped off the walls of the house from all four corners at once. Job's children were crushed under the walls and killed. Within minutes, everything which Job had to bring him rejoicing in his day-by-day work and life had been wiped out. Gone were this world's harvests, his family, and the results of his creativity and hard work.

Job's reaction was a terrific victory for God in this battle in the heavenlies. Remember that Satan was trying to prove that all Job cared about was what he had, and that he would curse God to His face if his possessions were taken away. Job did not know anything about the challenge and was in ignorance of how important his reaction would be to God. Job truly loved and trusted God and bowed before Him in worship as his first reaction to the wave of shocks. He humbled himself in the most lowly things he could physically do—by shaving his head, tearing his clothing, and falling on his face before God. What he really did was worship God, to adore Him. Job didn't quote anyone else. He couldn't look up an appropriate verse. Job was original in his prayer as he communicated to God his honest thoughts and reactions to all the terrible things that had happened. He said, "Naked came I out of my mother's womb, and naked shall I return thither: the Lord gave, and the Lord hath taken away; blessed be the name of the Lord" (Job

1:21). Job attributed all his prosperity to the Lord's blessing, and in this way recognized in a proportionate way that there had been a protective hedge around him. However, he didn't know what we know as we read the account, because the curtain had not been pulled back for him. Job was in the dark, in a fog, as to what was going on, but he trusted God without seeing. "In all this Job sinned not, nor charged God foolishly" (v. 22).

In the second chapter of Job, we see Satan once again appearing before God. And, as God points out that Job has not wavered in his fear of God and in his integrity (in spite of the deluge of disasters), Satan comes back with further thrusts in his accusation of falseness in Job's love for God. "Just do something to his health, his flesh. Then You'll see that he won't go on this way. He'll curse You if he has pain and troubles in his flesh!" is the gist of what Satan says. Once again God says, "He is in your hand." This is a removal of the protective hedge, but *God* is not afflicting Job. It is Satan who is doing it to try to cause Job to curse God. It is Satan's method of getting at God. This is what we are being allowed to know about, to help our understanding.

The physical ailment which Satan chose to send upon Job was boils. We see then that Satan has the power to work in other people—to incite wars, assassinations, violence of person against person. In some measure he also has power over the elements and can bring tornados and lightning. Now he directly sends disease. As the "prince of this world," he definitely has a certain degree of power for the battle. Job's boils appeared "from the sole of his foot unto his crown," in other words, on every inch of his body! (2:7). He sat in ashes and scraped himself with a "potsherd" (a piece of broken pottery). A dismal, painful picture. And he hasn't read the Book of Job! The only help he has is a wife who stands looking at his miserable condition, saying: "Why don't you curse [renounce] God, and die?" Yet there continues his certainty that he can trust God. We are told that he did not "sin with his lips." Job really endured to the end. He remained faithful in the midst of tribulation, affliction, and suffering. What is more fantastic is that he remained faithful to the Lord in the midst of the criticism and needling of his "comforters." Job couldn't raise his eyebrows and think for his own satisfaction, "Oh, they're just 'Job's comforters.' " That relief wasn't available to Job himself.

What a gigantic task he had in the battle in the heavenlies, not only the one he was personally involved in, but also all the ones that were coming in subsequent history. No amount of imagination could bring Job to recognize a fraction of what victory was going to flow forth from his sitting in the ashes. What an unglamorous task: sitting in the ashes covered with boils, full of all the varieties of pain which a person can have—physical pain, emotional pain at tragic loss, the sorrow of having one's children all die at once, psychological pain at the isolation from the understanding of wife or friends, the loneliness of being misunderstood, as well as the misery of having a lifetime of success turn into total loss within hours. Yet the victory which was being won by Job in the midst of all that—unseen by him—was a reality in the ongoing battle in the heavenlies. The stream of victories which have flowed forth from Job's example—and from God's explanation as He pulled the curtain aside for the writer—is something it will take us eons of time to discover.

In the middle of his anguish, Job couldn't imagine his life having any meaning at all and cursed the day he was born. In chapter three, Job very eloquently wishes he had never been born, or that he had died at birth. But Job never curses God in all this outpouring of frustration and agony. It is interesting to note that God doesn't scold him for longing for death. Discouragement and depression are not equated with cursing or blaming God. Job's lack of hope for any relief in this life does not erase his expectation of a solution in resurrection and a life ahead.

For thirty chapters there is an argument between Job and his friends. The friends declare that all trouble comes from chastisement, that if Job would confess his sin, everything would change. Their dogmatic statement is that Job must have sinned some specific sin for which God has sent this series of troubles. Job says there is no special sin that caused his troubles. In chapter eight, Bildad states a simplistic formula: that sin always results in trouble and that the righteous always prosper as a cause-and-effect happening which is easily recognizable by everyone. Zophar insists that a confession will put it all right immediately (Job 11:13–18). Job argues that robbers prosper (12:6), and he declares that life is "full of trouble" (14:1). He goes on to point to a solution which is ahead:

O that thou wouldest hide me in the grave, that thou wouldest keep me secret, until thy wrath be past, that thou wouldest appoint me a set time and remember me! If a man

die, shall he live again? all the days of my appointed time I will
wait, till my change come.

Job 14:13, 14

For I know that my redeemer liveth, and that he shall stand
at the latter day upon the earth: And though after my skin
worms destroy this body, yet in my flesh shall I see God:
Whom I shall see for myself, and mine eyes shall behold, and
not another; though my reins be consumed within me.

Job 19:25–27

Job's cry here shows an understanding that there is no balanced
solution until the resurrection, even as David prayed: "As for me, I
will behold thy face in righteousness: I shall be satisfied, when I
awake with thy likeness" (Psalms 17:15). And in another Psalm, the
"balancing" is described as in the future, not to be seen easily in the
things of the present: "But God will redeem my soul from the power
of the grave: for he shall receive me. Selah. Be not thou afraid when
one is made rich, when the glory of his house is increased; For when
he dieth he shall carry nothing away: his glory shall not descend
after him" (Psalms 49:15–17).

The discourse goes on and on, in great detail. The overall importance is seeing that these friends had one string to their violin, one
tune to play, one theme: that the wicked always suffer in this life.
Job says that you can't tell the wicked from the good by their ease of
life or ease in death. At one point in the beginning of chapter 22,
Eliphas says that God doesn't care about a man anyway. But the
whole story shows that God *does* care, that man *does* have a part in
the battle of the heavenlies in a central way, and that this is a portion
of the demonstration that man is not a machine, but rather that each
person matters to God.

Elihu is better than the others in seeing that the elements can be
for either chastisement or for mercy, but he sees nothing at all of the
third possibility of the battle in the heavenlies having results, or
causing changes in events of history. He doesn't see the possibility
of Job's being involved in this warfare. Job himself doesn't know
what is going on in the battle, nor does he have any idea of the
revolutionary understanding which his story will open up to future
generations. *His* trials and tribulations, *his* agonies and struggles, *his*
longing for death, and *his* trust in God will mean much to those who

will follow. He declares to God: "Though he slay me, yet will I trust in him: but I will maintain mine own ways before him. He also shall be my salvation: for an hypocrite shall not come before him" (13:15, 16). Although his words are heard by his friends, he does not realize that they are indelibly written for generations and centuries to come. When he calls out, "Oh that my words were now written! oh that they were printed in a book! That they were graven with an iron pen and lead in the rock for ever!" (19:23, 24), little does he know that indeed this would take place!

There is a wide diversity of pioneers and heroes. A great variety of teachers is needed, and one of the most important ways which God has given His children to be used in the area of teaching is to simply *live* with reality whatever they are faced with. The teaching comes without being verbalized in some of the central and basic truths to be taught. Yet God knows that verbalizing emphasizes what has been lived through, so that those coming along in subsequent generations can have light and encouragement along the path. Job lived through a terrible period of time, not knowing whether there would be any relief before death or any change until the resurrection. He lived through it without knowing how much his longed-for "printed book" was going to mean to God's people in removing for them some of Satan's camouflaged attacks. From Job's time on, people could say, "Just like Job . . ." in the midst of being attacked, and they could visualize Satan's taunting of God. It is not that every child of God remembered to do that, but something had been made clear, which should never have been forgotten. The problem is that people constantly drift into a simplistic lack of balance and are in danger of joining Job's comforters.

When God speaks to Job directly, he does not chide Job for his sin, but does chide him for having a lesser view of the greatness of God than he should have had. We stand with Job as God speaks, for He speaks to us, too. Do we really bow as created beings before our Creator? Do we really let God *be* God in our communication with other people and with God Himself? We must read and reread His Word—to help keep ourselves in our place. God is saying that Job hasn't enough knowledge to see and understand his situation in the framework of total history. God says that if you can't know *all* about Creation, how can you know the more subtle things!

Who is this that darkeneth counsel by words without knowledge? . . . Where was thou when I laid the foundations of the

earth? declare, if thou hast understanding . . . . Whereupon
are the foundations thereof fastened? or who laid the corner
stone thereof; When the morning stars sang together, and all
the sons of God shouted for joy? . . . Hast thou commanded
the morning since thy days; and caused the dayspring to know
its place . . . . Knowest thou it, because thou wast then
born? or because the number of thy days is great? Hast thou
entered into the treasures of the snow? or hast thou seen the
treasures of the hail . . . . Gavest thou the goodly wings unto
the peacocks? or wings and feathers unto the ostrich? . . .
Doth the hawk fly by thy wisdom, and stretch her wings toward
the south?

Job 38:2–7, 12, 21, 22; 39:13, 26

All the diversity and detailed marvel of the Creation, God points
out, is completely beyond Job in every aspect and completely beyond *any* human being. His point is: "If you can't understand these
things, then do you not recognize that you are not full of enough
knowledge to comprehend all that is happening to you at this moment of history?"

Job bows before God and acknowledges that he has not enough
knowledge to judge his own place in total history. God makes clear
to him that only God can judge in this final fashion. Job shows that
he now realizes he is completely a "creature" and that God is
completely Creator. It is at this point that God turns to the friends
(although Elihu is left out) and says, "You have not spoken of Me as
Job has. You have not spoken correctly. Now you must go to My
servant Job and make a burnt offering, and Job will pray for you"
(*see* 42:7, 8). In other words, Job is going to take the place of a
go-between, doing a priestly work for his friends. There is an amazing forgiveness shown in Job's willingness to pray for his friends,
rather than to gloat over them. It would do us good to think about
this carefully in our prayer times, and to recognize the opportunities
that we have time after time to pray for people who have hurt us.
We should pray with a desire that others may come to an understanding of the truth of God's balanced Word, rather than with a
desire that they be proven wrong. The difference is in an inner
attitude which God knows about as we pray for those who have in
some form "railed against us."

The friends did do as God told them, which meant a humbling
kind of acknowledgement on their part that they had been wrong.

Job did pray for them, and God must have been pleased with the motive and inner attitude of Job as he prayed, because we are told: "And the Lord turned the captivity of Job, when he prayed for his friends: also the Lord gave Job twice as much as he had before" (42:10).

The realization by Job that he now knows God—in a way he never had known Him before—means that he feels a deeper love and trust than he did when he said, "Though he slay me, yet will I trust in him." There is a tremendous contrast with the statement: "I have heard of thee by the hearing of the ear: but now mine eye seeth thee" (42:5). Job feels now the kind of thing we each have felt in a minor way when, for instance, we have heard of the Swiss Alps all our lives, and then suddenly have the moment arrive when, on a day of crystal-clear air and sparkling sunshine, we awaken to a breathtaking view of snow-capped peaks. We marvel at the dark evergreens mixed with the lighter green of hardwoods which grow right up to the grassy pastures where the cows are grazing in the summer and flocks of sheep are tinkling their smaller bells. We take a deep breath and look at the high rocks, the blue sky that seems too blue to be real, and we say, "I imagined what it would be like, but I didn't know it would be like this. It was too much for any imagination. *Now* I have seen what before I only heard about." We look at our feet as we walk and see the gentians with their deep blue cups set in dark green leaves right on the ground, and wonder how such beauty and perfection could grow wild in dry, rocky soil.

It is hard to put into words the contrast between one stage of knowing *about* something and the higher stage of really "knowing." Job's reaction, when he came to know God in a fuller way, was to hate himself and want to repent in dust and ashes. Why? Because, although he had endured much in a very real and practical way and had not cursed God, he still regretted very thoroughly that he had not trusted *more,* and had not more willingly gone through all the afflictions, trials, and tribulations of those weeks and months. The repenting in dust and ashes was a way of saying to God, "I wish I had trusted more thoroughly. Forgive me for the imperfection and weakness of my trust."

This repentance was a way of saying:

Oh, God, my dear Heavenly Father, I didn't really know how great and marvelous You really are. You are so magnificent, so wonderful, so great, so beyond anything I was able to imgaine You to be. I did worship You and I did trust You, but it was such a tiny fraction of what I should have done, had I realized more completely just what You are like and how perfect You are. Oh, God of the Universe, Master and Creator, there are not sufficient words in the human language to express the difference between You and me, and I want that expression so very urgently that I must make a visible and feelable difference by shredding my clothing and putting dirt on myself, so that I can feel I am bowing before You in a state which demonstrates the difference to myself more clearly.

Job, while in the land of the living, had a glimpse of what we are all going to experience when we meet the Lord face-to-face in death—or at the return of Jesus Christ to gather us up, changing our bodies to be like His glorious resurrected body, "in a twinkling of an eye." Job was a pioneer in living through a series of tragedies and painful physical disease as his part of the heavenly battle. God gave him a very hard "work," but one which was to have far-reaching results in helping each generation and you and me personally. However, in Job's lifetime he experienced afflictions which none of us may experience. Job was gently given by the Lord an opportunity to actually see his God and Saviour and thus come to a clearer understanding. The time of terrible tribulation was followed by sufficient explanation so that it could be helpful to all of us to live with a measure of understanding. For Job, it was also an amazing happening—with a completeness which all of us will experience at death or at the Second Coming of Christ.

As a special "reward" for his particular piece of work, Job was given the clarity of view which he had when God talked with him. He also experienced the balanced perspective of seeing his friends' need for intercessory prayer, and thereafter was warmed by the healing emotion connected with his forgiveness of his friends and his earnest, faithful prayer for them. Then Job lived through another step, which was the Lord's material answer to his prayer. God had given Job the most important thing first: the spiritual understanding he needed. Now this was to be followed by what family and friends could see, taste, smell, and share physically. "And the Lord turned the captivity of Job, when he prayed for his friends: also the Lord gave Job twice as much as he had before" (42:10). The "turning of the captivity" refers to the fact that God no longer allowed Satan to hit Job with his fiery darts. God no longer allowed Job to be the center of the battle—the battleground between God and Satan. God not only put up the protective hedge again, He "prospered" Job. There were evidently "brothers and sisters" who had not come around during Job's hard times, but who now came to bring him comfort now that it was all over. They brought all sorts of gifts. Job began to gain property and flocks and herds of animals again, and the accounting which God wants us to have carefully numbers the sheep, oxen, and asses into the thousands. In fact, what Job was given was double what he had before.

Why double? It seems to me that we are having still another glimpse of what awaits us. Does that mean that I think that after we have "come through," then all our afflictions, tribulations, illnesses, and losses will be made up to us by double of everything: material possessions, health, strength of relationships with family and friends? No. *Not in this life.* I don't think we have any promise that can lead us to claim a copy of Job's experiences in *this* life. Naturally, the diversity of our personalities (and the fact that we are individual people who matter to God as individuals) enters into consideration. But, putting that aside for a moment, I think that Job's life was a picture which God placed in all its completeness in the land of the living. Job's life pictures the total completeness for each of us—with the momentary removal of the wall which separates heaven from earth and separates the life we will have in our new bodies from the life in these present bodies. Job had *in this life* a "moment of seeing." He saw God and himself, the totality of life, and the spoilage of the world due to the Fall in a new perspective which was a great contrast to the view he had had before (although he had been a faithful believer).

There was a climactic moment of fresh understanding. Right after this came a new sense of perspective which enabled him to see his friends with the right kind of pity and to pray for them with honesty and reality in his requests. Then came a restoration of everything that had been burned, looted, slashed, and taken from him with violence—including his health. What Job had in the latter part of his life is what we will each have in heaven, except that heaven's portion will be so far beyond the "twice as much" that it is only a tiny illustration of what is ahead. We look forward to a time when our perspective will be balanced, after seeing "face to face" rather than "through a glass, darkly." We look forward to a time when the troubles we are going through now will seem like nothing when contrasted with what the Lord has prepared for us. Job's double reward is meant to help us to understand this. Job's story is meant to encourage us and help us to keep on without giving up, whatever the struggle is that assails us right now.

It is interesting to find, as we come to the end of Job's story, that he had three new daughters and seven sons born to him. What welcome must have been given to those babies! Yet they did not "replace" the other ten who had died. For any who have children who are now in heaven, it is very important to remember to keep counting them as your children. A child who is in heaven is still your child and has not gone out of existence. One day (if they were all believers) the "double family," that is, the *twenty* children of Job, will receive their new bodies and demonstrate that God who is a God of detail did indeed give double of everything which Job had lost. We are told that Job lived 140 years after this, so his health must have been restored in double portion, too. We are also told that he saw four generations of his own children—that is, children, grandchildren, great-grandchildren, and great-great-grandchildren—so he had twice the number of generations to get to know and enjoy. Far from dying when he felt too miserable to go on, he was to know life to its fullest, without ever facing that same stream of misery again. Job came out "on the other side of the avalanche," so to speak.

We have personally lived through an avalanche of flowing mud, rocks, trees, and a great variety of debris. It is frightening to hear the thundering sounds, to feel the wind and the icy air mingled with a threatening descent of matter too enormous to do anything about, except feeble efforts which could make no difference to the relentless onrush of danger. To live through an avalanche for a week is more like looking back on months of fear and danger and alertness to sounds. Time loses its normal, even progress during periods of difficulty, fear, pain, danger, or excruciating sorrow. In a certain sense, time stands still. Short periods of time seem to last forever when the pain is the most violent, when the waiting is filled with fear of what is ahead, when a harsh uncertainty envelops one's being like the shrill shriek of wind in a hurricane. It is hard to keep a perspective or a balanced view of things when the solid earth is breaking up in an earthquake or an avalanche, or when the floating hotel of a ship suddenly pitches and tosses like a piece of bark. When the "normal" solidity of earth or water, houses or boats, governments or families, begins to break up and fall apart all around us, it is hard not to get a twisted perspective.

God did not use Job as a piece of theater, a puppet, or a chalk drawing to illustrate a truth to help us keep our balance in an upside-down period of history or in the attacks Satan will make on us personally. The life of Job was real. The challenge by Satan to God, in which Job was the human being attacked, was a real part of history. It did not take place just to be written about. In His gentleness and fairness to us, God prepared His Word to include the portions of history which would bring sufficient balance and give us understanding for this life. We have an eternity ahead to increase our knowledge and understanding. What we need now is just enough to live by. We have been given understanding, but also warning. The account of Job's life (which tells us more than Job knew) is a warning to us. We are meant to grasp that warning sufficiently to help us see how worthwhile are periods of our lives which seem to be a waste. We are meant never to forget—no matter how shrill the wind, how violent the storm—that there is meaning and purpose in our lives. This involves us as individuals, involves other people (future and present), and involves God Himself, as well as Satan as he tries to "win."

Our reactions, and what we actively do as a result of them, cannot only change a piece of history but can bring glory to God. "Whoso offereth praise glorifieth me . . ." (Psalms 50:23) is speaking of a praise that is deep in action and reaction, that is, in both outward behavior and inner responses to all the situations of life. The glorification of God by us—as imperfect, sinful, finite creatures in all our weakness—is a staggering opportunity set before us. It is a fabulous possibility for us to contemplate that we can really do anything which will glorify the Living God, the Creator of the Universe. What could we possibly do? Paint the greatest picture, write the most outstanding symphony, design or build the most magnificent building, change a piece of land into the most beautifully landscaped garden, care for the poor and destroyed people of the world in some practical and specific way so that there will be a difference before they die? Yes—all these things we can do with special love for Him whose Creation we so appreciate, and for whom nothing is too hard. The enormous projects we may think of might be out of our reach. Prison cells, hospital beds, concentration camps, and wheelchairs bring limitations, even as does lack of talent or lack of money or land. However, there is unlimited possiblilty for glorifying God—moment by moment, hour by hour, every day in every situation.

How? By offering praise, not with our lips and throats in repetitive cadence, saying the words while our minds and emotions are filled with other thoughts and feelings, but by actually loving and trusting God when there is pressure being brought upon us to not trust Him. Job gave us a demonstration of one person's fulfilling that kind of faithfulness which did bring glory to God. The demonstration which Job gave had sufficient effect to be worthwhile for that result alone. Job brought sufficient glory to God, and sufficient victory in the heavenly battle, to have his period of agony be worthwhile in history without any other results. However, no "incident" stands alone in history. Job has been the teacher, a source of discovery, an encouragement, a person to relate to—for countless people in many generations, including you and me. He has helped us to know something of the variety that there is in praising God.

We need to be very careful not to let Job's lesson get lost in a flood of "spirituality" which is bounded by legalistic tape measures. This would divert our attention from what Satan is really hitting us with when he turns our minds to repetitive following of a list of petty rules and regulations. We need to be reminded and warned constantly that our enemy is a crafty one. He repeated Scripture verses to Jesus, although he knew the Scripture was written by inspiration of God and that Jesus knew it very well. He tried to trip up the Second Person of the Trinity with Bible verses twisted into a seemingly logical reason for doing something which would have been sin for Jesus. Satan does the same to us, only we are much more vulnerable. Jesus answered Satan with verses in proper context from the Word of God. We certainly need to be filled with the Word so that the twisted version presented to us in various circumstances will not throw us into a situation where we do just what Satan is setting out to make us do in the battle.

Remember that Satan in his false work tries to turn aside the trust in God on the part of God's people and change it to the trust in some false promise of a "thing." In Job's case, there was the promise being handed out by his "comforters" that *if* he would just repent of sin, the immediate result would be that everything would be fine. Satan tries to twist people into thinking of the "things" they want, and offers them those things with a series of false promises. He so tempted Jesus in the wilderness:

> If thou be the Son of God, command that these stones be made bread . . . . If thou be the Son of God, cast thyself down: for it is written, He shall give his angels charge concerning thee: and in their hands they shall bear thee up, lest at any time thou dash thy foot against a stone . . . . Again, the devil taketh him up into an exceeding high mountain, and sheweth him all the kingdoms of the world, and the glory of them; And saith unto him, All these things will I give thee, if thou wilt fall down and worship me.
>
> *See* Matthew 4:3, 6, 8, 9

Notice that all these temptations were promises of things which Satan thought would be just what Jesus wanted. In each case, Satan promised a "shortcut" to having attractive things. He tried to make the false promise sound pious and genuine by connecting it with something true—and also by constantly using the needling note: "If thou be the Son of God . . . ."

Satan will do the same thing to us, over and over again. As part of the battle, he chooses the affliction he attacks us with and then he himself whispers the temptation to us to get out from under it, to simply "bow" to another god or put our trust in some formula or person, and we will then be relieved immediately. Satan says to God that he accuses Job of wanting only the good things that God gives him, not loving and caring about God himself, but only loving the pleasant things in themselves. This is Satan's opinion of *all* people. He thinks it will not be hard to turn our trust into a trust of things or to any kind of formula for relief. "If you are a good Christian, you should not be suffering at all," he says.

Jesus knew what Satan was trying to do to Him. Jesus also knew well clear passages of Scripture which warned against a turning aside to false solutions. The Old Testament warning was given:

> If there arise among you a prophet, or a dreamer of dreams, and giveth thee a sign or wonder, And the sign or the wonder come to pass, whereof he spake unto thee, saying, Let us go after other gods, which thou hast not known, and let us serve them; Thou shalt not hearken unto the words of that prophet,

or that dreamer of dreams: for the Lord your God proveth you,
to know whether ye love the Lord your God with all your heart
and with all your soul. Ye shall walk after the Lord your God,
and fear him and keep his commandments, and obey his voice,
and ye shall serve him, and cleave unto him.

Deuteronomy 13:1–4

We are warned that Satan will not only tempt us to complain
against God when afflictions come, but will also try to turn us into
getting rid of the affliction in a wrong way. Satan can do "miracles"
or "wonders," and can give power to people to do them.

Today we have constantly increasing dangers from the super-
natural traps which Satan is setting through false prophets seen
multiplying all around us. We are tempted to get rid of afflictions
through shortcuts promised by a cult. Thus we may try to relieve
tenseness and depression by getting relief from Transcendental
Meditation, try to cure illness by going to a Buddhist healer, or
blindly seek "more exciting" spiritual experiences. The danger of
not glorifying God in the midst of affliction is more prevalent than
ever in our "post-Christian" culture, where every day's newspaper
influences us to water down our resolve to "Put on the whole
armour of God, that ye may be able to stand against the wiles of the
devil" (Ephesians 6:11). The "wiles of the devil" were pitted against
Job in his afflictions. Those "wiles" are continuing today. The devil
"dishes up on the same plate" both the affliction and a false way of
getting rid of it, so that we face a double temptation: cursing God
and complaining against Him, and then turning away from Him
toward something or someone else.

Jesus overcame Satan for us. Jesus resisted sin, and His resisting
is given to us (as if we had done it) when we believe in Him and in
His substitutionary death for us. Jesus shed His blood for us, so that
it would be possible for us not only to have eternal life but to know
some measure of "overcoming" in this life. Job overcame Satan in
his victory. How? He looked to the Redeemer in the limited measure of understanding he had at that time. The Blood of the Lamb is
the only way in which "overcoming" can ever take place in the life
of a human being. "And they overcame him by the blood of the
Lamb, and by the word of their testimony; and they loved not their
lives unto the death" (Revelation 12:11). Someday these swelling
words will be accompanied by a crescendo of music, as the moment
comes when we will be a part of the great singing chorus of believers

and angels in the presence of the Lamb Himself.

Shut aside other things for a moment, when you can take the time, and come along into the next chapter with nothing to distract your thoughts except the sounds of birds, rushing water, and tinkling cowbells—or even city traffic flowing below your windows. Shut yourself into contemplating the *fairness* of God in His marvelously personal attention to us as individuals, now throughout all this life and on into eternity.

4
The Museum in Heaven: Rectangle A

It was a spring day in Holland, and the flower-filled fields and gardens and the flower stalls on many street corners brought a fragrance into the very air. Sweetness and light drifted through the streets and canals of Amsterdam, seeming to permeate even the dark corners. It was before the drug scene had changed the center of the city, and the old beauty and charm were yet unspoiled. We turned into the path leading to the hospital steps and entered the halls, immediately struck by the antiseptic odors and dim quietness—such a contrast to the freshness of the season outside. As we carefully opened the door to the room to which we had been directed, we were reassured that it was the right one. Mrs. Van der Weiden was standing by a window, and her husband, with bandages swathed about his head, turned his face a tiny bit toward us and managed a look of welcome in his eyes, as he recognized us.

Such a short time before, this couple had been at L'Abri, happily taking part in all the study, discussion, and lectures there, and having meals with us in our chalet. Mr. Van der Weiden had loved the last Sunday High Tea he had eaten with us before they had to return to Holland for a doctor's examination. After months of pain and treatment, he thought he had some sort of sinus trouble. But a brain specialist had diagnosed the need for an operation to remove a brain tumor, and the operation was now over. The report had been a terrible shock—it had been cancer in an advanced stage—and there would be only a few days before Mr. Van der Weiden would die. There it was: a blow with nothing to soften it. A starkly definite reality.

As Fran and I stood there beside him, gently squeezing his hand for contact and to give unspoken sympathy and communication of

67

loving concern, Mr. Van der Weiden began to speak in jerky and raspy spurts. It was an effort to communicate through his pain and weakness, and it was to be his last verbal communication before he died three days later. What he said was easily understood: "Before—I—everything—could—do.   Now—I—nothing—can— do." He was referring to all our times in Amsterdam, when he would arrange for discussion groups from the University of Amsterdam at his store, Arti-Home, and other places. We would come to Holland to have discussions at Professor Rookmaaker's home with students from Leiden University, and then have one evening in Amsterdam in Mr. Van der Weiden's interior-decorating store. The Van der Weidens arranged a very tasteful grouping of lovely Scandinavian furniture as a "living room" for those attending. They served coffee with delicious little sweet things early in the evening, and about midnight, in another complete set of Dansk pottery, they served tea and little salty tidbits of cheese and crackers and other savory things. Candlelight and flowers completed the preparations, and the whole atmosphere was one which they felt brought an evening of "L'Abri" to Amsterdam. Now Mr. Van der Weiden was feeling the "waste" of dying. He was feeling that now, in our last time with him, he had been reduced to doing nothing at all for the Lord. I am sure that he also felt that his lifetime had been all too short to do what he had hoped to do for the Lord. He made another labored statement in which he made clear that he regretted not doing something he had someday intended to do. "I—wanted— to . . ." he began.

As I stood there looking at the distress in his face about being shut off from doing anything more for the Lord, I suddenly realized that there *was* something to say, something that would have immediate value and would not be a trumped-up "pat on the head" of meaningless comfort. I suddenly had a flash of recognition that perhaps the next hours and days would be the most important ones of Mr. Van der Weiden's life—a part he could still have in the battle in the heavenlies. When *time* is given us for a particular task, if we turn away from it at that time, that particular task can't be repeated. As time was slipping away for him, I felt an urgency to explain something which was like a searchlight to me, lighting up a fresh understanding of the whole problem of suffering. This insight could highlight the importance of winning a victory exactly at the point where Satan is challenging God: "accusing the brethren," trying to prove to God that one of His children does not really love Him at all.

I looked in my purse for two clean handkerchiefs which I had tucked there, and spread them out on the coverlet under the ill man's chin. His head was propped up sufficiently to see them. I then proceeded to go into a description of what I wanted so badly to give him as a positive reality of refuting his statement that he could now do "nothing." I honestly felt spurting within me a deep fountain of excitement that there was really still something he could do—a "something" that perhaps would be the most important victory of his whole lifetime of actively doing things for the Lord. The wonder of the fairness of the Lord overwhelmed me, as I began to talk.

What I gave that dying man for his final days was something to use as a weapon against Satan's present attack on his trust and love of the Lord. Naturally, the thoughts of his large family of nine children whom he felt needed his care—and the all-too-human feeling that "fifty years old is too young to die"—would open up a vulnerable area into which Satan could send his "fiery darts." What I gave Mr. Van der Weiden that day I also gave to myself, without knowing it at the time. I was doing the groundwork for the talks which I later labeled "The Two Rectangles" or "A Museum in Heaven." I would use this illustration in widely separated parts of the world, for individuals, small groups, or huge auditoriums full of people. I would later use two rectangles drawn on a blackboard or on a sheet of paper and then projected onto a screen, or rectangles sketched on a piece of paper for an individual or small group sitting around a table. Sometimes I used just two separate pieces of paper, or even two handkerchiefs laid side by side, as they were that long-ago afternoon in the hospital in Amsterdam.

When we ask the Lord, "Please put Your words into my mouth for this person, for this situation. Please give me Your strength in my weakness in this specific need," so often His answer becomes a seed in our own thinking and understanding which goes on and grows as the years pass. This has been one area in my own experience of the reality of "My cup runneth over." When one asks for help in meeting another person's need for the moment, so often there is a "spilling over" of truth which continues to be practical in a diversity of future situations which could not be counted!

I have drawn two rectangles (see next page), a first step in trying to unfold this explanation which I feel is necessary for a complete, balanced view of affliction, suffering, persecution, and martyrdom. It seems to me that this illustration provides a framework for the

Rectangle A

Rectangle B

understanding of affliction, although there are also other aspects which need to be remembered. This illustration weaves together the understandings we are given in Job, Hebrews 11, and an important verse in Revelation. Without understanding what part the battle in the heavenlies has in the whole question of affliction (and the part each of us has in the important victories in that battle), we have a lopsided understanding. A lopsided understanding is a lopsided vehicle in which to take our journey along the path of life. What a discomfort and insurmountable hindrance to progress it would be to ride in a horse-drawn cart with both wheels missing from one side!

Each rectangle pictured represents all geographic space ever lived in for all time—from the first man and woman until that block of time is cut off by the Judgment. These two rectangles represent all space and time, but in a small enough area for us to comprehend in our finite and limited imaginations. As we consider (to the extent that we are able to conjure up such a space/time grouping) all the people of God from the beginning until the end, we are imagining those who came to God in His appointed way, as did Abel and Abraham, as well as Peter, Stephen, and Paul. The grouping includes any of us today who look back to the substitution of Christ on the cross as the sacrificial Lamb of God who took our place and made it possible for us to have the second birth. In other words, these rectangles represent all the people throughout history who have been, are, and will be the people of God: the sheep of His pasture, the bride of Christ, the redeemed hosts. Pictured in tiny stick figures are all those we will be knowing throughout all of eternity. We are all there, in our particular moment of history, just as each one has been and will be until Jesus comes back.

Each rectangle represents the same space and the same time and the same people. We are each in *both* rectangles in varying incidents in our lives. We find ourselves in Rectangle A at one time, and in Rectangle B at another, because the rectangles differ in representing the two kinds of victory which can be won by the people of God. We will study Rectangle A in this chapter and Rectangle B in the next. Rectangle A represents the victories in the heavenly battle which have taken place in the midst of unchanging circumstances. At the top of the rectangle, the large dot represents God, looking over space and time and regarding the people who love Him and trust Him. The small dot represents Satan "accusing the brethren," coming before God and pointing out each one of us at various moments of our lives. He says, in essence: "That person does not love You, God. That person only loves his or her comfort [or possessions or health or land]. There is no trust of You that would continue in that life if I . . . ." Here something would be mentioned as being "the impossible thing to endure."

It seems clear to me that the accusation of Satan comes specifically so that he would be pointing to an individual and saying, "Seth [Katie, Matthew, Dick, Rebecca, Elizabeth, Francis, Regina, John, Priscilla, Jeremiah, Natasha, Hannah, Andrew, Fiona, Joanne, Ranald, Margaret, Naomi, Hannah, Deborah, Udo, Susan, Kirstine, Gian, Samantha, Jessica, Bill] would not continue to love You or trust You if I . . . ." And then he mentions one or more "fiery darts" with which he could afflict that individual.

Go back to Job, and think of how the battle was waged then. It was a battle in the heavenlies and demonstrated that the action and reaction of a human being has significance in the victory that takes place in the heavenlies. Satan attacks God through attempts to make His children stop trusting their Heavenly Father and start complaining and murmuring against Him. Satan's planned afflictions are aimed at getting the people of God to criticize Him in a variety of ways and in different intensities. This took place in Job's time, and the curtain was pulled back for all who lived after Job to have some measure of understanding as to the source and meaning of affliction in their own lives. We are meant to understand that one very important victory we are meant to have is a series of repeated "overcomings" in a variety of difficulties. We are meant to understand the total fabric in which each individual child of God is a thread. This fabric is to be complete—without the "holes" or "ravelings," which would present Satan with a possibility of saying, "*There* is a thing that no child of God can endure and still continue to trust God."

We know that this battle will someday be over. The final victory will one day be won and the fabric will be complete. Satan will one day never again have access into the presence of God with his accusations. The Book of Revelation tells us of this glorious day, still in the future:

> And the great dragon was cast out, that old serpent, called the Devil, and Satan, which deceiveth the whole world: he was cast out into the earth, and his angels were cast out with him. And I heard a loud voice saying in heaven, Now is come salva-

tion, and strength, and the kingdom of our God, and the power of his Christ: for the accuser of our brethren is cast down, which accused them before our God day and night. And they overcame him by the blood of the Lamb, and by the word of their testimony; and they loved not their lives unto the death.

Revelation 12:9–11

We look forward with excitement to that day, but this passage can add much to our understanding of today's affliction. It can help us to recognize the importance of our task right now, when we are meant to be occupied with "overcoming by the blood of the lamb." What does it mean? It means overcoming Satan's thrusts, his darts, his temptations, his attempts to draw us into a variety of sin and to push us into directly sinning against God by complaining against Him, cursing Him, or murmuring against the afflictions that come to us by declaring, "It isn't fair."

Peter was in danger of just this thing when Jesus asked him whether he loved Him. When Peter kept declaring that he did, Jesus indicated that Peter was going to face a martyr's death at the end of his life. Peter was full of the wonderful victory of Christ's Resurrection and the marvel of eating and talking with the risen Lord. His thoughts were all in the direction of victory over the terrible death on the cross which he had seen Jesus go through, and the promises of the Second Coming of Jesus and fantastic glories ahead. Peter was not thinking of afflictions and persecutions immediately ahead of him, nor of martyrdom as his ending in this life. Peter's thoughts of victory were not in the area of trusting the Lord and loving Him (as he so firmly declared that he did) in the midst of horrifying circumstances. His immediate reaction was to look to John, the disciple he remembered that Jesus had especially loved, and to ask, "Lord, and what shall this man do?" (John 21:21). Jesus was very emphatic in His answer to Peter and to us: "If I will that he tarry till I come, what is that to thee? follow thou me" (v. 22). He did not say that John would live until He came back again, but that if He willed that John should live that long, it should not affect Peter in the least.

Peter had one important thing to do, and that was to follow Jesus in the midst of whatever would be *his* special circumstances in life. For Peter to have victory in the midst of tribulation as well as in times of triumph—and a final time of suffering martyrdom—was the series of victories which *only* Peter could have.

It is plain that the *individual* matters to God. Peter could not have a duplicate of John's life, because not one of us can have a duplicate of any other Christian's life. We are not carbon copies turned out of a machine. We are not mass-produced in a factory. We are individuals with significance in history, so immensely important that no one else can live our lives or die our deaths for us. No one else can have our joys or bear our pain for us. It is not possible for anyone else to win our victories for us in any area. Satan attacks us individually, and we must as individuals cry out to God for help in defeating Satan as he tries to put a wedge between God and us. When Satan attacks believers, he is trying to put a barrier between an individual child of God and God the Father. Satan attempts to get people to curse God, to blame Him for their troubles, as well as to stop loving God. Satan indirectly attacks God by a direct attack on one of God's children. The victory for God against Satan is when—one by one—God's people continue to love Him and trust Him in the midst of unchanging circumstances.

Here is how I explained the truths of that first rectangle to our dying friend:

There is no one else in all history, Mr. Van der Weiden, who has had your combination of life experiences. You lie in a hospital room after a brain tumor has been found inoperable, knowing that you have nine children of certain ages. Your present combination of agonies right now is unique. No one else has had the exact life you have had or the same business, nor has had to say good-bye to the wife you have and the children you have. You are a person in the sight of God—and of Satan. You are really one definite individual, not just a statistic, and perhaps the next hours or days are the most important in the whole succession of time in your life. You still have perhaps your most important work to do now, as you face the temptation to spend your remaining hours in wishing it could be otherwise, or blaming God. Instead of that, you tell God you really trust Him implicitly and love Him in the midst of this circumstance. No one else has this particular portion of the battle to take part in, nor this particular victory to win for the Lord.

You see, I believe that—in spite of similarity of troubles, illnesses, pains, difficulties, afflictions, persecutions, and sufferings—no two people have exactly the same combinations of circumstances to be lived through. In my imagined rectangle where Satan confronts God throughout all time and space, I picture Satan as saying to God, "If a woman had five sons who died in a war, she couldn't keep on trusting You." God would then reply, "There is Mrs.—— whose five sons died in World War One, and she *did* keep on trusting Me." And then Satan might say, "Ah, but if a young man lost his wife and child during the first year in the mission field, that man would stop trusting You." And the reply would come: "There is Mr.—— who went through exactly that in 1906 in Africa and still loved Me."

Satan: "But if a woman had her first son born dead, and then her husband died three weeks later, she would become bitter."

God answers, "Look at Jessie Green who went to Bible school and prepared for work in China in 1896, although she had just gone through these tragic losses. She loved Me and spent her life trusting Me in China." Satan: "If a young man saw his parents and friends tortured and killed in Cambodia, he could never trust You and love You." God says to this accusation: "There is a sad Cambodian boy in 1977 who is going on after just that experience, trusting Me, and continuing to ask Me for help." Another challenge by Satan: "If a woman prayed for her alcoholic husband to change, and he kept on beating her for fifteen years, she would stop trusting You." And God would point out exactly the woman who had gone through that combination of frustrated sadness, and yet still remained faithful to Him.

Read slowly and think carefully: The death of Jesus on the cross was to give three distinct kinds of victory to each one who believes in Him. His death was sufficient for complete victory. First, when a person accepts Christ as his or her Saviour—after sufficient understanding of the reality of God's existence (and of what true guilt means before such a God) and what the death of Christ on the cross accomplished—that person has *victory over the penalty of sin.* There will be no penalty to pay. Christ's death produced perfect victory for each one who believes on Him, and the penalty is wiped out. Second (this is really the third victory chronologically), there is *victory over the presence of sin.* One day every one of us will be glorified. This is absolute and certain after we have been justified through believing in Christ. The death of Christ brought forth a victory over what Satan had destroyed in the Garden of Eden. The extent of this victory is so glorious that we may be sure of not only being in heaven and having eternal life, but of being separated entirely from the presence of sin. There is also a *day-by-day, moment-by-moment victory* which Christ died to make possible—a most important one in the continual battle by Satan against God. This third kind of victory is meant to take place over and over again in the period of time we are still in the land of the living. The death of Christ on the cross was sufficient to provide a victory that was complete. Christ's death has opened the way to us to be immediately forgiven and justified when we accept Him as Saviour. His death assures us of immediate entrance into heaven whenever we are "absent from the body." His death, however, was also to give the possibility of victory over Satan in this present day-by-day life. One of Satan's great campaigns against God is in the area of trying to break down our trust of God. We have seen it in Job, and we know from the Book of Revelation that Satan is, has been, and will be doing that "day and night."

I believe that there is to be an historic fulfilling of proof that the death of Christ *was* sufficient for *every* kind of victory needed to make the reality complete. There will be no individual in heaven who *perfectly fulfilled,* moment by moment, a constant trust and love of God. Each one of us falls into Satan's traps from time to time, some more frequently than others. However, I believe that there will be no type of affliction or suffering that someone has not lived through with victory supplied on the basis of the shedding of the blood of Christ. I believe that "They overcame him by the blood of the Lamb . . ." will be demonstrated as having included a fantastic diversity of "overcomings" throughout history. It seems to me that the "cup of victory" will be complete. There is titanic meaning and purpose in our individual afflictions, since the particular one Satan is hitting us with today has not been lived through before at any time in history—nor will it be again. There is no general type of affliction by which we can be categorized. We are individuals, and our afflictions are individual, because of our own personal history, circumstances, and surroundings, and our personality with all its strengths and weaknesses. No one has ever had the "set of afflictions" you and I have, and no one has experienced the same particular kind of frustrations or agonies. Our own happenings are unique, even if they sound like someone else's. The similarity is that we all do have afflictions of some variety, and that we can't know what the next one is going to be.

An absolutely breathtaking discovery comes to us in the middle of considering this rectangle and thinking of the little stick figures as representing not only all people in history, but all the incidents, including all the attacks of Satan as he tries an endless variety of combinations. The wonderful discovery is that our finite, weak, imperfect, human actions and reactions—the attitudes of our minds and emotions and the things we whisper to God, as well as the things we do—matter to God. This is a discovery that can change all of life for us, when we begin to realize fully that we can have a part on God's side of the heavenly battle, bringing joy to God and defeat to Satan—while we lie in a hospital bed or spend a lifetime in a wheelchair; as we sweep up the broken glass on a floor, sweat uphill with a heavy load, or wait on someone who is unloving; when we sit in a prison cell and feel the rough hand of a guard on our shoulder, stand in a courtroom to answer unjust charges, or feel the crack of a whip against our flesh or the crack of harsh criticism whipping into our sensitive feelings; and at the moment of facing a telegram with crushing news or discovering that we are going blind. We can whisper, whatever the circumstances, "God, I don't understand, but I love You and I trust You. Don't let me flinch; don't let me let You down in this area of the battle."

This to me is the fabulous "discovery of all discoveries"—that God is so fair that He enables us each to have the opportunity to have outstanding things to do in His total history of victory through the ages. Here is the vandal Satan, trying to destroy all of God's Creation and trying to smear and devastate the beauty of love and trust and the continuity of the relationship between God and His people. You and I and each of the people of God through the ages have completely different and individual things to do which are equally important. Christian evaluation of work as "important" or "unimportant"—"outstanding" or "unnoticeable"—is all out of balance so much of the time, because the perspective is all wrong. None of us can have God's perspective. However, He has given us small glimpses, hints, open windows here and there in His Word, so that we might have some idea of His fairness, which is so marvelous that the unknown and unheard-of slave in some obscure village of the world, beaten and bashed around, may have the most titanic victory in the heavenly battle that has ever been had.

On the day when the believers' rewards are given out, we will be craning our necks to see who is being given a shining reward and some special treasure. I am sure that we will be astounded at the things that were counted "the greatest" and the things that were counted "the least." There is no one who is shut away from having a victory (or even a whole string of victories in the heavenly battle) because of wheelchair lives, hospital walls, prison bars, concentration-camp barbed wire, desert abandonment, nursing-home loneliness, mundane work in some wilderness spot, or absence of another human being over miles of lonely farmland to be worked on a tractor. None of us can know which shock or illness (headache or operation, disappointment or disillusionment with a friend, criticism or other human attack, loss of job or loss of house and land, news of a close loved one's death, or totally destructive earthquake) will turn out to be the most important opportunity we are ever going to have to honestly love God and truly trust Him in a way which will bring Him joy and defeat Satan. We cannot know which is the most important moment in our lives. Its arrival won't be announced with a blast of silver horns or a blare of an orchestra's full crescendo. Our most important moment can come when no one but God and Satan are aware of it, when our response to the Lord is one which wins at once a battle which could have left a horrible tear or hole in the fabric of history.

It seems to me that there are people watching. How many? How constantly? We aren't told, but we *are* told that there are those who are concerned about how we get on with our life in the midst of the battle. It is not a matter of doing the "biggest" thing there is to do, nor yet of doing the "most humble" thing we can think of doing. It is not a matter of conjuring up the most splashy way we can discover to serve the Lord, nor of planning to follow the life of a hermit so that we can be sure we are not seeking notoriety. We are to keep on the course which the Lord lays out for us individually and seek to do His will hour by hour as we follow that course. However, in the midst of it all, we cannot tell what is Satan's sharpest aimed arrow or dart or what is the most important victory. Satan will try to come up and hit us when and where we least expect it, and not only are we in danger of not recognizing the attack as *his* attack, but of not realizing how important our victory is.

Who is watching us? The answer is in the Book of Hebrews:

Wherefore seeing we also are compassed about with so great a cloud of witnesses, let us lay aside every weight, and the sin which doth so easily beset us, and let us run with patience the race that is set before us, Looking unto Jesus the author and finisher of our faith who for the joy that was set before him endured the cross, despising the shame, and is set down at the right hand of the throne of God.

Hebrews 12:1, 2

This description of being surrounded with witnesses puts our lives into a kind of stadium where (it seems to me) we are running a race in front of onlookers who have gone before us and care about the outcome of our individual races. It seems to me that the "wherefore" puts these lines into a relation with the preceding chapter of Hebrews. That chapter fits into my concept of the rectangles—or rather, my imagined rectangles were born out of Hebrews 11 as it came to my mind beside Mr. Van der Weiden's bed. This chapter is often called "the roll call of the faithful" because it names, one after another, all who have had faith in the Living God and have exhibited this faith in their lives:

By faith Abel offered unto God a more excellent sacrifice than Cain, by which he obtained witness that he was righteous . . . . By faith Abraham, when he was called to go out into a place which he should after receive for an inheritance, obeyed; and he went out, not knowing whither he went . . . . By faith they passed through the Red sea, as by dry land: which the Egyptians assaying to do were drowned. By faith the walls of Jericho fell down, after they were compassed about seven days. By faith the harlot Rahab perished not with them that believed not, when she had received the spies with peace. And what more shall I say? for the time would fail me to tell of Gedeon, and of Barak, and of Samson . . . of David also, and Samuel, and of the prophets: Who through faith subdued kingdoms, wrought righteousness, obtained promises, stopped the mouths of lions, Quenched the violence of fire, escaped the edge of the sword, out of weakness were made strong, waxed valiant in fight, turned to flight the armies of the aliens. Women received their dead raised to life again: and others . . . .

Hebrews 11:4, 8, 29–35

Is the *measure* of faith always such miracles as described above? Is faith as defined by God that which brings visible results in the flow of life—results of constant victory over difficulties and troubles? Is faith demonstrated by a list of healings, material goods supplied, obstacles removed, police turned away from the door, persecutions and afflictions stopped miraculously? Is faith present when circumstances suddenly change for the better immediately after prayer, but missing if the circumstances get worse or remain the same?

The cloud of witnesses which Hebrews 12 describes as watching us as we live day by day have evidently all been through the things spoken of in Hebrews 11. Thus far we have read a list of fantastic miracles and answered prayer which changed circumstances. But the list is not yet complete. The chapter continues with no break:

> And others had trial of cruel mockings and scourgings, yea, moreover of bonds and imprisonment: They were stoned [we think of both Stephen and Paul, among others], they were sawn asunder, were tempted, were slain with the sword: they wandered about in sheepskins and goatskins; being destitute, afflicted, tormented; (Of whom the world was not worthy:) they wandered in deserts, and in mountains, and in dens and caves of the earth. And these all, having obtained a good report through faith, received not the promise: God having provided some better thing for us, that they without us should not be made perfect.
>
> Hebrews 11:36–40

The demonstration of faith has taken place, even as it did in the case of Job, in a whole succession of people who had sufficient faith to demonstrate to Satan, God, the angels, and whoever else could see that they loved God and trusted Him in the midst of titanic affliction, without being bitter about that affliction not being removed.

I believe that the sufficiency of the grace of God on the basis of the blood of Christ, shed to give victory in the battle against Satan, has been and is being and will be proven to be not just academically "sufficient." This grace will have been, in instance after instance, historically proven to have been sufficient indeed in every conceivable kind of affliction and suffering, in every kind of trouble and persecution. Not only is it possible that the victory which Christ died to give us in day-by-day life in the midst of the battle *could* carry us through situations without blaspheming God, but there is some factual, historical happening in some real individual's life to prove that this was possible. My pictured Rectangle A spreads out in my imagination every single one of the people of God through history, and I believe that the combined experiences in which there has been victory—or a variety of kinds in a variety of lives—will make up a total "full cup of proof," so that Satan will be totally defeated. Satan will not be able to find a single thing for which the grace of God has not been sufficient for *someone—somewhere—*at *some time.*

An art museum demonstrates what has taken place in art through the years. A museum in one country usually has more of that country's art than a museum in another country, so one goes to Florence to see the history of Italian art and to Amsterdam to see a concentrated history of Dutch art. Some museums are more international or wider in their scope, but each is limited in some way. There is no museum which has everything which has ever been painted or all the sculpture which has ever been made. Natural-history museums or music museums are specialized in their own way, but are also limited in bringing together all that has taken place, even in their own fields.

In my own imagination I walk along with you through the woods and fields of my own "Narnia" portion of the new heavens and the new earth (or perhaps in the heavenly city), and we come upon a fantastic building which is a special kind of "museum of history." This would cover the history of the *victories* in individual lives. How would the victories be displayed? I don't know; but I visualize some kind of visual record, portraying the diversity and tremendous scope of the completeness of the victory of the death of Christ in overcoming Satan's attempt to separate the love of God's people from God. We are told that nothing shall separate us from the love of God (*see* Romans 8:35–39), and I do believe that it shall be proven that the grace of God is sufficient, so that there is to be a demonstration that the *opposite* is possible on the basis of the blood of Christ. Nothing should separate *our love* for God from Him. Not one of us will perfectly love God and trust Him in every circumstance; but some of us will show forth that trust and love in the midst of one difficulty, and others in another. I think this is a two-way kind of list and should be thought of in that way. We may think, "Thank God that none of these things will separate Him from me," but we may also *pray*, "Please, God, don't let me fail You when these things come. May my love and trust be firm for You when Satan is trying to turn me away."

Who shall separate us from the love of Christ? shall tribulation, or distress, or persecution, or famine, or nakedness, or peril, or sword? As it is written, For thy sake we are killed all the day long; we are accounted as sheep for the slaughter. Nay, in all these things we are more than conquerors through him that loved us. [We are not separated from His love, and we can be conquerors in the battle which revolves around us when Satan is trying to separate God from our love.] For I am persuaded that neither death, nor life, nor angels, nor principalities, nor powers, nor things present, nor things to come, Nor height, nor depth, nor any other creature [created thing], shall be able to separate us from the love of God, which is in Christ Jesus our Lord.

Romans 8:35–39

Read this with Revelation 12:10, 11, as you think about my museum of important victories:

. . . for the accuser of our brethren is cast down, which accused them before our God day and night. And they overcame him by the blood of the Lamb, and by the word of their testimony; and they loved not their lives unto the death.

It will take us eons of time to wander through this building and to marvel over the power of the Blood of the Lamb in overcoming Satan's attacks.

We have read in the Bible the record of Job, so we won't be surprised to see *his* part shown there, and we know a good bit about Jeremiah's agonies and victories, as well as David's and Joseph's. We have our minds full of Paul's long list of afflictions, but we will be interested to find out just what his "thorn in the flesh" actually was. Remember that after that long list of terrible things which Paul had lived through (2 Corinthians 11), he tells us in chapter 12 of his own "last straw"? We learn of a fabulous experience he had, of being caught up into paradise and of hearing such things that created a danger of exalting him above measure. In other words, he could have become so excited and overwhelmed over the things he had heard concerning the future that he couldn't have gone on with what he needed to do next. This is followed by:

. . . there was given to me a thorn in the flesh, the messenger of Satan to buffet me, lest I should be exalted above measure. For this thing I besought the Lord thrice, that it might depart from me. And he said unto me, My grace is sufficient for thee: for my strength is made perfect in weakness. Most gladly therefore will I rather glory in my infirmities, that the power of Christ may rest upon me.

2 Corinthians 12:7–9

What is Paul saying? Paul, who had known such a succession of afflictions, is now troubled by some physical problem that is in the center of his thoughts and he cries out for relief. He asks God, not once but three times, to please heal him, to take this thing away, to give him relief, to change these circumstances in which he finds it difficult to go on. If his faith had been great enough, would he have had an affirmative answer? Do we dare suggest such a thing? Could no one else have prayed for him? Are we led to think that some formula is not being properly followed here, so that God has not heard the cry at all?

No, a thousand times no! One of the most central sentences God has given for our comfort and help in a variety of times of need was spoken to Paul right then. Even as we say, "Thank you, Job, for encouraging us in your way," we need to thank Paul for having another hard experience on top of all the rest. The very wonderful answer he received to prayer was God's clear statement of fact, which is at the same time a promise: "My grace is sufficient for thee, for my strength is made perfect in weakness." Paul's answer is not one of accepting "second best." There is no indication that this answer which Paul was given is inferior to healing. Quite the other way. Paul makes it clear that he accepts God's answer as an answer indeed, and helps us to recognize that there is miracle and wonder in being given sufficient grace to go on in the midst of an unchanging circumstance. It is as much a miracle as any immediate healing would be—this demonstration of the sufficiency of the grace of God, and the reality of His strength as "made perfect" in a variety of people, in many different kinds of weaknesses. In fact, to put it in another perspective, it is a much "harder" miracle. Paul goes on to speak in a crescendo of recognition that he is able to have a special "thing to do" in demonstrating the reality of God's strength being available in his weakness: "Therefore I take pleasure in infirmities, in reproaches, in necessities, in persecution, in distresses for Christ's sake, for when I am weak, then I am strong" (2 Corinthians 12:10).

Paul was in Rectangle A as he had victory in that place of the battle—where winning by faith was to be through experiencing the "sufficient grace" without the thorn being removed. This historical happening which people can look back to (and which will remain in the museum which portrays the variety of attacks which Satan has made) was a portion of Paul's living by faith, which could have been one of the most important portions of his life. We know from history that Paul was later martyred. It is said that he was beheaded, so he experienced something similar to what John and Betty Stam later experienced. However, it was different. There are no exactly duplicated experiences, because we are *individuals*. Paul's death as a martyr was his last moment of trusting God, and his victory was in experiencing God's strength in his weakness.

What price did Jesus pay for enabling us to have such victory—over and over again in a diversity of situations, afflictions, attacks, and sufferings? His own death on the cross and all the suffering that entailed? Yes, but stop a moment and go back to the Garden of Gethsemane. Jesus Himself experienced the struggle you and I face when we long to be rid of an affliction, a pain, an approaching tragedy, or a fear of the unknown that looms up in front of us. Jesus went through an honest and very real struggle—not some kind of dramatic acting—in the Garden before His approaching death on the cross. The price He paid for the victory He is able to give us over and over again, as we ask for His strength in our newest form of weakness, was the costly price of going through an agony which enables Him to know very completely what we are feeling, fearing, and longing to push away from us. "In all their affliction he was afflicted . . ." (Isaiah 63:9) has this detail of reality. He was afflicted at that time with the feelings we experience when God's answer to our prayer is to provide help to continue living through the pain and sorrow, rather than to remove the source of suffering. Jesus cried out—not once but three times—sweating not just drops of perspiration but blood, as He asked God the Father, "If it be possible, let this cup pass from me." I have paraphrased these words in another book, as Jesus asking, "Oh, Father, isn't there another way for them to be saved?" I believe that Jesus was there asking the question which comes to so many—*Are there several possibilities for salvation?* The answer that God the Father gave not only makes it conclusive that there is no other way: Jesus had to go on through the historic reality of the awful beatings and mockings, the taunting of men as He hung on the cross, as well as the physical pain that He had to bear. But the startling thing that should stop each of us in a sudden silence of amazement is that Jesus in the Garden experienced a shrinking back from suffering and made a request: "If it be possible, remove this 'cup,' this terrible affliction and suffering ahead of Me. Please take it away." And Jesus knew what it felt like to get a negative answer which pointed Him to the necessity of keeping on. He did this that we might go to heaven, have eternal life, be forgiven of our sins, but also so that we might be given victory through having access to His strength in our weakness when troubles assail us. He did this so that the answer to our cries could be: "My strength is made perfect in weakness . . . . My grace is sufficient for thee."

Think for a moment of the fact that Jesus not only had to continue on the path of agony and suffering without relief, but that in the middle of it He was accused of not being truly the Son of God because He did not come down from the cross. Those "If You are the Son of God, then prove it" tauntings were the worst kind of temptation we can imagine. Satan repeats himself constantly when he brings that kind of mocking in haunting forms with jeering faces or sarcastic voices, as human beings say to us: "How can a Christian have that kind of trouble? If you were really a child of God, you wouldn't have such a succession of difficulties!"—"You say you fainted at a baseball game and were carried off by policemen to a hospital for an emergency operation? How could a Christian have such an experience? Surely, if you were a child of God, He would take care of you in a more dignified way than that!"—"But you can't be a Christian mother if you have twins born so deformed at birth. You'd better find some way of proving you are a Christian. These sons should be healed!"—"Prove it! Prove it! Prove it!" say all kinds of voices in all sorts of forms. Had Jesus "proved it" that day by coming down from the cross and calling upon legions of angels to appear immediately, the men would have been thrown off their feet—true. But the result would have been a total loss of victory. The "proof" would have been the most gigantic *defeat* in all of history, affecting every single believer from Old Testament times until the end. The "proof" would have destroyed salvation and the final victory over all death.

Our individual attempts to slide out of what we are told we will be given strength in our weakness to live through—our individual temptations to "prove it" in our own way (or someone else's suggested way), rather than asking God for His definite will and then His strength to go on—will not bring as complete a defeat for all history as Jesus faced in His period of being jeered at and told to prove that He was the Son of God. However, each individual defeat—where we insist on proving our closeness to the Lord by some false "pushing aside" of the affliction, instead of willingly accepting His answer and His subsequent grace to go on—will also have far-reaching results in a negative way. We cannot live unto ourselves, nor die unto ourselves, and that includes every incident. We do cause ripples that never end. Thank God for forgiveness and for fresh starts daily, but the fact that He does remove our transgressions from us does not mean that we have not affected history. The approach to affliction is very delicate when seen in this light. It is important not to allow the loud noises of people (who clamor for us to "prove it" by having a miracle change the circumstances) drown out the answer that the Lord gives us as we pray in a field, under a tree, on a rock in the woods, by the shore as waves lap against pebbles, or in a closed closet in our little apartments. If His answer is to change the circumstances and give us relief, then we thank Him and worship Him who is "able to do all things." But if His answer is as it was to Paul, that the "thorn" is not to be removed, but that He will give His sufficient grace to go on, a moment at a time, then we are to answer as Jesus did, "Thy will be done." Or "Not as I will, but as Thou wilt." Which is the greatest victory?

The utter fairness of all this is that one day we will have more understanding of where the greatest battles were won, where the greatest miracles of victory took place. No one is shut out of having an outstanding moment in his or her life which can be recorded as a victory in that imaginary museum I picture—or in whatever way God records these proofs that the death of Christ was sufficient for every kind of affliction.

In 1950 Professor Wong came to study at Cambridge University before going back to continue teaching in his native China. It was the year the Communists were to take over and, although he did not realize it, he was not only never going to return to China in his lifetime, but he would never see his wife and daughter again, this side of heaven. It was a sudden shock when Professor Wong found he could not go back, and it was a terrible piece of news when Professor Wong was told that his wife and daughter had been captured and were in prison because of being Christians. A lifetime cannot be lived in a moment, or an hour, or a day. Professor Wong was to become Pastor Wong and start in London a tiny gathering of Chinese which was going to grow into a really strong church in that city. Here many Chinese were to be given the truth of what is the real meaning of life, that there is a Personal and Infinite God. They were to be born again, these Chinese who might never have heard the Gospel but for Pastor Wong. Out of that there was to flow forth a ministry among the Chinese in Paris and other European cities.

One time when I was talking to Pastor Wong, he said it had been twenty years since he had seen his wife. She was still in prison, and at very infrequent intervals he had some bits of news from her, with a lapse of years in between. Yet she was still trusting God, loving Him, and asking for His strength to go on, hour by hour. She could not be hindered from praying, nor could prison bars shut out the sufficient grace of God—sufficient for her in her physical pain and discomfort, her lack of enough food, her frustration at being shut away from life. The prison bars could not shut her away from repeated victories in the heavenly battle. Only God knows how many times she had a victory which counted and which defeated Satan and brought joy and glory to the Lord. I hope we will see an exhibit of Mrs. Wong's victories in the "museum in heaven." Who can know what a force she was in praying for her husband and all that he was doing (even if she could not have news of it all)? Who can know, except God, which was the greatest demonstration of faith? The exciting thing about God's fairness is that the dear Mrs. Wongs of history, shut away to oblivion in a tiny cell, can have a shining array of "battles trophies" and a long list of results from their prayer lives—results taking place thousands of miles away in the lives of people whom the Mrs. Wongs won't meet until they are introduced in heaven. It is so fair that the just God gives opportunities for important service for every one of His children in a strategic place and time.

Who was given the greatest opportunity in that particular twenty years? Pastor Wong—who was suffering loneliness, sorrow, and frustration at being exiled, and yet who went on and did day by day what God gave him strength to do there in London? Or Mrs. Wong who lived that same twenty years in prison, praying and perhaps even helping other prisoners, certainly winning victories by just loving and trusting God? No one of us can judge.

There is no time while we are still alive that we can say, "Now—I—nothing—can—do." And there is no way of measuring importance, since our measuring tapes are inadequate and twisted. Whatever your circumstance is right now, and whatever mine is, we have the immediate opportunity for defeating Satan and bringing glory to God. How? First, by whispering to Him, "I love You and trust You," and asking that He increase that trust and love. Second, by longing for an increase of truth within us as we say. "Not my will but Thine be done" in the middle of *this* period of exhaustion, *this* anxiety, *this* particular shock, *this* prison, *this* wheelchair, *this* set of bandages on our eyes, *this* kind of frustration, *this* pile of dirty dishes, *this* lack of understanding, *this* attack by friends, *this* disappointment, *this* accident, *this* unbearable, dull monotony, *this* unending succession of changes. Whatever the immediate "now" is made up of, it is not "after this is over" that we will have an opportunity to do something important for the Lord. Our place in Rectangle A—in the museum of victories—involves the immediate set of circumstances, in the "now."

5

The Museum's Other Section: Rectangle B

What about the other handkerchief under Mr. Van der Weiden's chin? Or the other rectangle I have pictured on cardboard or paper napkins, all with drawings of little stick figures? First, let me remind you that all the people in that second rectangle are the very same people as in the first. The second rectangle represents *all space* (geographic space identical with the space in the first rectangle)—and *all time* (the same historic period of time: from the first person who lived until the last person before the end of all that will take place before the final Judgment and the entrance into the new heavens and new earth). So Rectangle B squashes into our limited imagination all the same people in the same space and time, with God again represented by the large dot, and Satan (the small dot) once more standing before Him. What is different? Since you and I are in this rectangle, too, we need to know.

When Jesus died on the cross, the victory that He died to give included the staggering victory over the destroyed relationship between God and His people which occurred when Satan tempted Eve and Adam to believe him. Marvelous conversation took place in the cool of the evening in that perfect garden, with no plant blights, no curled-up leaves, no crawling green bugs making rose stems alive with ugliness, no places less perfect than other places. The air was filled with the sounds of gurgling brooks, soft whispers of leaves swaying in the breeze, and an endless variety of evening songbirds—making a symphony so gorgeous that we will hear nothing so flawless until we have our ears filled with what God is preparing for the new heavens and the new earth. The possibility of conversation with God was broken off at the time of the Fall, as were the background symphonies of perfect sound and beauty in an

90

unspoiled Creation. There will be no perfection until Jesus returns to give us our perfect bodies in the resurrection, and no flawless sight, sound, smell, taste, or feeling either, until God introduces us to the restored Creation in the Millennium, the marvels of His New Creation in the new heavens and the new earth. There will be a different level of communication in eternity, too, and we can only guess with feeble imagination as to the wonder of that communication. Now we "see through a glass, darkly." When your windows are streaked with dirt, paint, varnish, putty, or splashes of rain and dust, think of this as a fine illustration as you vigorously wash and scrape and polish to reach a contrast of sparkling clarity through which to see the view. However dirty the glass—whether a windowpane, spectacles, or the lenses of a pair of field glasses—nothing in the realm of dirty glass compared to clean glass could ever fully portray the contrast between either our imagination of the future (our present understanding of the wonders which God is promising us) and the reality of that one great day when we will step into the actual experiencing of it all forever. Although there will be no perfect conversation, communication, or talking with God until all the hindrances are forever removed, yet we are meant to experience something very real and tangible, very definite and practical, in restored communication *now,* on the basis of the victory which Jesus died to make possible. One of the results of our accepting Christ as our Saviour is being indwelt by the Holy Spirit; another is that we can have communication with the Heavenly Father at any time, through Jesus who died to make this possible and through the power of the indwelling Holy Spirit.

The second rectangle, Rectangle B, represents a victory that is just as important, but no more important than the first rectangle in demonstrating that we have been communicating with God. All the instances in history as shown in Rectangle A represent the occurrences, situations, problems, happenings, tribulation, troubles, illnesses, afflictions, persecutions, attacks, disappointments, crises, needs, fears, distresses, confusions, weaknesses, doubts, and worries when we cry out to God. These are the times when we verbalize our need, ask Him for help, pray for specific things, and plead with Him for a change or relief or immediate guidance and His answer comes: "Wait," or "Trust Me without a change," or "My grace is sufficient for you, and this is a time when I am going to answer you with My strength made perfect in your weakness, but there will be no change in the circumstances. This is your time to stand with Paul and Job."

Rectangle B represents the instances throughout all history where it is shown that the things in themselves were not impossible for God to change—for nothing ever took place that was too hard for God to answer His child's cry with a complete change in the circumstance. The second rectangle, as I imagine it, is also a "full cup of victory." The second rectangle demonstrates that the victory of Christ on the cross was sufficient to open the way into God's presence for His children, with changes taking place in history as a result of the requests made. The death of Christ was sufficient victory over the broken communication between God and His people so as to open the way into the presence of the Holy of Holies for salvation through eternity, and also to open the way for a moment-by-moment relationship between God and His people. That relationship includes answers to requests. There is no promise that *all* our requests are to be answered by a change in the circumstances, because the Bible so very fairly gives us a balanced understanding that the faith which asks and receives the answer of "sufficient grace" to go on without a change is no greater than the faith which asks and receives an answer whereby mountains are removed and cast into the sea. There are to be answers to prayer which demonstrate that a child of the Living God, a sheep of His pasture, a servant of His vineyards, a slave of His household, a friend of His Son, and a fellow heir of His Son has real *access* to God the Father and to His power to do all things.

I believe that there is nothing in the first rectangle that has been lived through in the lives of God's people—and has demonstrated to Satan that Christ's victory is complete in history—which will not have its counterpart in the second rectangle, or in the other section of the museum. I believe that, wherever God can point out to Satan one child of His being stoned and dying with unbroken love for Him, He can point out another being stoned with as many stones and yet being protected from dying in answer to prayer. When God can point out to Satan one woman still trusting Him during fifteen years of suffering violence at the hands of an alcoholic husband, He can point out another just as "impossible" a case where the man has been changed, born again, and become a new creature in Christ Jesus, living a different life altogether. Where one has died of an incurable disease, God can point out another who has been healed. God can point to Paul's thorn in the flesh and his ability to continue with that because of the sufficiency of grace given him. Very likely, God can also point to the same disability which was healed for someone living at the same time as Paul (perhaps because Paul was instrumental in praying for him).

It seems to me that there will be—not in any one life but in the combination of all that has taken place in history in answer to prayer—an historic incident which will demonstrate in actuality, not in theory, that the death of Christ gave complete victory: "If you ask *anything* in My name, I will do it." I don't believe that the "anything" means for each of us as individuals that *all* our answers will be a change of circumstance, and that *none* of our answers will be the "sufficient grace" to go on without that change. But I do believe that there will be a literal fulfillment of the "anything" in the total collection of all the answered prayers in all space and time. It will be demonstrated that, in the total collection of incidents throughout all the eons of history's centuries in all of our lives (we who are the people of God and who have looked to Him, feebly and imperfectly, but with a measure of faith and trust and love) Satan will be defeated by *some* life at *every* place where his devices have been attempted, at times with the most horrific tortures and most ghastly combinations of events. Satan's traps have ensnared each of us at some spot, his prison bars have enclosed us at some moment, and his disguise as an "angel of light" has succeeded at some point in the personal histories of each of God's flock—but Satan can show no total victory! The total victory will be Christ's, and I think the museum will display that victory in two parallel sections—parallel as to incidents. I do not mean that any one of us will have a life of total answers to prayer in positive and exciting changes coming, or that any other one of us will have a life that will be totally full of the seemingly negative answers of "Wait!" or "My grace is sufficient." I believe that each life has a different combination of answers, some in each section of the museum, some in each rectangle.

Then came the word of the Lord unto Jeremiah, saying, Behold, I am the Lord, the God of all flesh: is there any thing too hard for me?

Jeremiah 32:26, 27

[Jeremiah prayed:] Ah Lord God! behold, thou hast made the heaven and the earth by thy great power and stretched out arm, and there is nothing too hard for thee.

Jeremiah 32:17

Moreover the word of the Lord came unto Jeremiah the second time, while he was yet shut up in the court of the prison, saying, Thus saith the Lord the maker thereof, the Lord that formed it, to establish it; the Lord is his name; Call unto me, and I will answer thee, and shew thee great and mighty things, which thou knowest not.

Jeremiah 33:1–3

There was no one who knew more affliction than Jeremiah, no one who had a harder period of history in which to proclaim truth to scoffers and those who physically and in every other way tried to squash and blot out both the man and the message. But it is God's words to Jeremiah (and to us through Jeremiah) which give us courage to ask the "anything" which Jesus later commands us to ask in His name. Jeremiah trusted the Lord, but not only for future answers to promises such as God gave him in 33:10, 11:

Thus saith the Lord; Again there shall be heard in this place, which ye say shall be desolate without man and without beast . . . The voice of joy, and the voice of gladness, the voice of the bridegroom, and the voice of the bride, the voice of them that shall say, Praise the Lord of hosts: for the Lord is good; for his mercy endureth for ever: and of them that shall bring the sacrifice of praise into the house of the Lord. For I will cause to return the captivity of the land, as at the first, saith the Lord.

Jeremiah was not to see this in his lifetime, but he believed it to be true and expected the victory of the Lord in this "impossible situation" that was surrounding him at that time.

It was after this bright hope for tomorrow which Jeremiah had been given and believed, and looked forward to, that this description is given: "Then took they Jeremiah, and cast him into the dungeon of Malchiah the son of Hammelech, that was in the court of the prison: and they let down Jeremiah with cords. And in the dungeon there was no water, but mire: so Jeremiah sunk in the mire" (38:6). How vivid and bright do you suppose Jeremiah's hope was there in the mire—icky, gucky mud—with no food and no drinking water and pain and discomfort which must have been what we would call "unbearable"? Come to Lamentations that we may experience something of Jeremiah's struggle *along with him:*

> I am the man that hath seen affliction by the rod of his wrath. He hath led me, and brought me into darkness, but not into light. Surely against me is he turned; he turneth his hand against me all the day. My flesh and my skin hath he made old; he hath broken my bones.
>
> Lamentations 3:1–4

Dear Jeremiah was in the place of Job—despondent and suffering the physical pain of being in that horrible place and the desolate feeling of being deserted. Here there is real struggle which is akin to the kind of struggle which Jesus was later to have in the Garden of Gethsemane. Agony suffered and the temptation to give in to it are very real parts of the battle. Of course, there would be no result to compare with what would have been the result of Jesus' turning away from the cross when He agonized there in the Garden, but Satan's fury against God is nevertheless unleashed against God's people throughout the entire battle. It is a conflict which has no lull. Jeremiah was sorely tempted to give up. Read on:

> And thou hast removed my soul far off from peace: I forgat prosperity. [Have you ever felt this way? So low you can't even remember the good times, so full of struggle you can't remember the peaceful feelings? So full of hard days that you can't remember what prosperity was like?] And I said, My strength and my hope is perished from the Lord: [When you feel as if your situation is never going to change, and there seems to be no crack in the darkness, and your hope is like a flame which is flickering with an "almost out" kind of flicker, then you can relate to Jeremiah in his feelings in the dungeon, almost buried in mire.] Remembering mine affliction and my misery, the wormwood and the gall. My soul hath them still in remembrance, and is humbled in me.
>
> Lamentations 3:17–20

Are you discouraged about your answers to prayer ever liberating you or taking you away from the place or the thing that has you "down"? Are you worrying that perhaps you don't even belong to the Lord because of your affliction? Do you think that your up-and-down feelings show such an instability that you can't properly have a place among the Lord's servants or His people through the ages? Read Jeremiah's record of struggle, and remember that this is an inside sharing of his desperately difficult place as a prophet. Was he living in a bubble which protected him from affliction as he gave his message and did his work? Because he was in God's will did he live a "charmed life" without affliction?

Who was Jeremiah? He was one of the greatest figures in the whole of biblical history. His work was to make truth known to a sinful and stubborn people, misled by all kinds of false prophets and heathen religions which infiltrated their thinking and actions. He was witness to their doom! He stood alone in circumstances of a heartbreaking variety, faithfully and without flinching declaring the Word of God—although the words contained a prophecy of crushing judgment. It was to Jeremiah that God said: "Before I formed thee in the belly I knew thee; and before thou camest out of the womb I sanctified thee, and ordained thee a prophet unto the nations" (Jeremiah 1:5). It was Jeremiah who then replied that he could not speak! Jeremiah drew back and said that he was only a child. And it was to Jeremiah that God declared that he should go to all the people to whom God would send him, and that he should speak everything that God told him to speak. God told Jeremiah not to be afraid of the faces of the people, because He, God, would deliver him. God also promised to put His words into Jeremiah's mouth.

And then where was Jeremiah? Struggling fearfully in the dungeon. Can't you see the battle? Can't you feel the strength of Satan's attack? "Where are all those promises now, Jeremiah?" was certainly the question with which Satan tempted the man. And we are allowed to discover that Jeremiah had his downs as well as ups. We are to be comforted because God shows us so frankly what affliction is like. And then we are to be comforted by the honest picture of what took place in the worst kind of time, inwardly and outwardly. No change had come in the circumstances. Jeremiah was still in the hard place, but listen to him now in the very next sentence he spoke:

> This I recall to my mind, therefore have I hope. [Ah, something had just stirred in his memory—all the things which God had told him before, and the experiences of how God had met his needs in the past. Suddenly Jeremiah was reviewing the wonder of the sufficient grace of God, rather than the awful-

ness of his own condition and his own despair. He was recalling the wonder of who God is—and how great His power and compassion.] It is of the Lord's mercies that we are not consumed, because his compassions fail not. They are new every morning: great is thy faithfulness.

Lamentations 3:21–23

Next time you lustily sing this hymn in church or conference—"Great is Thy faithfulness, Great is Thy faithfulness, Morning by morning new mercies I see"—remember that it was what Jeremiah said to the Lord, right after he had been expressing his despair and depression, and while he was still in the same unchanging affliction. We are apt to sing that hymn and think of fresh dew on the morning grass or rose garden (or even of beautiful food spread on a snowy-white linen cloth), without remembering that Jeremiah gave the Lord this praise after he had just been talking about being desolate and being the laughingstock of the people as they tortured him. It was both the memory of the past and the hope for the future that made Jeremiah able to say those lilting words of praise to the Lord. It was trust in the Lord, kindled by rethinking who He is, and faith in the ultimate victory of the Lord that enabled Jeremiah to break out into song, somewhat in the way Paul and Silas did while they were in prison in Philippi. Listen to the bubbling forth of the words of praise and trust which brought joy and glory to the Lord in the midst of the battle, as Jeremiah continues:

The Lord is my portion, saith my soul: therefore will I hope in him. The Lord is good unto them that wait for him, to the soul that seeketh him. It is good that a man should both hope and quietly wait for the salvation of the Lord . . . . For the Lord will not cast off for ever: But though he cause grief, yet will he have compassion according to the multitude of his mercies. For he doth not afflict willingly nor grieve the children of men.

Lamentations 3:24–26, 31–33

And then later in the same chapter we have Jeremiah's prayer in the dungeon, and his declaration that God answered him:

They have cut off my life in the dungeon, and cast a stone upon me. Waters flowed over my head; then I said, I am cut off. I called upon thy name, O Lord, out of the low dungeon. Thou hast heard my voice: hide not thine ear at my breathing, at my cry. Thou drawest near in the day that I called upon thee: thou saidst, Fear not. O Lord, thou hast pleaded the causes of my soul; thou hast redeemed my life.

Lamentations 3:53–58

Now we go back to the Book of Jeremiah and find that his prayer *was* answered, and in Jeremiah 38:10 we find that the king ordered thirty men to rescue Jeremiah from the dungeon before he died. "And Ebedmelech the Ethiopian said unto Jeremiah, Put now these old cast clouts and rotten rags under thine armholes under the cords. And Jeremiah did so. So they drew up Jeremiah with cords, and took him up out of the dungeon: and Jeremiah remained in the court of the prison" (vv. 12, 13).

Jeremiah, as well as Paul, knew many experiences of answered prayer and of God's clear direction as to where to go and what to say. Certainly, if we think of the two sections of the museum—the two rectangles—Jeremiah would have many "exhibits" in both. But his tremendous answers to prayer never meant the end of affliction for the rest of his life. After being lifted out of the dungeon, Jeremiah was in the court of the prison until the fall of Jerusalem, and then he was carried off to Egypt. Tradition tells us that he was finally martyred in Egypt and that his experience of martyrdom was that of being sawn in half as he was placed in a hollow log. Hebrews 11:37 tells us: "They were stoned, they were sawn asunder . . . ." Perhaps Jeremiah was one of those being referred to there, even as Stephen who was stoned. The reason the eleventh chapter of Hebrews groups the miracles of answered prayer—as God reaches down in space and history to reply to the requests of His people and as they display miracles of love and trust for Him during their martyrdom—is that they are equally important and a balancing of both is needed to make up an historically complete victory.

The Triune God—Father, Son, and Holy Spirit—has given sufficient explanation about His majesty, power, might, infiniteness, and wisdom to help us have the courage to take action on the basis of His promises and commands. As human beings, we are made in His image so that we can think and understand a great diversity of ideas in our minds and experience the meaning of choice and creativity. Likewise, we know what love means (in that it causes us to prefer doing something for someone else rather than for self) and what communication means, as we search for vocabulary to make ideas take a form which can be transformed to the thinking of another person. Thus God not only told Jeremiah that nothing was too hard for Him, but He made this fact clear, over and over again throughout His Word:

We will not hide . . . from their children, shewing to the generation to come the praises of the Lord and his strength, and his wonderful works that he hath done.

Psalms 78:4

Ascribe ye strength unto God: his excellency is over Israel, and his strength is in the clouds.

Psalms 68:34

The Creator of the Universe is able to do all things. Jesus rebuked the Pharisees for being so proud of their birth by saying, "And think not to say within yourselves, We have Abraham to our father: for I say unto you, that God is able of these stones to raise up children unto Abraham" (Matthew 3:9). And when blind men came to Jesus, asking to be healed, Jesus asked: "Believe ye that I am able to do this?" (Matthew 9:28). In Romans 4:20, 21, we are reminded that Abraham truly believed that nothing was impossible to God, and he trusted God with a real measure of faith which God calls *strong.* "He staggered not [that is, Abraham] at the promise of God through unbelief; but was strong in faith, giving glory to God; And being fully persuaded that, what he had promised, he was able also to perform."

When the disciples came to Jesus and asked why they had not been able to cast the demon out of a child who was being troubled, Jesus answered: "Because of your unbelief [or little faith]: for verily I say unto you, If ye have faith as a grain of mustard seed, ye shall say unto this mountain, Remove hence to yonder place; and it shall remove; and nothing shall be impossible unto you" (Matthew 17:20). How can *nothing be impossible* to any human being? Only in one way and at specific moments for each individual—but with a totalness through history. It seems to me that the "anything" we are to ask is very much connected with the "nothing shall be impossible to you" in the area of prayer. There is nothing a human being cannot ask of God. God is able to reply to any kind of prayer. However, as we read the whole Bible, we see that not every prayer of God's greatest giants of faith was answered. My deep comfort in this area of wondering why is that God has not promised that any one of us will have a life of ease and perfection. Therefore, the

"anything," I feel, must mean the reality that "anything" is answered in some instance in some life in history, making a total of
answered prayer that will fill that section of the museum.

When Jesus was explaining to the disciples the case of the rich
young ruler who turned away from God because he had so much
wealth, he added that riches make it harder to enter into the Kingdom of God. The disciples asked with deep agony (I feel sure):
"Who then can be saved?" Jesus answered: "With men this is
impossible; but with God all things are possible" (*see* Matthew
19:25, 26). This striking statement demonstrates so clearly that
there are no "bars"—of poverty or wealth, of ignorance or the
wrong kind of education, of sickness or health—which might make
it impossible for a human being to come to the reality of the new
birth. Couple this with the stated fact that God has also demonstrated in physical birth that the physical "impossibilities" are no
barrier to Him. Abraham and Sarah's case of having their promised
son after their bodies were "too old" has its similar parallel in New
Testament times, as Zacharias and Elisabeth experienced the marvelous miracle of giving birth to John the Baptist. Elisabeth, prepared by the "impossibility" which had taken place in her own
body, spoke to Mary with utter belief and acceptance of what had
happened in Mary's body and praised God in this belief by calling
Mary "the mother of my Lord." It was the angel who told Mary that
she should consider that her cousin Elisabeth was going to have a
baby in her old age—and that the God who could do this could also
perform the most unique miracle of having Mary bear the baby who
would be Jesus, without a human father. For Mary, the Virgin Birth
was more difficult to believe than for anyone. Yet to her the statement was made by the angel, which gave her the kind of recognition
of who God is and helped her to bow her head in belief and acceptance of the truth of what would take place. The angel said, "For
with God nothing shall be impossible. And Mary said, Behold the
handmaid of the Lord; be it unto me according to thy word. And the
angel departed from her" (Luke 1:37, 38).

What has all this to do with prayer and with taking seriously the
promises concerning prayer? *Everything.* It is the God of the impossible, the Creator of the Universe who is able to do everything, who
has said:

> Ask, and it shall be given you; seek, and ye shall find; knock,
> and it shall be opened unto you: For every one that asketh

receiveth; and he that seeketh findeth; and to him that knock-
eth it shall be opened. Or what man is there of you, whom if his
son ask bread, will he give him a stone? Or if he ask a fish, will
he give him a serpent? If ye then, being evil, know how to give
good gifts unto your children, how much more shall your
Father which is in heaven give good things to them that ask
him?

Matthew 7:7–11

Verily, verily, I say unto you, He that believeth on me, the
works that I do shall he do also: and greater works than these
shall he do; because I go unto my Father. And whatsoever ye
shall ask in my name, that will I do, that the Father may be
glorified in the Son. If ye shall ask anything in my name, I will
do it.

John 14:12–14

The picture being given us is that when we come into the family
of the Living God through the new birth, by accepting what Christ
accomplished in His death on the cross in our place—as He took
our sins upon Himself and became our substitute—then a part of
what He paid for was a moment-by-moment access for us to the
Infinite God. Each of us has been given another portion in the fabric
of history which our individual thread is meant to weave. We are not
only to affect history in the geographic spot where we are meant to
be in God's plan, and to have victory in the heavenly battle as we
trust God in the midst of affliction and persecution right up to martyrdom, but we are to be having results two feet away from us in
prayer—and also two thousand miles away. It is also a part of the
battle that we "make our requests known" in the faith that God will
hear and can and will answer our "intercession," as we take our
places as a nation of priests interceding for all those who are not part
of the people of God. Among the many things that prayer is (and it
would take a separate book to write about prayer with any degree of
fullness), it is a means of fulfilling the victory which I have tried to
picture in those two rectangles. I believe that, at some point in
history in some individual life, any kind of request could be pointed
out as being answered. The "whatsoever ye shall ask in my
name . . ." will have practical, historic proof as having been done.
The total fabric will show this, or the complete museum will exhibit
it, or history related in some fashion will make it complete.

Turning back to the eleventh chapter of Hebrews, we find that there is something that is labeled "impossible" for us: "But without faith it is impossible to please him [God]: for he that cometh to God must believe that he is, and that he is a rewarder of them that diligently seek him" (Hebrews 11:6). It is after this that a record is given of the many who did believe that God existed and that He would answer their requests and fulfill their needs—Noah, Abraham, Isaac, and so on. Each one exhibited faith not only in prayer but by doing things based on believing in God. It is impossible to please God without caring about living by faith with some degree of reality. Habakkuk states this clearly: ". . . but the just shall live by his faith" (2:4). "Living by faith" means living with one's communication with the Lord as a very central portion of life. It is impossible to live with a human being with any degree of harmony without having communication. One asks concerning both big and little things, discusses, and makes decisions. If we have a Heavenly Father who is real to us and our relationship is growing, we talk about many things to Him—and, among other things, we make specific requests. Our specific requests and His direct answers are to be a portion, a part, an historic succession of happenings, proving the reality of the victory of Christ on the cross, which opened the way for human beings into the presence of God. Our answers to prayer are to fulfill historically the prophecy that Jesus made when He said: ". . . hitherto ye shall ask in my name."

In what realm can one expect answers to prayer? In *all* realms. God cares about His people as individuals and has a gentle, tender love for us. We are told that some of His answers are that our "joy might be full" and "that the Father may be glorified in the Son." There is no doubt that the people of God are meant to have answers to prayer. There is no doubt that we are meant to pray, believing that He is able to answer. We should have a growing history—like a trail of footsteps behind us in an unbroken field of snow—which will bring to our minds that great reality which Jeremiah was reminded of as he looked back and spoke forth with great conviction: "Great is thy faithfulness . . . ." Likewise did the faithful ones among the children of Israel look back and see in their memories the turning back of the Red Sea and the marvel of the manna which fell every day to feed them. As the early church people were suffering in prison, they could thank God with vivid memory for Peter's release from prison, as well as the release of

Paul and Silas by an earthquake. There should be a personal trail behind us—like wet footprints on the sand, or a line of grass clippings which slip out of our grasp as we carry them along a path, or ski marks on unbroken snow down a mountainside. We should be able to look back and gain courage to go on because of the trail of answered prayer. It should be a very definite part of the fabric of life.

It is wrong to shrug off the possibility that specific and positive answers to prayer are an expected part of the Christian's life, just as it is wrong to dismiss the reality that God's grace and strength are able to be given with adequate "sufficiency" to really make it possible to go on despite affliction. Both victories are meant to be gathered in a complete whole to defeat Satan with finality, as he attempts to put wedges between us and our dear Father. It is tragic to watch the ugliness of someone trying to turn a son or daughter against a good and loving father or mother, but what Satan is doing is far worse—as he attempts to "cool off" the relationship between the Heavenly Father and His children.

The constant temptation that comes to human beings is to try to be more than "creatures." People want to understand as much as God does, and (although we don't define it that way) the attitude of "I am only a finite, weak, sinful human being, and God is perfect and all-wise and has His sovereign plan, so there is no use praying . . ." is a turning away from what God has commanded—just because we lack an infinite understanding. We are meant to obey His commands and admonitions to "ask, " as much as we obey His other commands. When we are told specifically not to worry but to make our requests known, it is something which enters into our bedrooms at night—as we lie in the dark with a whirl of indecision about some crisis or change in our lives, or a fear that surrounds our thoughts about our children or someone else who matters very much to us. The command is to literally or figuratively get down on our knees and begin unfolding it all to the Lord, making specific requests as He has told us to do. Why? Isn't He able to do things without our asking? One clear reason, it seems to me, is that communication with God was important enough for Jesus to die to make it possible, and the Bible makes it clear that it is important to have it take place day by day in the "now" of our lives. We are not to sit and talk half the night about whether or not prayer is worthwhile. We are to talk directly to the One who told us to ask Him. "Ye have not because ye ask not" is not a meaningless sentence. It is meant to prod us into moment-by-moment communication in the areas of spiritual and intellectual needs, psychological and emotional needs, physical needs, the need for help in our work or creativity, the need for guidance, the need for planting and tending a crop and harvesting it—in our local gardens and farms, as well as in the realm of teaching or answering questions in the "gardens" which consist of people. We are meant to be asking for strength to go on, not just once in a while but throughout all our days.

There can be no closeness to the Lord without the two-way communication which is available by listening to Him as His Word speaks chapter by chapter to us in our reading of several places in the Bible—especially when we intersperse our reading with prayer. We come to know the Lord as we spend time with Him. However, nothing is a more real knowledge that we have had contact than the answers that come to our prayers. Sitting in a hospital room beside a son or daughter, a sister or brother, a mother or father, or an aunt or uncle or cousin whom we love, we wait, do bits of nursing care, grow weary and discouraged—we read: "Hast thou not known? hast thou not heard, that the everlasting God, the Lord, the Creator of the ends of the earth, fainteth not, neither is weary? there is no searching of his understanding" (Isaiah 40:28). Right there we can stop and talk to the Lord, the Creator, and say: *Forgive me for trying to go too far in searching Your understanding. Forgive me for trying to be more than a creature and for forgetting that You are the Creator and that I need to agree actively and consciously that You are God indeed.* Perhaps, if we remember, we will add these words from Psalms 147:5 to our prayer: *Great is our Lord, and of great power: his understanding is infinite.* We go on to tell the Lord that we are sorry for trying to approximate His infinite understanding and thank Him for letting us know the difference.

Then we might read on in Isaiah: "He giveth power to the faint; and to them that have no might he increaseth strength" (40:29). We reply to this by saying something like this: *Oh, thank You, God, for such a description of me. I am faint right now, and right now I have no might. Thank You for saying that I'm the kind of person to whom You give power and strength. Right now is when I need it so badly.*

We continue in Isaiah: "Even the youths shall faint and be weary, and the young men shall utterly fail . . . ." And we respond: *Oh, Heavenly Father, thank You for reminding us that youth is not the answer, that even Olympic runners have fatigue, that very young people can also grow physically, psychologically, and emotionally weary. Thank You for not putting us into an age category in this promise, but only into the category of being finite human beings. Thank You—that I fit in here.*

Then we read with growing excitement or hope or eagerness (or interest, at the very least) and come to the climax: "But they that wait upon the Lord shall renew their strength; they shall mount up with wings as eagles; they shall run, and not be weary; and they shall walk, and not faint" (v. 31). We plead: *Please, Lord, in whatever sense You mean us to "wait upon" You, let me right now have some "mustard seed" measure of sincerely and honestly waiting. I know I can't do it perfectly, but I am sure You have given this conditioned promise for us to have as a frequent help in our lives. Right now I am waiting upon You in the context of Your Word, asking that You will give me renewed strength to go on.*

What does the "going on" consist of, there in the hospital room? It may be a husband's need for a new surge of alertness and energy to continue rubbing his wife's back and encouraging her during her long labor while they are together in a natural-childbirth situation, awaiting the birth of their baby. At the bedside of a husband and father dying of a stroke, it may be the wife's, daughter's, and son's needs for renewed strength to keep watching the breathing and being aware of when a nurse or doctor might need to be called. It may be a dear friend who is sitting there with a piece of ice wrapped in cloth, gently moistening the lips of a loved one whose mouth is dry and lips are cracked after coming out of anesthesia. The ministering friend may be longing not to faint from exhaustion and hoping to be enabled to "stick it through" as long as needed.

However, there are a million different combinations of situations in a lifetime when these four precious verses can be combined with other verses and discussed with the Lord, can be accepted as true, can be the encouragement to you and to me of the "just who live by faith" in practical reality. One may feel faint and have a roaring headache just before scheduled to step out on a platform in front of several thousand people—and one can then kneel on the dusty floor of the backstage drabness and call upon the Lord in remembrance of what He has said in Isaiah. One may be just about to drop from a pain in the neck and a dizziness, deciding to relax in bed for an hour or so, when the doorbell or phone rings and it is someone in deep need, from whom one cannot turn away. What to do? Get the Bible and read the words in black and white once more, saying honestly: *I can't, Lord, but You have said that You can do it through me. You told Jeremiah that You would give him the words. Please put the words in my mouth for this one person, but it must be along with Your renewing my strength, so that I can feel the surge of air rush past me as I "fly with eagle wings."* Perhaps you aren't imaginative enough to think of yourself "flying" in any form whatsoever as you sit in one spot, speak to a crowd, or talk to one person. But within the limits of our own personalities, we visualize the wonder of what God—He who is able to do all things, who has said that nothing is impossible to Him—can do to fulfill His own promise.

Is it just in life's crisis moments that we can ask for His strength? In a hospital, before crowds, or talking to someone who has just had a death in the family or a sister in prison because of a drug charge? No. Hour by hour and day by day, we are the children of a Father who has told us to call upon Him. It is not just Israel or Isaiah or some other outstanding prophet to whom God is talking when He says: "Fear thou not; for I am with thee; be not dismayed; for I am thy God. I will strengthen thee; yea, I will uphold thee with the right hand of my righteousness" (Isaiah 41:10).

Day by day—when we have a drastically crushing load at the office or problems that seem to have no solution in our business; a crop to bring in from the fields or garden and then vegetables that need freezing far into the night before they spoil, or jelly or jam to be made before the fruit goes moldy; a broken pile of glass to sweep up and then carefully gather in wet newspapers, more on-the-knees care to get all the slivers in wet paper towels; a sick child who gets us up in the night when we are too tired to even finish the day's work before going to bed; noises shattering the air during our period of needed rest; a blast coming at us from a critic whom we had thought of as an understanding friend; dropping the grocery bag, leaving the most expensive bottles broken and the other things a soggy mess; in little and big situations of dismay and dismal awareness of our weakness and inadequacy for taking one more step in life—we can speak to the Lord, enter His presence in the context not of our imaginations but of His Word, and bring our need of having His strength given us in the immediate situation.

Does all this mean that we who are Christians are to fly six feet above the ground with perfect ease? A thousand times no! My attempt is to show the battle and the *balance* within the battle, as Rectangle B displays instances of answered prayer.

There will be, I believe, answers to prayer in the realm of the provision of material things, such as the entire story of George Muller's work makes clear, as well as the life and work of Hudson Taylor and Amy Carmichael. The L'Abri story tells some instances of our own answered prayer in the material realm through the first years. Of course, all these things are just tiny dots in the entire history of God's people, and all these answered prayers will be gathered into a whole. We are told that prayer itself is as the evening incense to God. When God's children pray, there is a sweet odor that is pleasing to Him, describable as whiffs of fragrance. Of course, prayer is to be worship, adoration, an expression of thanksgiving and love. Of course, prayer is to contain details about what we marvel about in God's Creation and how appreciative we are of His love and compassion. This is not a book on prayer, so all this is just a brief introduction to what prayer involves. However, as we think about the victory which Jesus died to make possible, we realize that prayer and answers are involved in *both* rectangles. The first involves prayer through which we receive the "sufficient grace" to continue with nothing outwardly changing. The second involves prayer which receives an answer which is exactly what has been pleaded for, asked for, called for, requested. It seems to me that the wide diversity of answers to prayer will include people being released from prison or taken down alive from crosses, the fire going out at the stake, the disease healed, guidance given clearly in the midst of utter darkness, a government's inner offices coming to a change of decision, as well as a diversity of provision of material needs. And through it all, in addition to the total victory which is being fulfilled, the trust and faith and love that brings God's children to the place of asking with confidence is to Him a joy, a sweet-smelling fragrance.

When Elijah asked that God send down the fire upon the altar on Mount Carmel—so that the surrounding Baal worshipers and the prophets of Baal could see it take place in response to Elijah's prayer—the desire, the motive, and the reason for Elijah's request was not a desire to point to himself as outstanding, but: "Hear me, O Lord, hear me, *that this people may know that thou art the Lord God,* and that thou hast turned their heart back again. Then the fire of the Lord fell . . ." (1 Kings 18:37, 38).

It really would be wrong to talk about the whole rectangle of answered prayer without making sure we realize that the motive is important, among other factors. We need to ask God to help us to really want His glory, His victory, and His existence to be known. We need to honestly want people to come to discover how great God is and how wonderful He is. We need to not just sing: "Wonderful Counselor, the Mighty God, the King of kings, the Prince of Peace . . ." but to pray that the gorgeous attributes of the Living God may somehow be made known to others touched by the ripples of our lives. So we pray for relief, restoration of energy to meet a need, material provision, endurance to keep on, a help in not flinching, and willingness to do His will, because we want others to get a glimpse of the wonder of our lovely Lord, who is "chiefest among ten thousand," dazzling in His glory.

Return a moment to Isaiah:

> When the poor and needy seek water, and there is none, and their tongue faileth for thirst, I the Lord will hear them, I the God of Israel will not forsake them. I will open rivers in high places, and fountains in the midst of the valleys: I will make the wilderness a pool of water, and the dry land springs of water. I will plant in the wilderness the cedar, the shittah tree, and the myrtle, and the oil tree; I will set in the desert the fir tree, and the pine, and the box tree together: That they may see, and know, and consider, and understand together, that the hand of the Lord hath done this, and the Holy One of Israel hath created it.
>
> Isaiah 41:17–20

Whether or not you believe this passage will be literally fulfilled in Israel in the Millennium, certainly we who are in the family of the Living God, the Holy One of Israel, the Master of the Universe, are to base something of our present life on God's promise to *hear* and to *do in reply* that which will enable people (all human beings who care to observe) to see, to know, to consider, and to understand together that the hand of the Lord has done "this"—and the "this" is to cover the "anything" which Jesus promises we can ask in His name and "receive."

We each have an individual part in both rectangles. We each need to be given the help of the Lord to recognize the "sufficient grace" and to not complain against Him or compare our lot with others. We also need to turn away from that peculiar form of bitterness and unbelief which is mingled with the "What's the use of praying?" kind of attitude. We will be tempted by Satan in his peculiar type of accusation which can take two forms. (Of course, Satan tempts in a diversity of other ways, also.) *Form one* is an attempt, as in the case of Job, to cause us to complain against God or even to curse Him and turn away from Him because of our deluge of afflictions. *Form two* is to tempt us to take an academic view of prayer, excusing ourselves, by hiding behind God's sovereignty, from ever asking anything in the wide areas God has specifically told us to ask—with faith as a grain of mustard seed and expecting changes in history as titanic as the removal of mountains. Both attacks are against the victory of Christ's sacrificial death— attempts by Satan to spoil, mar, devastate, and vandalize the perfection of Christ's victory. And marvel of all marvels—without understanding how it could be—*we matter in the battle!* We matter to God, moment by moment, day by day, and through the months and years in the hidden places of our own thoughts or our own tiny cave or tent or room or in the places where we stand in confrontation as Elijah did. We matter to Him as individual human beings, created in His image. He loves us enough to have planned the salvation which involved His knowing what affliction meant within the Trinity. He treats us fairly by letting us know as much as we could possibly understand with our finite minds as to what suffering is all about, and He asks us to remember that He is God and to act on that fact practically, not just in theological discussion.

"This people have I formed for myself; they shall shew forth my praise" (Isaiah 43:21) should be combined with Paul's prayer in Ephesians 3:14–21:

> For this cause I bow my knees [pray] unto the Father of our Lord Jesus Christ, Of whom the whole family in heaven and earth is named, That he would grant you, according to the riches of his glory, to be strengthened with might by his Spirit in the inner man; That Christ may dwell in your hearts by faith; that ye, being rooted and grounded in love, May be able to comprehend with all saints what is the breadth, and length, and height; And to know the love of Christ, which passeth knowledge, that ye might be filled with all the fulness of God. Now unto him that is able to do exceedingly abundantly above all that we ask or think, according to the power that worketh in us,

Unto him be glory in the church by Christ Jesus throughout all ages, world without end. Amen.

Don't read that over and say, "Oh, yes, that is a benediction I've heard many times." Think of the fabulous tie-up given there. This Paul, who had experienced so much affliction that we almost faint thinking about it, was making clear that he had had victories "in both rectangles" and was praying for the dear flock of Christians in the Ephesian church and for us, too, as their descendants, that we would be strengthened. For what? For both kinds of answers to prayer—the kind that is given when we need more and more of the "sufficient grace" to go on breathing without being bitter, and the kind that makes people see that the God to whom we have prayed is *able* to do far, far more than we have asked, that He is able to answer by filling our pail or cup with an overflowing answer. Paul is not giving just a fancy, high-sounding benediction; he is giving a tremendous summary which God means us to have for our courage. Put out your hand and grab hold. We aren't going to drown! Instance by instance, there is eternal purpose, and whatever is going on counts and matters in a perspective beyond ours . . . .

There in the hospital room, as I finished telling him the truth of the rectangles, I felt that Mr. Van der Weiden grew quieter and that he had appreciated the fact that he *still* had something to do that was important. As for myself, after talking to him in that urgent situation, where there was such a short time for understanding and acting upon that understanding, I realized that I had learned something very central to my own living. Since then, it has seemed that my need to relate this to others multiplied. This is how God works. He always gives something for one person as if no one else existed—and then allows it to become known by multitudes who need the same help.

6

Cracked Teapots

In the Word of God, we are often compared to clay. As we watch the potter work—molding, whirling the wheel and throwing his pots and dishes, shaping, changing, firing—there is much to think about. The verse that has been a help to me many times, when I am accosted by someone who thinks I should have perfect health because I am a Christian, is Paul's clear picture as given in 2 Corinthians 4:7: "But we have this treasure in earthen vessels, that the excellency [greatness] of the power may be of God, and not of us." As I read that, I see cracked teapots, still usable despite a chip in the spout, a crack in the lid, or a wobbly handle, and still lovingly used by the one who knows its history! I see favorite old dishes with the breaks glued together or the chipped edges not mattering as we arrange our freshly washed plums, apricots, a few grapes, and some leaves to set them off in a bowl that has had several bad falls. "Earthen vessels" describes us. What are the "treasures" we have? Paul has just spoken of "this ministry" we have. What ministry? The ministry of making truth known, of making the Gospel known, of letting the light shine forth through us because God gave light to us so that we ourselves might have "knowledge of the glory of God in the face of Jesus Christ" (v. 5). What a treasure is this important knowledge! What an important reality we have been given in the moments, hours, days, weeks, and months we have lived through since becoming a part of the people of God, the sheep of His pasture.

Yet we are reminded that we have this pearl of great price, this priceless treasure, "in earthen vessels." And following that declaration, lest we spiritualize it away and not relate it to our own difficulties, we are told: "We are troubled on every side, yet not distressed; we are perplexed, but not in despair; Persecuted [pursued], but not forsaken; cast down [smitten], but not destroyed; Always

111

bearing about in the body the dying of the Lord Jesus, that the life also of Jesus might be made manifest in our body [mortal flesh]" (vv. 8–10). This ties in the earthen vessels very strongly, firmly, and definitely with our flesh, our bodies.

We can understand ourselves better if we think of ourselves as earthen vessels and repeat from time to time, "There's another crack!" Or "Oops! There goes my spout." It lifts the tension or the disappointment and brings some relief in the midst of frustration or despair, if we remember that we have been given, in ten-foot-high letters, brightened by a spotlight, the fact that we are not to expect anything like perfection now. We are "earthen vessels"—made of chippable, breakable, and crackable earth. The promises of perfection are for a time ahead. Right now we are to have a very specialized opportunity, that of holding within us and giving out to others the priceless treasure of truth as opposed to falsehood, light as opposed to darkness, knowledge as opposed to ignorance. Our own cracks, chips, wobbly handles, and marred beauty are not in any way to detract from the perfection and wonder of the "excellency" or greatness of the power of God. No one gives us a second glance, so to speak, because of the glory of the One of whom we speak, whose existence is in some very real way shown forth in the very contrast of His strength being made perfect in our so-evident weakness. Our earthiness makes evident that the power is coming from a Source that cannot be our own bodily and physical perfection.

With this in mind, let me relate to you some very real examples of answers to prayer which will help to clarify with specific instances some of what we have been discovering in the last two chapters. These are only a tiny number of instances of what we will all be sitting about remembering to tell each other during eternity, as we look back over the wonder of how God has woven together the threads of our personal histories.

About six years ago my dentist wanted me to have one of my impacted wisdom teeth extracted. Now to me this was a very traumatic piece of advice. I had held a special terror of wisdom-tooth removal since early childhood, when my eldest sister had had a horrendous experience with such a case. To tell you the truth, I had left one dentist for another, any time the subject of my four impacted wisdom teeth ever came up! They didn't bother me, so "Let's leave them there!" was my philosophy, and I searched for dentists who agreed with that solution. However, at this time one X-ray showed a dark spot, and I finally decided that I was being childish and foolish. What did I know about it anyway? So I made the big decision: "All right. Go ahead."

The dental surgeon I was sent to at another office thought it would not take long and had great confidence from his training and experience, which was good. However, as he began to slash and hack, he remarked that he couldn't find the tooth and then quickly reassured me: "*Fait pas du souci. Je le trouverai.* [Don't worry. I'll find it.]" For a brief time I was left alone while he sought consultation, and soon I was being worked on by two men conducting a kind of treasure hunt in my mouth. Local anesthesia is something to be thankful for in the middle of such a time. However, one sees, hears, and feels a variety of not-so-easy-to-bear pressures while the excavation takes place. After an hour and a half, there was a triumph in two pieces, held up and displayed to me. "*Tien, tien. C'est droll, ça . . . .*" Very strange—there was no decay where the X-ray had shown a dark spot. "I'll have to show this to my class at the university tomorrow!" was the next remark. I could have the satisfaction of adding to the fund of dental knowledge the fact that an overconcentration of dentine in a tooth could be dark enough to look exactly like decay. My bleeding, gaping hole was carefully packed with all the proper antiseptics and the antibiotic that would avert infection. I had the various bibs and apparatus untied and was released from the ordeal with a pat on my shoulder.

Fran and I walked out together, first to find a drugstore where we got cotton and witch hazel to hold something cool against my jaw. Then we found a taxi for the half-hour ride back to the apartment where we were staying in Montreux. That evening Debby and Franky, feeling the need of rallying around, came all the way down from the mountain to minister to me with ice packs and aspirin and sips of something cool through a straw! I look back to their special care with great appreciation because, unknown to any of us, I was stepping into a very long period of changing but continuing "affliction"—this was to be a pretty lasting crack in the teapot that is me! You *see*, in that hour and a half in the dental surgeon's office, in spite of all the normal precautions, an infection had crept in unseen—where there had been no infection before. The results of this infection were to baffle dentists in a scattered number of places. My pain continued along with high fever for too long a time, and I had antibiotic injections given by our doctor in the mountains. The fever departed, but *we* also had to depart! That is to say, we had a speaking trip in the United States ahead of us which seemed impossible to cancel. Some people remember my speaking in Oakland at that time, speaking with apparent strength (the Lord's, not mine) and then disappearing from the banquet table, unable to chew, seeking ice and aspirin for my excruciating pain. Dentists in various parts of the United States were visited, and they usually diagnosed the problem with the same conclusion: "It is an abscess on your second molar. Have it out." I declined, saying I would wait until I got home to the dentist who knew my second molar very well and would have a background of dental history to consult. The pain kept on, and the lump which was diagnosed as an abscess moved up into my face and was movable. Weird! But no one was sure of what was going on, except for the reality of the pain.

To make that long painful eleven months come to an end, come with me to a Swiss facial surgeon, who specializes in remaking people's faces who have been in accidents and also does very specialized tooth and jaw surgery. His immediate diagnosis was that an infection had formed a cyst or tumor which needed an immediate operation. By the next day I was in a clinic in Lausanne, the little hospital where he operated. My hair was in pigtails, tied at the ends with black velvet ribbons, and I bounced up onto the table with energy that was soon to be demolished! A major operation from the inside of my mouth skillfully removed the tumor which was wrapped around my facial nerve. The surgeon touched the nerve but did not sever it. I could have had a completely paralyzed condition on one side of my face. As it was, I had a new affliction commence and a new crack take place! At first those who visited me turned away from the door with a gasp, not recognizing this person swathed in bandages, who looked with black eyes and swollen face as if "it" had been in a prizefight. When the swelling went down and natural color started to emerge from the purples and greens and yellows, I discovered that I couldn't spit! This was when I was finally able to wash my teeth. I found that my mouth went down on one side. I couldn't manage my food properly and found it an effort to speak without my lips behaving strangely.

Why? Why a mistake at all? Why the infection? Why wasn't it perfectly healed? Why such a hindrance? Why this niggling difficulty and added pain on top of everything else imperfect that was already there? The *Whys?* that rush into people's minds have to be given not one answer but a whole book of answers, which combined together still do not comprise a perfect total. We need to *let God be God,* hour by hour, day by day, experience by experience, time after time. Our whisper, "I love You, God. I trust You now . . . ." covers a great variety of things, as we shall later see. The *Why?* can be that it is part of the battle, and it is—but it can also be some of the other aspects later to be discussed about affliction or a combination of things. And we lie there, praying that the Lord won't let us "waste" what is going on in any way: *Help me, Lord, to be what You want me to be in this, to learn what You want me to learn in this, to demonstrate what You want me to demonstrate in this, to show in this thing a flashing, vivid reality of the fact that the treasure You have given me is in an earthen vessel and that the greatness, the excellency, is all of You, God, not of me.*

Did this come at a time when I could go away for a long time into some out-of-the-way spot until I would be less embarrassed? No, after a very precious ten-day time of restoration on the island of Elba at a place which Debby and Udo arranged for Fran and me, we had to go off for a speaking trip which took us across the United States and then to Hawaii, Japan, Hong Kong, Singapore, Kuala Lumpur, and Bombay. This has been my only time in these places, and in each place it was necessary to speak for the first time to people I had never met before. The fresh "hole" in the side of my face, the dropping of my lip, and the weird sensation and often pain in that side of my face had to be my unhidden affliction. A humbling crack indeed! It continues to be my affliction, although much better, and it will be there until I get my new body. Because of this, I can relate to others who have things much worse to bear. Because of this, my understanding has been increased concerning the "earthen vessel" and the reality of what the excellency which is God's greatness can consist of. Oh, don't twist your head and pull up your eyebrows in scorn, saying something like, "How trivial!" Your problem may be much more severe, but we each have our "things" which day by day work together to help our understanding of what it means to be "perplexed, but not in despair." The satisfying thing is that we are not machines. There is variety, and we are not ten-cent-store pottery. We are handmade from real earth, and the colors are natural, placed there by the Master Potter who knows what He is doing with His beloved "vessels."

Some of you are saying, "But why didn't she pray for healing? Doesn't she have any faith? God can do anything." First I would need to say that God *did* answer prayer by giving me the attention of this skillful specialist who *did* discover what was wrong, and who *did* remove the cyst. Then there is a need to say that there was the relief and certainty of answered prayer when the report was returned from the laboratory with the finding that the cyst was not cancerous. There was the moment of being thankful for an anesthetist who had read some of our books and greeted me with kind interest as I was wheeled into the operating room. There was the thankfulness for a caring family, as I came out of anesthesia to find Fran there, a lovely note from Debby, flowers from Franky and Priscilla, and a letter from Susan. The thoughtfulness of the next days from various L'Abri people in the wider family could never have been experienced with any reality in a situation of perfect health and strength! There is a terrible tendency to disregard or to place a low value on answers to prayer which *accompany* a time of affliction, and to "kick" or "step on" the very definite evidences that the Lord *is* timing a variety of help in response to our cries or whispers to Him. We are so often in danger of being like small children who scream for one particular thing and push away or tear up other things being gently given them by a loving parent, who knows that if they'd turn their attention to the positive thing, they would feel the loving care as well as become involved in whatever was being given.

A totally different example is necessary to make it clear that we do believe that God heals physical disorders, at times directly in answer to prayer, even as He answers other prayers in amazingly direct ways. However, even as God gave manna to the Israelites during their time in the wilderness, He provides food for His people in other parts of history in other ways. Thus, farms and gardens are part of His provision to some of us, while earned money and stores where the money can be exchanged for food are another kind of provision. In one part of history, people whose eyesight began to fail could no longer sew or read books. In this portion of history, most of us can go to dentists to be able to have our teeth last longer, obtain glasses that help us to keep on reading, or have hearing aids to prolong the time we can take part in conversations.

Yes, God can do things directly in response to prayer, but He has a great diversity of ways of meetings our needs—and He has not asked us to sit and *not* read His Word because our eyes need glasses; He has not healed that disorder directly; nor does He make a law that we cannot have cataracts removed when we are going blind. Christian doctors have given their time to going to countries where there is tremendous need for lifesaving or sight-saving or hearing-saving operations, and this ministry is as much of the Lord's leading as the instances where God has used someone to pray for an individual's healing and that one has been made well. One does not cancel out the other, neither in our own lives nor in the history of God's people. Our problem so often is that we want to make up rules in a neat little list or make a box that we think holds everything necessary in a neatly stored place—and we try to limit God to that little list or that box.

My personal "different example" is something I have never written about before, and something I once thought ought to be kept between myself and the family and a few friends. However, to give a balanced view of the variety of answered prayer in our span of time in these "earthen vessels," this portion of my history needs to be included. While we were in America for a year, before L'Abri began, before our time of floods, avalanches, polio, rheumatic fever, and so on, we lived in a tiny little house, in Germantown, Philadelphia, with all our trunks and boxes of books stored in a tiny little cellar. My husband was away speaking a lot of the time, so one late hour, during a night while I was quietly working away at my typewriter and the children were asleep, I heard a strange bursting sound and then the sound of gushing water. A quick dash to the cellar revealed a broken, leaking hot-water boiler and a slowly rising flood on the cellar floor. Before thinking of trying to go to a neighbor's for help, I struggled with boxes and trunks to pull precious things back from the water, and in that few minutes of time I did something to my own body that was to be my "thing" throughout the following four years. A Philadelphia doctor diagnosed a hernia, which he said did not need an operation unless it became "strangulated" at some later time, and he gave me instructions as to how to care for it—wearing a girdle and a powder puff!! There was a certain amount of discomfort, and it was not very esthetic—that half-an-egg-sized lump, but life went on without much hindrance.

Four years later, with much history having been lived through, we were having an "afflicted vacation" from our busy life at L'Abri. What do I mean by "afflicted vacation"? This precious time at the

Italian seaside, so looked forward to, had nineteen hindrances in eighteen days! Such as—each of the children's coming down, one after another, with a flu accompanied by a fever of 103; my husband's having an abscess on a tooth; the curtain rod's falling down on his head one evening; and a basketball net, board and all, filled with a bowl of wine (at some Italian street festival) which fell down slowly and hit me a glancing blow on my head and shoulder while I was innocently standing on the sidewalk—spilling the wine all over my new white suit! Things like that—and the nineteenth thing was that my hernia would not be pushed back into place as normally, and the pain was very severe. I stayed in bed with my feet up, and the sun and beach were a tantalizing impossibility for first one reason and then another.

I came home, reticent and reluctant about seeing a doctor. Our doctor in Lausanne had often told me that the day was coming when I would have to have my hernia cared for, and had severely said, "That means rest afterwards for six weeks; none of your rushing around to cook for so many people, neither running up and downstairs nor traveling." I put it off for a few days. Then on our Monday day of prayer, as I was kneeling in the room we put aside for that time during those days, the pain stabbed me like a knife, and I tried to go upstairs but had to walk bent over double. This was it! We called the surgeon at the Aigle hospital and made an appointment for the next day. "Is it an emergency?" his wife asked anxiously. "He has a funeral to attend today." I said quickly, "No, no. Tomorrow will do." I had no very noble idea, just a desire to put it off. As I lay in bed in Mélèzes that day, various people came to get instructions for cooking and various things, and in between others my husband kept sticking his head around the door: "How do you feel?" At other times: "Well, this is it; you go to the hospital, then six weeks . . . . No L'Abri, no English trip. We'll just have to shut down."

My occupation that day consisted of making out menus and writing down various instructions for the house and the children and so on, but in between those things I read the Book of Mark—and prayed. I read so frequently how the Lord "immediately" healed and how the people "immediately" got up and cooked a meal or returned to their work without recuperation time. Fran and I were to go to England to be at Cambridge University, Oxford, and St. Andrews for times of discussion in student rooms, and I knew the students were very much looking forward to this. On top of what we called "the English trip," my work in L'Abri was to prepare a constant stream of meals, as well as talking to people who needed help as they peeled potatoes, weeded in the garden with me, or washed dishes. I also had a variety of things that seemed imperative for me to be doing as a mother those next six weeks. The more I read of Mark, the more I prayed. The more Fran stuck his head around the door and said gloomily, "This is it. We'll have to cancel England and shut down L'Abri for a while . . ." the more the *immediately* stuck in my mind. I finished Mark and, in talking to the Lord in between reading, I kept telling Him that I believed He *could* do anything and thanked Him for recording these things that He had done, for us to know about and be encouraged about.

Then I turned to Psalms. Number twenty was my Psalm for that day. It has just nine verses, and I read them several times:

The Lord hear thee in the day of trouble; the name of the God of Jacob defend thee; Send thee help from the sanctuary, and strengthen thee out of Zion . . . . Grant thee according to thine own heart, and fulfil all thy counsel. We will rejoice in thy salvation, and in the name of our God we will set up our banners: the Lord fulfil all thy petitions. Now know I that the Lord saveth his anointed; he will hear him from his holy heaven with the saving strength of his right hand. Some trust in chariots, and some in horses: but we will remember the name of the Lord our God . . . .

I took my pencil and wrote tiny words in the margin of my Bible—"Some trust in operations"—and began to pray: *Oh, God, I really trust You, and if You wanted to, You could do this operation instead of Doctor G.* It was just about that time that Fran stuck his head in the door again, made another pessimistic prediction, and then went out.

Now I must confess that I got mad—not a spiritual condition and not a good feeling to have. It would be untruthful to tell it otherwise. I thought to myself, *He can't talk like that. How does he know I have to have an operation? Only God knows whether we can go to England or not.* I should have had more gentle, loving feelings. I should have had patient, quiet thoughts, rather than annoyed, frustrated ones. But the Lord is very gentle and patient with us. He does not ask us to be perfect; He knows we are but dust and He remembers our weaknesses. He takes us where we are and is as an understanding Father to us. I prayed:

Oh, dear Heavenly Father, if You want us to go to England and if You want me to keep on cooking and caring for L'Abri after that as usual, then I know You can do this operation, and I won't need that time of recuperation . . . . I can get up and go "full speed ahead" like those people in Mark's time. But—if You want me in the hospital, if You have a purpose for me to go to Aigle and be in touch with those doctors and nurses, and if You want me to go through all that those six weeks of recuperation would mean—I am really willing, Lord. Help me to want Your will honestly. But please show both Fran and me Your will—and show Fran You can change circumstances instantaneously when it is Your will to do so.

I am not saying that my motives were perfect, but there was a measure, a degree, an amount of honesty and sincerity there. And I *did* believe God could do it. The next morning I got up to go to the bathroom, and for the first time in four years I looked down at my body and saw that the half-egg-sized lump was not there. At first I couldn't let myself think that it had been healed. I told no one, went back to bed, and asked that Joyce come over from Beau Site. Joyce was a trained nurse who was working with her husband at L'Abri at the time. She had consulted with me and had seen my condition as we talked about going to the hospital. My first question was: "Can a hernia turn inside out suddenly?" She examined me again and said, "I think it must be healed. I can't think of any other explanation." That afternoon I kept my appointment with the surgeon. He examined me lying down and standing up and made me run around the room, jump, and hop on one foot. Conclusion? "No hernia here!" and he gave me a bottle of tranquilizers which I never took. He thought that I must have been having delusions. The lump was never to come back, and there were later other doctors who confirmed that it had been healed.

I have no complicated explanation. God answers prayers. God does not answer our prayers in any predictable way. One of His reasons for answering prayer is as a part of His guidance. I am convinced that the English trip was of tremendous importance (subsequent history has shown that to be so) and also that my day-by-day work at that time was what the Lord wanted me to do as a mother and at L'Abri. He also gave that instance to me and to my husband—as evidence that He can and does still work in the area of reaching down into present history to change circumstances in response to requests from His children. We have had many instances in many varieties of situations that God answers prayer. However, there is no more—or less—wonderful *kind* of answer to prayer. There is no elite group which has better or more marvelous answers to prayer. We have not entered a comparison competition. We rejoice when we read or hear of what God has done directly in answer to His children, but we are not to demand a recurrence of an event in someone else's life or of an exact combination of situations.

Lazarus was raised from the dead. But Lazarus later died again. Lazarus may have had a cold or a headache, or lost a tooth only a week after he had been raised from the dead. One can be healed of one ailment, but that brings about neither perfect health nor everlasting life without going through death. One can be healed of one misfortune, only to have another very quickly. One can pray for a house and have a lovely home turn up to be bought or rented and furnished for a section of time during one's life, but there is no promise that assures us that we may not in the future face prison or concentration camp or the need to live in some very much changed circumstance. The "house" which is our body will be perfect one day, even as the "mansions" which God is providing and preparing for us will also be perfect. However, perfection is not promised immediately after we become the children of the Lord in this life. Sometimes people take the verses in Isaiah 53:5—". . . with his stripes we are healed"—to mean that *right now in this life* the suffering which Jesus went through, as He was beaten and then died on the cross, will heal us of our diseases in this life. As we read the whole Bible, we come to understand that God is not making that promise. Therefore, He has not broken a promise when Christians suffer accidents to their bodies, become very ill, have crippling strokes, or develop polio or heart disease. Indeed, the day is coming when our bodies will be perfect. Indeed, Jesus died to make this possible, and He rose again and walked about the earth for forty days in His resurrected body so that we could know what a resurrected body is like. We *will* be perfect. *But not yet.* Any answer to prayer that we have in the physical realm is only temporal, and our situation can change very suddenly again. Any answer to prayer that we have in the material realm is also temporal, and our situation can change. We do have a continuing, unbroken thing—and that is our communication with the Living God and our access to His ear at any time.

Come to 2 Corinthians 5:1, 2 and think carefully about what is being made clear to us here: "For we know that if our earthly house of this tabernacle were dissolved, we have a building of God, an house not made with hands, eternal in the heavens. For in this we groan, earnestly desiring to be clothed upon with our house which is from heaven." Combine this with Romans 8:22, 23: "For we know that the whole creation groaneth and travaileth in pain together until now. And not only they, but ourselves also, which have the firstfruits of the Spirit, even we ourselves groan within ourselves, waiting for the adoption, to wit, the redemption of our body."

The agony of waiting which is very starkly described in these two places is an agony with audible groaning which sounds like a hospital ward full of patients coming out of anesthesia or recent operations. Why the "groaning"? It is a longing for the return of Jesus, for the end of the battle, for the final victory over death. When we are told that the last enemy to be destroyed is death, I believe it is not just that no one will ever die again, but that disease, disability, the breakdown of cells, or the process of disintegration will never again take place. Perfection of the new bodies is a perfection which is beyond anything we have ever seen or heard of in this world. While still living in the midst of the ongoing results of the spoiled world with the abnormalities which have come after the Fall, we will still be affected by epidemics of a variety of diseases. We will still be stung by hornets if we step on them, and still have toothaches when decay comes. "Decay" has not been arrested yet, but we wait for, long for, and at times groan for the time when it will be—when Jesus returns and the change takes place in a moment, in a twinkling of an eye.

Jesus told of His Second Coming and of a time of Judgment during which He would speak as King and say:

. . . Come, ye blessed of my Father, inherit the kingdom prepared for you from the foundation of the world: For I was an hungred, and ye gave me meat: I was thirsty, and ye gave me drink: I was a stranger, and ye took me in: Naked, and ye clothed me: I was sick, and ye visited me: I was in prison, and ye came unto me.

Matthew 25:34–36

When the people asked, "When did we [and all the things are repeated]?" Jesus replied as King: "Inasmuch as ye have done it unto one of the least of these my brethren, ye have done it unto me" (see verse 40). Please forget other questions and discussions we might have in the context of these verses and think of the shaft of light that hits us concerning illness. We who are "earthen vessels" get sick, we who are "one of the least of these my brethren" *are* the people of the King, the sheep of His pasture, the brothers and sisters of Christ. We are meant to visit each other, take care of the poor, visit people in nursing homes and hospitals, in tumbledown cottages, palaces, tents, caves—wherever are the sick who are His brethren. We are to have no other opportunity of visiting Christ when He is sick! Does this hit us with a hard shock? He is not saying, "Heal the sick." He is talking about visiting with the idea of bringing comfort and love. This is coupled with the reality that there will always exist physically hungry children of the Living God who need money or a lovely meal—piping hot and beautifully arranged and carried into a hut or a run-down apartment house—served as if we were serving the Lord Himself.

Visiting the sick means that there will always be those who are sick. Feeding the hungry implies a personal involvement with someone who needs human and individual loving care, not just campaigning for a change of the political setup. Taking a stranger into one's home is quite different from giving money to keep a flophouse open. Going to a prison and visiting the people who are there is the only way we can visit the Lord in prison. The picture is powerful in its force, and we can't wiggle out of what it presents to us. However—with all there is to go on thinking about and praying about and searching our hearts and lives about in connection with this passage—we cannot miss the striking fact that Jesus says that the sick are to be cared for in some very personal way. We should check up on ourselves sometime: "Have I sent the Lord a card or a letter or a bunch of flowers in His sickness this week?" Day after day, week after week, instead of being tempted to say, "They shouldn't *be* so sick. What's *wrong* with their lives or their faith?" we are instead to be asking ourselves, "Have I failed to care *for the Lord* in some person's need when offered that opportunity?"

There is a great danger that an emphasis on healing can make some people hardened or insensitive to the gentleness and thoughtfulness and imaginative care they are meant to be giving to someone. And that lack can be very serious, in that there is no other way to "minister" to the Lord. Could He have put it more strongly in the negative? "For I was an hungred, and ye gave me *no* meat: I was thirsty, and ye gave me *no* drink: I was a stranger, and ye took me *not* in: naked, and ye clothed me *not:* sick, and in prison, and ye visited me *not*" (vv. 43, 44). It is given both in the positive and the negative and should make a lasting impression on us as we think over the people whose existence our lives could touch. Are we being practical in our believing that this is God's Word, and are we being balanced in our response? We need to keep telling ourselves that not only are we faced with the possibility of entertaining an "angel unawares," but that we are meant to be caring for people as our only way of caring for the Lord Himself. As long as we are *all* "earthen vessels," the opportunity is still with us. When we are all "changed," the opportunity will be at an end.

Paul advised Timothy what to do about one of his "infirmities" or sicknesses, when he wrote to him and advised him not to drink any more water at that time: "Drink no longer water, but use a little wine for thy stomach's sake, and thine often infirmities" (2 Timothy 5:23). Did Timothy have some sort of intestinal microbe or dysentery? Whatever it was, it came often or was one of many things which made him ill. Paul neither scolded Timothy for being a weak Christian because he was ill, nor told him he would always be well if he had enough faith—nor did he offer to heal him. He gave him a little "remedy" of that time, before any antibiotics were available to fight such microbes in water or air! Never mind about the remedy itself. The central point is that not every disease was healed. Jesus Himself did not heal everyone, nor did He heal any one person of everything that was wrong with him. The apostles were given a ministry of healing, but they neither healed everyone, nor were they themselves kept from affliction of physical pain and illness, nor were they preserved from the final bodily destruction in martyrdom.

We are encouraged and given comfort by finding that the Bible gives us a frank and clear balance in letting us know what to expect. At the same time, we are given much in the way of explanation and hope. There is a big enough purpose, a certain enough expectation, and enough help available to make it possible to go on. Our bodies are important and will be raised from the dead, but our bodies are not at the moment more important than our inward and spiritual growth as growing personalities, children born into God's family. We need to be very wary of a danger which Jesus pointed out when

He was preaching and teaching during His three years of public ministry. He had so many following Him in order to be fed, after He multiplied the bread and fish, and then so many flocking to Him for physical healing. He made it so very clear that it was neither the physical healing nor the physical bread that was the basically important thing. Nor was the provision of physical healing or physical bread the hardest thing to do. If people got out of balance and saw things in a wrong and twisted way, when Jesus, the Second Person of the Trinity, was Himself walking and teaching among them, how much more danger there is of getting things out of focus now!

As we live our lives with a blend of the answers to prayer which bring us sufficient grace and the Lord's strength in our weakness to go on—in the midst of pain, fever, disappointment, crushing shock, grueling work, fatigue that makes us long for escape, fear, storms, earthquake, famine, drought, fire, loss of a variety of kinds, despotism that affects us personally, and persecution—we need to recognize His grace and strength as answers that fit into the "museum" of the first rectangle, and fulfill a part which no one else has. As we also live our lives in the second rectangle, we need to recognize that these are answers of an equally important kind in our own life or others', and that we are living through a life that "fits in" to the whole and that matters. These are the same lives, with a blend of answers to prayer which brings relief in pain, diminishing of fever, tender and loving concern for our disappointment, help in the midst of the shock, a cup of tea and a wee gift to give a lift in the midst of grueling work, a glass of water in the midst of the drought, helping hands to fight the fire, the sharing that comes with amazing timing in the midst of loss, a friend or protector to push aside some temporary result of the despot's rule in which we are living, and rescue in the midst of persecution. We need to recognize these things before the Lord, remarking on them to Him, so that we won't be among the nine lepers who were healed and never said, "Thank You." In all the Lord's answers we need to see the danger of being just a retreating figure, showing our backs to the Lord as we hurry away, forgetting to say, "Thank You."

The perspective of seeing and feeling and knowing in our hearts and minds that we really have a treasure in our weak selves, a light that is not to be hidden within these earthen vessels, gives a whole new impetus to "endure to the end," whatever that enduring means. People who become children of the Lord's family early in life—with long years in which to do His will, to be what He wants them to be, to serve Him, and to make Him known—are often in great danger of "growing weary in well doing" and are in danger of becoming lax in their prayer lives, tending to forget the wonder and marvel of prayer. I have found in my own life that fervency in prayer is greatest when the *need* is most urgent. It is in times of affliction that the heights of reality are experienced in the sheer length of time spent talking to God and the earnestness with which one talks. It is when the need is sharply vivid that one searches one's own lazy use of time and becomes conscious of needing to ask forgiveness for not being verbal enough to the Lord about thankfulness, or frequent enough in true adoration and praise. It is then also that we realize the deep practical truth of the fact that we are never alone, and that His "I will never leave thee nor forsake thee" is true. We can observe God's most amazing tenderness in the detailed answers He gives in comfort and assurance to His children, when we review those moments of our own lives or hear of answers given to others.

One of my comforts ever since childhood was the Lord's tender answer to Honey II of Lisu Land. (His story is told in a book published by the Overseas Missionary Society.) This man was a native of the hills back of China where the Lisu tribe then lived. He had known nothing but heathen teaching all his life, but the "seeking" inside him was so real that he determined to find out whether there *was* a God that he did not know about. The little book about his life tells of how he found a torn page from a Lisu catechism on a mountain path one day (in the early days of Frazer's beginning work among the Lisu) and he read: "Are there more gods than One?"— "*No, there is only One God.*" "Should we worship idols?"— "*No . . . .*" As I remember it, the rest was torn and lost. On the strength of just this much information, Honey II went to his home and tore down the demon altars. He knew of nothing positive to do. Immediately his daughter became ill with a very high fever. While his child tossed and turned in a serious sickness, the neighbors came around to jeer and taunt. "Aha! You see what has happened? You have made the demons angry." Honey II knew nothing about prayer, but his thought was that if there was One True God, perhaps he could reach Him with his voice. So he climbed to the highest mountain peak in that area of peaks which were twelve- and fourteen-thousand-feet high. There at the top he turned up his head and raised his voice to a shout: "Oh, God, if You really are there and You are the One I am to worship, please make my little girl well again." His long trek down the mountainside took time, but when he got into his hut, his little girl was completely well, with no time of recuperation needed. Comparing the time as to when it happened, it seemed that it was just when he prayed that the fever left her.

God has promised: *If with all thine heart ye truly seek Me, ye shall surely find Me.* "He that willeth to do the will of God, shall know of the doctrine, whether it be of God . . ." (see John 7:17). God is gentle and tender with the truly honest and seeking hearts, the ones who want to do His will and be His children "if" He is there. There will be so many stories to compare with Honey II's that I picture us taking thousands of years to find out about them all. The compassion and the tenderness of our loving Heavenly Father will take forever to learn about; we will never get to the end. The tiny bit of knowledge we have about Him now is meant to show something of the brilliance of His excellence—His love which prompted the Gospel, which caused Him to plan the way of salvation through the affliction and suffering of the Trinity. Later Honey II was to find the Gospel of Mark, as translated by Frazer, in a Chinese marketplace to which he had walked miles upon miles. Still later he himself was to become a marvelous "teller of the Good News," taking the treasure of truth to many Lisu as he hiked up and down endless mountain paths. The Communists have scattered these people, and many new walls have been constructed to shut out the truth in this as well as so many other parts of the world. But the truth has not been stamped out! God is still hearing the cries of the seeking ones; and we who know truth are still carrying about the treasure in our earthen, cracked, chipped, broken teapots—in so many strange places.

7

"Tribulation Worketh Patience"

Tribulation, affliction, and suffering involve the whole person. Physical illness, persecution in a violent physical form, an accident which results in permanent physical changes in this life, onslaught of epidemics from a variety of viruses or microbes, and loss of energy or physical strength due to sickness or old age or crippling disease all affect not only the body of a person, but his or her whole being. The whole person is also affected by the psychological, mental, emotional, and moral condition. Tensions and worries brought about by our own mistakes (or other people's mistakes or thoughtlessness), stress in the midst of indecision or deep concern for others or in the midst of our own anger or other people's anger or jealousy or cruelty, and an endless variety of uncertainties and fears can affect each person physically, too. Personality as a whole is affected by the physical condition, and the physical condition is affected by the mental and emotional condition. There is an amazing interweaving of the physical, psychological, spiritual, and intellectual unfolding or growing of a person throughout life.

A child is affected by having parents who have no understanding of what is going on in "the whole child" when there is a sickness, a sudden bee sting, a terrifying fright, a crushing disappointment, or a deep uncertainty. It makes a difference in the child's growth into a person with balance in life, if the parents have understanding and wisdom in giving comfort, strength, attention, love, and careful explanations when these things are needed. Scars of various kinds can result from bewildered suffering, made worse by being screamed at: "Shut up!" "Be good." "Do as I say and don't ask me any questions." "Just stay in bed and take the medicine." "Who cares if anyone hit you at school." "No, I won't answer your question. I'm busy." A lap is needed. Arms are needed. A hand is needed, as is a voice speaking with care and the desire to give understanding. The imparting of confidence is needed even when explanations are impossible for the moment. It is so important for a child to know that "Mother and Father know about this, and they understand more than I do. They explain everything they can, and they care about me even though I have to stay in the hospital." This is so different from the total lack of assurance that the parents care at all, the feeling of being utterly deserted and forsaken in four walls that seem like a prison.

When we say to a little child, "Be patient," it must be spoken from a background of having lived together and known each other, with a growing amount of trust having developed in the child. Communication from parent to child—in a context of love and provision of needs, understanding, and a response to the longings of the past—prepares the way for a parent's response in stringent circumstances to be summed up in a few words: "Wait. Be patient a little longer. I'll let you know later, but right now this is where you have to be. I won't leave the building. You can count on me." The opportunity for the child to demonstrate his trust in a mother or father comes in the crisis moments, but there has to have been preparation for that trust. The child needs a memory to sustain him, communication to be remembered, assurance rooted in some realistic part of the past.

As children of *one family,* we who have been born into the family of the great and marvelous God of the Universe have a Heavenly Father who has given us sufficient communication. He has not spoken in short, broken, unconnected verses. His communication to us is a full and complete revelation of Himself (as complete as we can now understand), as well as guidance in times of stress. He has given us a memory of His work and care of our "relatives," our brothers and sisters in His family. He has also given us a memory of our own experience of having Him as a Father of our own, whether that time be short or long.

His statement to "[be] patient in tribulation" (Romans 12:12) is not an isolated harsh command to grit our teeth or bite our lips and summon some sort of patience to show to people around us that we are indeed living a Christian life. When we come to Romans 5, we must not separate the phrase in verse 3—". . . tribulation worketh patience"—from the rest of that chapter or from the whole Word of

God, and just sigh deeply with a feeling of desperation as we say within ourselves (if not to someone else), "It isn't working. It doesn't work at all. I have tribulation—and the very *opposite* of patience is coming out of it, in my feelings and actions." We can't just look up the word *patience* and plunge into James 1:3, 4 and lift out its message: "Knowing this, that the trying of your faith worketh patience. But let patience have her perfect work . . . ." We can't expect anything but more frustration if we have nothing more of the Word of God as a background, or have not lived through the reality of having had patience grow in us and work in us.

Patience is not a neat package to be received in a basket or bowl after paying a certain price for it, any more than *faith* is a single prize to be doled out by weight and measure from someplace where it is being awarded. Like faith, patience involves not just one isolated person but a horizontal or vertical relationship with someone else. Of course, the vertical relationship is possible only with God, on the basis of the death of Christ in our place—and in whose name we come—with the Holy Spirit dwelling in us to continually help us in our relationship. Horizontal relationships are those we have with other human beings. The element of patience does not stand out as separate from the whole picture: who we are and what effect we are having on history. It is woven into our whole person: our minds, with all the thinking and learning that is possible in that area; our emotions, with all the variety of feelings we can have about other people and God; and our actions, with all the things we are accomplishing for or against God's glory, and all the things we are doing to help or hinder the lives of other human beings. Patience cannot be applied like lipstick or a plaster on a mole and then removed at bedtime. It is interwoven with our moment-by-moment, year-by-year growing. We are not static as personalities, nor are we static in spiritual and mental growth. Something is always taking place in the way of change. It is the *change* going on in us that concerns our Heavenly Father, even as the change going on in our children should concern those of us who are parents (or teachers who are taking the place of parents). If our children, grandchildren, nieces or nephews, students, or foster children we love and care for are constantly changing for the worse—not only in morals, but in becoming more and more bitter, dull, static in the very "ruts" we fear the most—our longing is that they will come back into communication with us. Thereby we can try to point out the place of departure and see if we can help in any way to get them onto the stream or path or track or way where they can take up where they got off the right course.

We, as God's children, matter more to God than any human being does to another human being. We need to read and reread what He has told us about His concern for us:

> God is our refuge and strength, a very present help in trouble. Therefore will not we fear, though the earth be removed [changed], and though the mountains be carried into the midst of the sea; Though the waters thereof roar and be troubled, though the mountains shake with the swelling thereof. Selah.
>
> Psalms 46:1–3

> The Lord also will be a refuge [high tower] for the oppressed, a refuge in times of trouble. And they that know thy name will put their trust in thee: for thou, Lord, hast not forsaken them that seek thee. Sing praises to the Lord, which dwelleth in Zion: declare among the people his doings.
>
> Psalms 9:9–11

> Then they cried unto the Lord in their trouble, and he saved them out of their distresses. He brought them out of darkness and the shadow of death, and brake their bands in sunder. Oh that men would praise the Lord for his goodness, and for his wonderful works to the children of men! . . . . Whoso is wise, and will observe these things, even they shall understand the lovingkindness of the Lord.
>
> Psalms 107:13–15, 43

> But let him that glorieth glory in this, that he understandeth and knoweth me, that I am the Lord which exercise lovingkindness, judgment, and righteousness, in the earth: for in these things I delight, saith the Lord.
>
> Jeremiah 9:24

As we daily read the Word of God, as we talk to Him and thank Him specifically for letting us know of His loving-kindness and of His wonderful works for His children, among whom we are a part of the same family, our preparation for the growth of patience—as well as trust and faith—is meant to be taking place. We read the verse which is so carelessly quoted at times without deep thought: "For God so loved the world, that he gave his only begotten Son, that whosoever believeth in him should not perish, but have everlasting life" (John 3:16). As we read, we are not meant to think of theologians and their discussions but of the startling fact that the One who spoke these words was the Second Person of the Trinity, the "only begotten Son" Himself. With these words He was making clear to Nicodemus and to us something of the marvelous quality of love which God has for His people: all human beings who come, believing in Him. This familiar verse, which expounds in Jesus' own words the love of the Father, should be expanded by Jesus' words in John 15:9: "As the Father hath loved me, so have I loved you: continue ye in my love." We are still "continuing in His love," during our times of tribulation.

Without a rich background of understanding of the gentleness, compassion, kindness, goodness, and love of our Heavenly Father, the seed fertilized by tribulation will not begin to send down roots and put up shoots of the "plant of patience"! In this particular picture, one needs to recognize the continually necessary work of soil preparation. We do have something to do with the richness of this particular soil. We, the children of the Living God, are already in this picture. In this imaginary garden, in which I am one plot and you another, one of the things we are meant to be growing is a plant called "patience." The fertilizer for this plant seems to be carefully described to us as "tribulation." I would like to suggest, however, that before the fertilizer is added, the soil preparation needs to be an hour-by-hour, day-by-day digging into the Word of God. This preparation involves having as a part of our whole being a growing understanding of the love of God and of His marvelous kindness which surpasses any kindness we could imagine from our knowledge of human beings or ourselves. We need to be trusting Him in an increasing manner, so that our reactions and actions are slowly, slowly changing through the months and years. One of the points of discovery—akin to the discovery of the sprout of a most difficult seed to germinate in our physical gardens—is the discovery of patience starting to sprout!

There is a fertilizer that speeds up a spurt of growth, causes heads to form in the cabbages that were too loose-leafed, and peas to burst forth in their pods. Something has to be there to start with, but this is a "pusher" for fruitful growth. Tribulation, all by itself, without a ground to work in and without a seed planted there—without a "base," so to speak—would not bring about patience. There is a very basic need to be "rooted and grounded" in the love of God:

That he would grant you, according to the riches of his glory, to be strengthened with might by his Spirit in the inner man; That Christ may dwell in your hearts by faith; that ye, being rooted and grounded in love, May be able to comprehend with all saints what is the breadth, and length, and depth, and height; And to know the love of Christ, which passeth knowledge, that ye might be filled with all the fulness of God.

Ephesians 3:16–19

The Bible is continually giving us two things at once. Here we are told that as we are rooted and grounded in love we move along toward the place where we come to *know* the love of Christ, "which passeth knowledge." The "know," which applies to what we can understand in this lifetime, is only a part of the entire possibility. The complete love of Christ is beyond or "passeth" our finite, limited comprehension, but what we *can* know is very real and increases through life. This growing understanding of the breadth, length, depth, and height of His love gives us a growing confidence, trust, and faith.

However, before going on to think of the context of the thought that "tribulation worketh patience," we need to remind ourselves again that we are not only "cracked teapots" in our physical imperfections, but that not one of us is perfect spiritually, emotionally, intellectually, or psychologically. We need to take ourselves to Romans 12:3 where we are admonished not to think more highly of ourselves than we ought to think. This chapter points out very carefully that, although we are to give our bodies as a living sacrifice to the Lord and present our lives to Him as a reasonable thing to do, the forms which our lifework takes will differ tremendously. And whatever it is that He gives each of us to do, we are to do well, thoroughly, and with love. Love for the Lord? Yes, but the way of daily life outlined here is in the setting of loving each other and preferring other people's good, rather than fighting for our own rights. The goodness and kindness of our Heavenly Father is meant to be something we show forth to other human beings in practical ways that can be seen, felt, and noticed in a variety of ways. Practical things are outlined in this chapter as to what day-by-day life is to include—such practical things as feeding our hungry enemies and giving our thirsty enemies something to drink. Materially sharing our things with others of "the saints" is more personal than putting money in an offering, although that is to be done week by week, too.

In the very middle of this clear explanation of what to expect and what to do in living as a child of God, comes "patient in tribulation." Tribulation comes right in the middle: "Rejoicing in hope; patient in tribulation; continuing instant in prayer" (Romans 12:12). You are in the midst of rejoicing over the last letter you have had from your son, telling of his accepting the Lord—and suddenly comes the news of his suicide. What happens to your rejoicing? *You weep.* God has given the admonition in the same chapter: "Rejoice with them that do rejoice, and weep with them that weep." As you weep in the midst of this terrible shock—this awful tribulation of separation, this cutting off of any possible communication which could help you understand what happened—you should be joined by others who really weep with you. The weeping is needed. The weeping is right. The weeping is to be shared. The patience to be displayed is patience on the part of the stronger one toward the one that is more crushed.

There is no room for pride or for pious speculations as to what has brought on this particular "tribulation." We can go back to the first chapter and remember the battle. Not one of us can tell another the answer to *Why?*, but we know there is a battle and that cause-and-effect history brings about such things as sudden brain pressures, body imbalances, and even measles and mumps. When we are plunged into personal tragedy, sorrow, a series of afflictions and tribulations, it *is* a wonderful opportunity to trust the Lord and His love and to ask for His help in being patient in a growing way, an increasing-through-the-years kind of way. But there is also a constant and urgent need for us to learn how to be patient with *other* people who are in the midst of some kind of tribulation. Our patience is not supposed to be measured in minutes or hours or days. We are not meant to put a limit on our patience with others who need our comfort and help. Other people's tribulations should increase our patience with them, rather than causing us to grow hardened:

> We then that are strong ought to bear the infirmities of the weak [the failings of the weak], and not to please ourselves. Let every one of us please his neighbour for his good to edification [to build him up]. For even Christ pleased not himself; but as it is written, The reproaches of them that reproached thee fell on

me. [The insults of those who insult you have fallen on me.] For whatsoever things were written aforetime were written for our learning, that we through patience and comfort of the scriptures might have hope. [For everything that was written in the past was written to teach us, so that through endurance and the encouragement of the Scriptures we might have hope.]
Romans 15:1–4

I have given the King James translation, with the New International Version in brackets. It seems to me that this passage is clearly a confirmation of the basic fact that we are meant to prepare ourselves by reading and rereading the Bible, so that we may be taught by what has been written in the Scriptures in the past, and be ready for a reality of "patience" or "endurance." The source of help and encouragement is the Word of God, He who is called the God of "patience and comfort" (King James Version) and the God who gives "endurance and encouragement" (New International Version).

Don't you see that we are *all* weak, although there are differences among us as to physical health, intellectual abilities, and spiritual understanding? If one is stronger than another in one way or another, it is not to be a source of pride, but to be used to help the weaker person in that one's failings. However, in the very helping of another person, as well as in our own times of sorrow and trouble, we have Someone to call upon for help. We have a Heavenly Father who gives "endurance and encouragement." We are to call upon Him. Romans 12:12 in the New International Version says: "Be joyful in hope, patient in affliction, faithful in prayer." The prayer is to be constant—in times of joy as we are filled with hope, and in times of affliction, our own and others whom we are helping. The source of sufficient strength is to be reached by prayer. There is no "clogging of lines," no delay in communication. We can call out to Him in our dismay or bewilderment or shock and ask Him directly to supply our own immediate need and our need for having the right words to say or the right thing to do for the other person. There is a clear statement of fact here, as in so many places, that there will always be "the weaker person," even as there will always be "the poor" or " the lame and the sick," until Jesus comes back. Just as there will not be perfect physical health, no Christian will be perfect, and some will be weaker than others until Jesus comes back and we will all be changed.

Falling into Satan's trap, into one or another kind of temptation to sin, is an affliction of the deepest kind. We are given a shaking, a firm hand on our shoulder which gives us a strong pull to attention as we read:

> Brothers, if a man is trapped in some sin, you who are spiritual should restore him gently. But watch yourself; you also may be tempted. Carry each other's burdens, and in this way you will fulfill the law of Christ. If anyone thinks he is something when he is nothing, he deceives himself. Each man should test his own actions. Then he can take pride in himself, without comparing himself to somebody else, for each man should carry his own load.
>
> Galatians 6:1–5 NIV

Are you a bit dizzy and shaken up? This is strong speaking that leaves no shadow of doubt as to our responsibility. We are to be aware that there is a heavy burden in the area of falling into temptation, in the realm of struggling with the thing with which Satan is hitting us. All too quickly, people think of sexual sin or gambling or drinking or embezzling or destruction of property as the greatest kinds of temptation and sin. However, without considering all the areas—lack of love and lack of fulfilling the positive commands made to the people of God—there is the whole realm of falling into doubt and lack of trust in God, when Satan throws affliction into our faces like buzzing gnats or sprays of acid. When we consider the "burden" or "affliction" or "tribulation" of temptation, we must not narrow the items down to a trite little list, especially a list of things which do not affect us personally at all.

We are being called upon to act with gentleness when we feel we need to help someone to extricate himself or herself from some sinful thing. But we are warned sharply, as with a blast of a flute blowing its highest and loudest note right into our ear: "Watch yourself . . . ." Spiritual pride can be the worst pitfall. The very practical schedule of carrying out that watchfulness is outlined. We are not to compare ourselves with anyone else, but rather only with what the Word of God tells us we should be—and then we have a sufficient load! We have a burden of our own to be concerned about and to talk to the Lord about. In this manner, then, even though we are to help others, we are to discover our own burden and carry it. It seems to me that the place of honest humbleness (not a whining display of humbleness like Dickens's Uriah Heep) comes in carrying out, each time we pray for anyone else, the reminder to ourselves or the rereading of these words from Matthew:

[Jesus says:] "Do not judge, or you too will be judged. For in the same way you judge others, you will be judged, and with the measure you use, it will be measured to you. Why do you look at the speck of sawdust in your brother's eye and pay no attention to the plank in your own eye? How can you say to your brother, 'Let me take the speck out of your eye,' when all the time there is a plank in your own eye? You hypocrite, first take the plank out of your own eye, and then you will see clearly to remove the speck from your brother's eye."

Matthew 7:1-5 NIV

Anytime you or I pray for someone else's sin or fault or hindrance, we should first pray for eyes to see our own sin or fault or hindrance. We need to be really scared of rushing into the presence of God with such a request, without talking about our own weaknesses first. He who knows us inside out is not waiting for us to be perfect before we can intercede for anyone else, but He does require us to be aware of our own need to be cleansed, as we come with our requests for others. This is true in the case of anyone we are praying for, but especially for those closest to us. As a wife or a husband, a child or a parent, when we are praying about the "faults" of anyone close to us, we need to pause long enough to examine ourselves carefully and then ask for forgiveness and for greater sensitivity to our own "blind spots." The sin of someone else can be your affliction or tribulation—or mine. But the reverse is also true. We each can be, by our sin or faults—our stubbornness or insensitivities or selfishness—the affliction or tribulation of someone close to us. That portion of Matthew can be a practical help in our daily communication with the Lord, as we fulfill what He tells us to do before we pray for the other person.

Yes, of course we can pray with great fervency for our husbands or wives, our children or parents, our cousins, nieces, nephews, aunts, uncles, grandparents, and close friends. We pray for various kinds of "traps" to be opened, so that they may walk free of something which we feel is either hindering their spiritual growth or walk with the Lord or their recognizing His will for them. But—and the BUT should be in capital letters—we do not pray from a pinnacle of perfection, now or ever. When Jesus comes back, we won't have to pray in this way anymore, but until then we ourselves have further to go in our own growth. The "affliction" of a person greatly beloved to us—perhaps seeing that one go off into a divorce, drugs, alcoholism, bitterness, doubts, selfishness, and so on—should, of course, cause us not only to pray "once in a while," but to take sections of sleeping time for prayer or even put aside some meals for prayer. However, in it all, no matter what the agony of affliction we are living through, these times of prayer should be a help to our own growth. Otherwise, this kind of tribulation is not going to produce any growth of patience in us at all.

The evangelist Dwight L. Moody is reported to have once said, as he saw a drunk staggering across a bridge, "But for the grace of God, there go I." This is the attitude we are meant to have. There is a great difference between having a lax view of sin (or constantly lowering standard for oneself) and a recognition of the fact that not one of us has arrived in such a "high class" that we are incapable of some form of "addiction." Without patting ourselves on the back and praying as the Pharisee did when he thanked God he was not as other men, we should indeed thank God for what He has saved us from—and continually recognize that His grace and strength have been our daily help. The *patience* (in the tribulation of living daily with the burden of unchanging personalities or situations in the lives of people we love) comes in verbalizing to the Lord the recognition of our own sinfulness and of the areas in which we are still weak, inspite of all He has given us. This is one real source of "tribulation worketh patience."

In fact, it is a truism that patience and endurance are both qualities which cannot be evident or present unless there is something taking place which would naturally cause *im*patience. We all endure some kind of hardship. God had promised Abraham many descendants, which seemed humanly impossible, since Sarah, his wife, was "too old" to have children. Hebrews 6:15 tells us: "And so after waiting patiently, Abraham received what was promised" (NIV). Paul includes in his list of difficult things (which we can expect to live through in one form or another) some of his own experiences: "We put no stumbling block in anyone's path, so that our ministry will not be discredited. Rather, in every way we show ourselves to be servants of God: in great endurance; in troubles, hardships and distresses; in beatings, imprisonments and riots; in hard work, sleep-less nights and hunger; in purity, understanding, patience and kind-ness; in the Holy Spirit and in sincere love" (2 Corinthians 6:3–6 NIV).

The list in which *you* discover what patience and endurance are all about may read: "In having the washing machine break and empty water all over the floor; in being up all night with the baby's case of croup; in feeding eighteen people and being left with all the dishes; in having rain every day of a long-awaited vacation; in drop-ping the new lamp before it was once turned on; in having to cancel a precious hour of reading to talk to a weeping neighbor; in being deceived in the office by the cheating of someone on the staff; in learning patience and kindness under ever-changing difficulties." Every list differs from person to person and from day to day, but endurance and patience, accompanied by love and kindness, are only learned in some such catalog of happenings.

I love the account of Abraham in which we are told (although he was about a hundred years old, and Sarah was far too old to have a child): "He staggered not at the promise of God through unbelief; but was strong in faith, giving glory to God; And being fully per-suaded that, what he had promised, he was able also to perform" (Romans 4:20, 21). The basis for going on into the hard things—with an expectation of learning patience and endurance—is one of coming to know and love the Living God as the One who is *able* to keep His promises. Abraham believed God, and we are told in the next verse that it was "imputed to him for righteousness." There follows the explanation that the same righteousness is also imputed to us: ". . . if we believe on him that raised up Jesus our Lord from the dead; Who was delivered for our offences, and was raised again for our justification" (vv. 24, 25). That is the end of chapter 4 of Romans, and it is immediately in the next sentence that we find the theme of this chapter:

Therefore being justified by faith, we have peace with God through our Lord Jesus Christ [a lasting and exciting certainty, not dependent on how we measure up, but on what Christ did in His completed work on the cross]: By whom also we have access by faith into this grace wherein we stand, and rejoice in hope of the glory of God. [We have access to God in moment-by-moment prayer for help, as well as to all the other things this grace provides us with.] And not only so, but we glory in tribulations also: knowing that tribulation worketh patience; And patience, experience [character]; and experience, hope: And hope maketh not ashamed [hope does not disappoint us]; because the love of God is shed abroad in our hearts by the Holy Ghost which is given unto us.

Romans 5:1–5

Patience in the midst of tribulation, or as a result of affliction, doesn't spring from nowhere! It didn't for Abraham, and it doesn't for us. First, we must have become the children of the Living God by believing what He has made so plain in the Bible—that is, that Jesus is who He said He is and that He died in our place. That is what is meant by "believing God." That has to be the base. Then we need to grow in our knowledge of our new Father, our Heavenly Father, and grow to love and trust Him more and more. But we aren't left alone in this growth. If we were left alone, we'd be like babies left to starve in a hospital delivery room. We are fed daily as we read the Bible and we have access to our Father; so we have the love a growing baby needs. When the tribulation and affliction come, we have help in meeting them. The "plant of patience" has something to grow in.

As we read the list of the afflictions which "worketh patience," we may make the mistake of thinking we will graduate from a tribulation, as time goes on, and go straight up to hope with no further dips into troubles. It seems to me that if there is noticeable progress to us as we grow, it would be the *speed* with which we would move into patience, further growth of character, and hope. The hope doesn't disappoint us, and we don't need to be ashamed of having bright hope when things look so gloomy around us. The hope is going to be fulfilled, and one sweet day the fulfillment will arrive. When that day comes, the patience will no longer be able to be exhibited.

God is so very fair with us in His Word, as He makes clear that we are living through what can be expected because of the Fall and the abnormality of the world since the Fall. We need not be drawn into Eastern religions, trying to train ourselves into thinking that everything is a dream (a nightmare) and that nothing really exists—nothing material or intellectual, either in the past or in the future. We have been told very plainly that everything is real and has been real through generations—and that there is a very real future. Perhaps you say that this is no problem to you, but it is to an increasing number of people. The Word of God helps us to recognize the marks of reality in outlining the practical, day-by-day, tangible things we are going to have to face and deal with and live through. God's Word is very different from the word of a father or mother who says something like this to his or her child: "It won't hurt at all, dear. There really isn't any needle, and you won't bleed. Whatever you see or hear or feel will only be your own imagination." God treats us as would careful and understanding parents who say instead: "There will be a needle, one in your arm here, and then a prick on your finger here. The one that goes in your arm will bring out blood to put in a little bottle. And the prick will let out enough blood to put on a glass slide. It will hurt, but the hurt won't last long, and there is a fantastic reason for doing it. You see, your blood is made up of red and white corpuscles, teeny-teeny things; and in the laboratory they can find out whether you have the right number of each. There are so many things they can find out under microscopes and in test tubes. Then the doctor will have a better idea of what to do for you next. See? The thing to remember is that it won't last long, just a minute, and that there is a very real reason. There will be something worthwhile discovered."

The careful parent lets a child know that not all bleeding comes for such noble and good reasons. Some cuts and bruises come from an enemy who attacks on purpose. Some bleeding comes from a disease. Other bleeding results from an accident.• Here the *cause* may be running across the street when Mother has said to wait for help, and the *effect* is being hit by a car. Is everything we question explainable to us when we are three years old? No. Not only is our vocabulary not sufficient for everything we might have asked, but there are things in human knowledge simply beyond us for the moment. God has given us in His Word that which can be understood through the years, in varying degrees by a variety of His children—but sufficient to give His children the certainty they need as to the fact that Someone knows all the answers and that we can trust Him. We then turn our minds to using the brief period of time we have in trying to *live* on the basis of what He has given us and to learn as much as possible in the midst of the living. Patience, perseverance, and endurance (certainly not the only qualities that must become practical and real in our history) present us with enough reason not to be wasteful of the short time we have. When are we going to be finished with finding out all we can, before this time is over?

Let's go back to the hospital with the child. Does he follow the lab technicians into the laboratory and discover all there is to know about what is going on? There is a minimum of explanation needed, and only a small amount that could be given with any meaning to the child to make it clear that there is a logical purpose in what is taking place. Of course, given the human factor, mistakes can be made. An old-enough child can discuss this with you—the results will not be all-conclusive, since no human being can find out everything about anything. This, we point out to the child, is the difference about God. He really *does* know everything, although what He tells us is not everything, but rather all that we need at present, all that we can possibly understand. He is giving us a lifetime, however long that lifetime is to be, in which to do things and be things in areas which He tells us are important.

We may read a book on Zen Buddhism one day and find our minds boggling with the thought of people spending a lifetime concentrating on nothingness, on what they think is the empty nothing of no existence. The next day we may read an article on "Sociobiology" and come across such lines as: "Morality and justice, far from being the triumphant product of human progress, evolved from man's animal past, and are securely rooted in the genes" (*Time*, August 1, 1977). Zen would say there are no genes! Then we go back to the Bible and thank God that He has not given us a nebulous number of abstract ideas, but has fixed all that He has to tell us into history and the real world where it can be tasted, touched and felt, smelled, seen, and heard. Even the things we are told to consider important, such as patience and endurance and perseverance, are not allowed to float in an abstract cloud obtainable only by those who can sit and meditate in some "holy" position in a "pure" spot. The very spelling out of affliction, persecution, and tribulation in terms of stones and whips (as well as people's scorn in words) lifts the setting in which we find the reality of patience from an unattainable realm into the stuff of day-by-day life.

In my book *What Is a Family?* the fifth chapter covers the answer that a family is "A Shelter in the Time of Storm." The story of Marry Berg-Meester is told in that chapter. There is a sequel that fits our need for an illustration of continuing growth, not in "higher levels" without the tribulation, but down in the stuff which relates to *your* seven days a week (and mine). I won't repeat the details of all Marry had gone through up to the time I wrote about her afflictions. A quick summary can only gather together a background for you. Hans, Marry's husband, had known the most titanic kind of trouble in childhood: concentration camp in Indonesia and actually seeing his parents killed. He had loved God and trusted Him in the most amazingly vivid way and continued in all he had learned from his parents on into his married life. Their second child was born with an Rh-factor problem, causing not only cerebral palsy but deafness. My account goes on to give some detail of their lives with these two boys: Jaapjan—bright and healthy—and disabled Stephan, who needed constant care in his wheelchair and bed. I told of the day when dear Hans kissed Marry good-bye as he left to drive through the rain to work, and was instantly killed when a truck skidded and plowed into the front of his car. I told something of the balance which God has given Marry in her understanding of agony, sorrow, loneliness, longing for Hans, weeping, and hating the enemy, death. Through it all was her determination to go on, with God's moment-by-moment help, to make a home for her boys.

Did Marry's life then settle down to a stable pattern? Did life go on with no more crises—as she settled in an apartment nearer to the school for disabled children where she takes Stephan for four days a week, and she designed a special car so that she could manage Stephan by herself? (Let me tell anyone who might be interested, because of needing to transport someone in a 'wheelchair, that Marry got a very small pickup truck and had the manufacturer make windows in the back, and build a track and ramp, so that she could manage to wheel the chair up, fasten it, and then drive with her other boy on the seat beside her.) Did Marry's bright, creative ideas for designing clothing, which would be both attractive and practical for different kinds of disability, grow into a flourishing business? Is there an "And she lived happily ever after . . ." kind of ending to report?

No! A really huge "disaster" has been added to the various kinds of "gray days" and difficulties which any widow with two children, one disabled, could imagine. That is to say, many people would think it was one of the major disasters or afflictions they fear most. Marry developed what the doctor diagnosed as something which needed removal by surgery. She then faced the shock which many others have faced upon coming out of anesthesia—that it had been cancer and that "everything" had been removed, even a part of another organ. Lying there for weeks of recovery, with the heaviness of heart any loving mother has for her children, Marry had her only really close Friend by her side, day and night. The Lord Himself is the One whom Marry has come to know more and more through the years as "a very *present* help in trouble." His words— "I will never leave thee nor forsake thee"—were not blotted out by the seriousness of her trouble, but became more real than ever before. Just as shock waves come one after another in earthquakes, so very often the afflictions that come upon us follow one after another in waves. We may have just gotten the salt out of our eyes and the choking deluge of water out of our noses and mouths, so to speak, when another wave breaks, before we have had time to take a deep breath. Waves of the sea, earthquakes, wind, hurricanes, and fire are part of our experience of reality. But they also illustrate to us other forms of difficulty, tribulation, shock—the reality of a continuing set of circumstances which give meaning to the words: "Endure to the end!" or "Let patience have her perfect work." There is nothing abstract about these statements or commands.

Marry's next shock wave was the news which came to the hospital that her dear brother and his wife (who were caring for her boys) had had an accident with her specially built car. It was totaled! Lying there in that weak condition, the contemplation of going back to her life without that car was about as heavy a set of "buzzing bees" as could fly about in one's thoughts. How many times do you suppose she wept when no nurse or visitor was there to see? How hopeless and discouraged do you suppose she felt? These feelings are real. There is no mock battle going on inside us. Never mind Satan now, and his desire to make us stop trusting God. Yes, he is an enemy that is able to get past hospital doors and prison bars, but we face within us a struggle to take the step which God has given us to take. We lie there with the hot tears flowing; we turn to Him when there is no one there, and cry out, *Help me. Help me. Do Thou for me, Lord, the thing You know I need now.* We remember that He has said, "Do not be anxious about anything, but in everything, by prayer and petition, with thanksgiving, present your requests to God" (Philippians 4:6 NIV). Then the next verse promises that peace will follow along as a result. We have identified with Marry now; we lie there with her or on the bed of our own affliction, and slowly we begin to review the things for which we are thankful. We verbalize some requests. If we care about having a reality of *patience* along with the *peace,* we ask for a fresh measure of these things.

Let me read you a letter from Marry that has just arrived from Holland. She is back in her apartment now, but not well enough yet to do the necessary work to earn her living. But listen as she speaks for herself:

I am physically very well. I always have a fresh complexion (how thankful I am for that) but now I do feel strong and energetic (drinking Adelle Davis' tiger's milk is still a good way to feel good), though I do have days that everything seems just impossible. I am thankful to have the time to regain strength and do so many things I could not do when I had a full-time job . . . . Right now I am making a leather jacket for Jaapjan, from an old coat someone gave me and with brown sheep's-wool sleeves knitted for it. It will save a new winter jacket. One learns such a lot by turning to small things. In this jacket I put all my love for him; a bought one would not have one stitch of it.

What a marvelous thing to write a book about affliction. I know that lots of people don't understand affliction, and ever so often think that the persons in question must be very sinful or at least unwilling to follow the Lord. They don't know that it brings afterwards "utter peace and endless trust in the Lord," "a walking with Him, a constant clutching of His Hand." I would not want to miss these periods of my life, yet going through it is not easy, I think it is hard and most painful and wet with tears. But ours is not an easy life on this earth, yet riches are stored away and treasures hidden in heaven, safe for ever and ever. Some people think that this is mysterious and the right way to live. But I see it as a long, hot walk with blisters on your feet, an empty watersack, and maybe one piece of chocolate left, yet you know that after the next turn you will see the mountain and on top of it the house with all its lights burning, and your loved ones waiting. It is worthwhile to climb up and reach it. It is not all that far and difficult, and besides that, your Father walks with you. Because of your hunger and thirst and blisters, you become more aware of the things around you, the small flowers and the big sharp stones. Besides that, it is very important that you remember that many people have to walk this same road with the same pain and thirst.

Perhaps I should have saved that portion of Marry's letter for the chapter on comforting each other, because I must say that Marry has been a comfort and encouragement to me, all along the path, during the seventeen years I have known her since she was in bed so often with liver trouble as a young L'Abri Worker. When people go to comfort her, it is they who come away comforted. A "perfect" person? No—no such one exists, but Marry is one who is able to demonstrate that *patience* followed by *hope* can actually be seen to follow one another in the midst of the waves of tribulation. Far from abstract concepts!

There are so many, many kinds of afflictions. (This, of course, is why I personally imagine a whole museum of the total incidents—complete with all the possibilities in which either prayer is answered and situations changed, or the "sufficient grace" is visibly given as people see patience and endurance becoming a reality.) Among the diverse sorts of afflictions, First Peter mentions the frustrating one of being attacked and hurt for doing a good thing. Physical attack can be violent and devastating, and our newspapers are full of instances of twentieth-century unfairness in the violence done to completely innocent people. Attacks upon people through the saying of un-truths can be as stinging as the lash of a whip. Such persecution can be given by people close to one, or by people in a circle one thought of as "friends," whether as individuals or nations. There are people in government circles who attempt to do what they think is really right and are then fiercely attacked for it—as well as individuals who are deeply hurt by their own family members.

Many kinds of situations are summed up by Peter: "For this is thankworthy, if a man for conscience toward God endure grief, suffering wrongfully. For what glory is it, if, when ye be buffeted for your faults, ye shall take it patiently? but if, when ye do well, and suffer for it, ye take it patiently, this is acceptable with God" (1 Peter 2:19, 20). The passage goes on to remind us that Jesus, who had never done anything wrong, suffered in our place and bore our sins as He hung on the cross. The reason this is pointed out to us is that we are to recognize that if we are criticized, shot at, thrust into prison, or martyred for doing what the Lord has in His plan for us, doing what God then would describe as "well" is especially "commendable" in God's sight.

What age person do you consider as being spoken of in James, when he tells us that "the trying of your faith worketh patience"? Do you think of a young person, a middle-aged person, a little child, someone just ready to retire, someone who has been in an old-folks' home for years? Do you think of a king, a street sweeper, a pastor, or a surgeon—or a student preparing for a wide variety of things? What age, what stage in life, what stratum of occupation do you visualize being filled in on the "file card" which you might prepare to record "patience," the kind which James is talking about. Is it some other age group than your own? Are you past it? Have you not yet come to it? Let us read this passage in the New International Version. ("Patience" in the King James reads "perseverance here." I think you can use it interchangeably with the nuances of meaning that are helpful in your present situation.)

> Consider it pure joy, my brothers, whenever you face trials of many kinds, because you know that the testing of your faith develops perseverance. Perseverance must finish its work so that you may be mature and complete, not lacking anything. If any of you lacks wisdom, he should ask God, who gives generously to all without finding fault, and it will be given to him. But when he asks, he must believe and not doubt, because he who doubts is like a wave of the sea, blown and tossed by the wind. That man should not think he will receive anything from the Lord; he is a double-minded man, unstable in all he does.
>
> James 1:2–8 NIV

You may say he is writing to adults. I would say that there is no age eliminated here. A child can have as many trials as an adult and can be as much of an example of patience as anyone has ever known. I remember our daughter Debby, as a child in bed for a very long time, singing through the hymnbook for her own pleasure. Her larklike voice carried notes through the house and into the garden, which were not only a joy to hear, but an audible sign that something called "patience and perseverance" was being produced within her. Any of you who have worked in children's hospitals or with handicapped children will know what I am talking about. The reality of patience coming forth in the midst of tribulation is not restricted to a chosen section of life.

One of my regular correspondents is a ninety-three-year-old man in an old-folks' home. His name is Mr. Secrest. I love reading his letters, because they are so full of a very active patient endurance, with a real measure of joy. His wife died in that same home some years ago. He has recently had an operation and must walk with a cane when he goes outdoors. But what fills his letters? He counts the cloudy days, the sunny days, and the cloudless days, and once gave me a list for the "last five years." Another time he told me he had just taken his 3,437th walk since he came into the home. He has scarcely missed a day, except when he was in the hospital. Sometimes he sends me the menu and tells me what he chose to eat. He reads every afternoon to a blind woman and also to another person who cannot read. Mr. Secrest is very concerned that so many people in the home are wasting their days, doing nothing, talking about nothing, and not even caring to come to Bible classes. His patience is not just a matter of "waiting to die," but in using the time as thoroughly as will all who believe that they are where the Lord wants them to be for a reason, a purpose—*right now.*

The "patience" in the Word of God is nothing like the passiveness of a grazing cow waiting to be hit by lightning or a falling tree—or simply waiting for the evening to come without making a fuss! The patience that God unfolds to us, in passages covering tribulation and difficulties, is an active, purposeful flowing of prayer and action that affects ourselves and other people and makes up a part of the important victory that matters to God. This patient endurance is acceptable to God, commendable to God, because in some tiny way we are following the example which Christ gave us when He told us that we were to follow in His steps.

Within the limits of our own talents and personalities, within the confines of our circumstances (hospital, prison, concentration camp, school, office, old-folks' home, tent in the desert, city slum, whatever), we are to have an increasing number of opportunities, of finding that "tribulation worketh patience."

8

The Refining Process

In the midst of my writing about affliction, the evening arrived for our special "family time together" at a concert. Sitting in a balcony almost directly above the orchestra, we could see not only each instrument and the fingers of the artists (along with their faces, or backs of their heads, shoulders, or arms), but we could watch the conductor's movements and facial expressions as he "played" upon the whole orchestra as *his* instrument. He brought out the best from the musicians, hushing some as he brought out others more vividly—always conscious of the proper place of every note in the "whole" as a unit. It was the Chamber Orchestra of Vienna, but the guest conductor was the American Kenneth Klein. The Mozart was deeply satisfying, and the Beethoven First Symphony was gorgeous. One felt that ears could not be more satisfied! The soloist for the evening was Alexandre Lagoya, a classical guitarist who played the Concerto d'Aranjuez with the orchestra. It is hard to put the musical experience into words, but one couldn't imagine that a guitar could bring forth such variation and beauty from one man's fingers, nor that the violins could sound so like a breeze in young spring leaves. The notes of the flute were so exquisite that it was almost too much to bear, yet the cellos and bass viols and every other instrument were in such fantastic blend of musical perfection that singling out one instrument was scarcely fair.

So much then came to my mind to illustrate the wonder of our Conductor who is also our Creator. Music such as we heard that night does not just flow forth by chance. No accidental blending produces such sheer satisfaction. Nor does it come by gathering together a few experienced solo players. Long hours of practice has to be added to the natural talent of each individual, but there must also be hours of practicing *together*. However, forgetting the artists for a moment, think of the instruments. A truly excellent instrument

149

takes a long time to make. I am no expert on the making of musical instruments, but I do know that wood must be tempered for years, and that time for mellowing and refining is necessary for the variety of materials involved. The blend of the instrument and the artists playing that instrument is a very special combination of long hours of work, much of it sheer drudgery and some of it even painful. The bringing forth of something which sounds close to perfection has had a background of each individual's periods of squeaky, squawky mistakes, and of the "togetherness" often being spoiled by several people veering off in their own directions, rather than following the director's leading. The ears of the artists themselves, to say nothing of the director's, have suffered through many a false note, and discouragement has been frequently experienced in some form or other. The glow and excitement of the night of a concert that is really good brings forth a "Well done!" in the pleased smile of the conductor, as well as in the clapping and at times thunderous foot stamping of a delighted audience—who may not be as capable of making a musical judgment, yet nevertheless have been watching and listening with varying amounts of understanding and appreciation.

One wonders who feels most deeply the reality of "Well, it was all worth it." People sigh as they go out into the ordinary noises of chattering human beings and car motors starting up. A glimpse has been had (if ears can be said to have "a glimpse") of sound that excels most of the sounds ordinarily heard by our ears. Do we hope for more? Do we look forward to more? Is there something even more wonderful to be heard? If so, will we be able to have tickets and time to be in on it? Will we have trained ears, prepared to hear?

No illustration is perfect, but only partial. However, the first thing I think of in hearing the sweetness and strength of an orchestra—the *pianissimo* and the *crescendo,* the rising tide of climax, and the soaring notes of a soloist—is the absolute excitement of the Bible's balance and blend which so many people seem to miss. How is it that one note seems to be played as if on a stuck record? Have you ever scratched a favorite record and, before getting to the other room to stop it, grown frantic at hearing the note repeated over and over again until you could almost scream? Anything wrong with that note? Should it be removed from the music? No, no; it is meant to be heard in balance, and the time spent in listening to it has been proportioned in the whole. It is to come forth as a triangle or drumbeat, the introduction to a cello solo or the last blast of a trumpet before a softer measure is to be played. The balance has been established by the composer.

The worth of a particular instrument, the portion that instrument is to play, or the worth of the section of music (whether it is the *allegro con spirito* or *adagio* or *larghetto* or whatever) is not to be determined by how long it goes on, or by comparison with some other instrument or section of the symphony. The worth of either the instrument or the portion of the music or the artist playing it is by being where it should be at the right time—whatever that time is—and by its proper blending into the whole, so that nothing will be missing. It seems to me that when one thinks of the Bible as a fantastic orchestra of God's true truth, some people are in danger of getting stuck on one note of one instrument and never hearing the balanced whole at all. It would be like listening to someone going over one bar of music endlessly on one instrument and then trying to describe that as the whole symphony. The Bible is a fantastically balanced whole. We cannot understand it all perfectly, but we can grow in our understanding and in our "hearing" in a balanced way. If anything is out of balance, it is not the perfect, all-wise, completely compassionate, holy, sovereign, eternal, and wonderful Counselor who is our Creator, our God of love. He is also Judge, but He gives us a balanced view of who He is—and then of what He expects of us and what He wants us to know.

As we grow in understanding some small measure of all that the Bible tells us about suffering, affliction, persecution, and tribulation, it is extremely important to listen to another "movement," so to speak, if one is thinking of our study as a piece of music. There is another aspect to be considered, in order to reach a more balanced understanding.

Not only are our times of victory—in our sufferings, hardships, sicknesses, disappointments, frustrations, worries, stresses, strains, accidents, and sorrows—important in what I have pictured as the battle. But we are really significant in history (with perhaps that imagined museum of mine recording the moments of significance in answered prayer or in the reality of "sufficient grace" being given to endure). Not only do we recognize something of what is going on as we see behind the curtains in the Book of Job (and realize that we, too, are imperfect "cracked teapots" in every way), but we see something of the fact that in the pain and drudgery of it all, one thing is emerging—patience or endurance. There is much more to that theme before we reach a base for balance.

All through the Word of God there runs a thread of silver that speaks of a very real preparation within us. We are being prepared for something ahead, but the complete scope and the richness of what it is all about are beyond us. We are given hints, but only hints. It seems clear that, whatever God is preparing for us, He describes it as:

> But as it is written, Eye hath not seen, nor ear heard, neither have entered into the heart of man, the things which God hath prepared for them that love him. But God hath revealed them unto us by his Spirit: for the Spirit searcheth all things, yea, the deep things of God.
>
> 1 Corinthians 2:9, 10

God is preparing things to hear, beyond the greatest symphonies we have ever heard; things to see, beyond the greatest beauty of sunset on sea or lake or Alpine hillside ever seen; things to imagine, beyond the fancy of the most exquisitely imaginative person who has ever lived. What God is preparing for us is greater than anything He has yet given us to experience. However, it seems clear that He is letting us know that He is not only preparing something *for* us, He is preparing *us* for something.

You may say, "What on earth do you mean? Hasn't the Blood of Christ cleansed us perfectly? Aren't we dressed in His righteousness, so that we can be presented perfectly at the throne? Aren't we completely forgiven, and isn't it true that no works can be added? Didn't Jesus say that the work we were to do was just to believe on Him whom God had sent? And isn't it true that we are not saved by any kind of works, 'lest any man should boast'?" Yes, all that is true, very true. Yes, we are to glory in the Lord. Yes, the weak are the ones whom the Lord chooses to "confound the mighty." Yes, the work is all *His* work, but a part of His work that He tells us about is a work that He is doing in us—and that has something to do with our further understanding of affliction.

Proverbs 17:3 gives a hint of something that is going on in true preparation: "The fining pot is for silver, and the furnace for gold: but the Lord trieth the hearts." The need for heat to bring out the impurities of silver means that there is a special refining pot that the silversmith uses. Heat is also used to purify and prepare gold, and a special furnace is needed for that. In comparison with the purification of silver and gold, we are told that God Himself is "trying" (or doing something important) to human hearts, to the hearts of His people. In various contexts, purity is compared with the purity of refined silver and gold. Listen to Psalms 12:7, where the words of the Lord are described as pure, without imperfections, in this way: "The words of the Lord are pure words: as silver tried in a furnace of earth, purified seven times." We are to be reassured as to the perfect wholeness of His Word, by being told that it is as pure as silver purified seven times in the heat of the silver furnace. His perfect Word gives us a blending together of notes which make up a theme we need to listen to in the midst of our times of trouble. In addition to all other explanations, we can whisper in our prayer: *Please let me come out of this closer to You, more mature as Your child, with a skimming off of some of the impurities which are spoiling the reflection of Your face as You look at me.* Fanciful ideas? Let us look at various portions of what the Bible brings out in this theme—this movement, if we are still thinking of the whole Word as a symphony orchestra.

And I will bring the third part through the fire, and will refine them as silver is refined, and will try them as gold is tried: they shall call on my name, and I will hear them: I will say, It is my people: and they shall say, The Lord is my God.

Zechariah 13:9

Here God is speaking to His people, Israel, but I believe He also speaks to us, we who are spiritual Israel, the spiritual children of Abraham through faith in Jesus Christ the Messiah. There is a very real thing that is going on inside us, a moment-by-moment, daily refining process, comparable to the refining of silver and gold. Speaking of the coming of the Lord, Malachi lifts up a flute note with the same theme:

But who may abide the day of his coming? and who shall stand when he appeareth? for he is like a refiner's fire, and like fullers' soap: And he shall sit as a refiner and purifier of silver: and he shall purify the sons of Levi, and purge them as gold and silver, that they may offer unto the Lord an offering in righteousness.

Malachi 3:2, 3

What is the meaning of the "refiner's fire"? Have you heard that a silversmith who sits over his "finer's pot" heats the silver to a very intense degree and then skims off the impurities that float to the top of the melted state of the silver? Have you heard that the silver is not pure, not considered ready for use until the silversmith himself can see his face reflected in the liquid silver? What a picture we have been given! Our dear Heavenly Father, who is also our Silversmith who is purifying us for some special use (surely an exciting use, a breathtaking secret that is ahead of us), is skimming off impurities as we are going on—day by day, week by week, and year by year—with a variety of "heat" which melts us time after time. We have a number of things to pray for when trouble hits us.

Lord, please give me the strength to go on loving You and to just defeat Satan, as he tries to depress me and make me blame You and rail against You.

Lord, I know I am far from perfect. Please skim off whatever is making scum on the surface, as I am being melted by this "heat."

Lord, may this tribulation bring a new step of patience, a quality of patience I haven't had before.

It doesn't all need to be understood by us in one fell swoop. We are given a lot to listen for and to recognize.

What kind of things are we to search for, as we ask for the scum to be skimmed off or the "beam" or "plank" to be removed from our eyes? Malachi points out some very practical advice, not a thing that is airy-fairy, intangible, mystical, in the area of our abstract thoughts. He goes on, as God directs him to write, with this:

> . . . Return unto me, and I will return unto you, saith the Lord of hosts. But ye said, Wherein shall we return? Will a man rob God? Yet ye have robbed me. But ye say, Wherein have we robbed thee? In tithes and offerings. Ye are cursed with a curse: for ye have robbed me, even this whole nation. Bring ye all the tithes into the storehouse, that there may be meat in mine house, and prove me now herewith, saith the Lord of hosts, if I will not open you the windows of heaven, and pour you out a blessing, that there shall not be room enough to receive it.
>
> Malachi 3:7–10

Each of us needs to remember that the places in which we are fooling ourselves can be in the practical areas of not being hospitable, not caring for other people before ourselves, not visiting the sick and washing feet, and not sharing our material things, at least to the one-tenth portion which is commanded here in the Old Testament. The reality of what theologians call "sanctification"—or the demonstration of the victory which Jesus died to give us in the day-by-day battle against Satan—is a reality that we can find "hitting us in the face" in various times of "heat." What are the recognizable things we are neglecting to do, which have been commanded—and what effect coming from this neglect is hindering inward growth?

In Isaiah, we have a few sentences which help us to remember that we are in the position of being representatives of the Lord here on earth. We are His ambassadors, and we can (just as earthly ambassadors can) either bring glory to the One we represent, or bring shame to Him. "Behold, I have refined thee, but not with silver; I have chosen thee in the furnace of affliction. For mine own sake, even for mine own sake, will I do it: for how should my name be polluted? and I will not give my glory to another" (Isaiah 48:10, 11). The staggering thought that God's people can "pollute" His name by their actions and deeds brings a further emphasis to our need of asking for cleansing and help. Ezekiel 20 tells of the false worship of the Israelites, as they became enmeshed and mingled their worship with that of Egyptian idols. God speaks of bringing a cleansing which is to put a stop to this: "But I wrought for my name's sake, that it should not be polluted before the heathen, in whose sight I brought them out" (v. 14). So there is a double danger to be remembered: our danger of going on needing the scum skimmed off, that we might be continually changing, and so becoming more what the Lord would have us be in preparation for a time ahead; and also our danger of becoming involved in that which would pollute *His* name.

Just as in Malachi—where the refining process of the Lord, as He prepares His people for His coming, is linked with the evidence of seriously considering the Lord's admonitions as relevant to the use of both our material possessions and our time and thinking—so Paul points out that generosity is one form of test we can apply to ourselves to measure our growth. The King James Version speaks of "a great trial of affliction," while in the New International Version we have:

And now, brothers, we want you to know about the grace that God has given the Macedonian churches. Out of the most

severe trial, their overflowing joy and their extreme poverty
welled up in rich generosity. For I testify that they gave me as
much as they were able, and even beyond their ability. Entirely
on their own, they urgently pleaded with us for the privilege of
sharing in this service to the saints. And they did not do as we
expected, but they gave themselves first to the Lord and then
to us in keeping with God's will. So we urged Titus, since he
had earlier made a beginning, to bring also to completion this
act of grace on your part. But just as you excel in everything—
in faith, in speech, in knowledge, in complete earnestness and
in your love for us—see that you also excel in this grace of
giving.

2 Corinthians 8:1–7 NIV

What has all this to do with affliction? A great deal. There is a
refining process going on, and one of the ways of recognizing that
something is taking place is that, in the midst of trials, these Christians in Macedonia are sharing their very meager goods with others.
In other words, they are thinking more about other people's needs
than their own, giving evidence of a work of the Holy Spirit taking
place within themselves, as natural selfishness in the time of suffering is turned to generosity. The polishing process is not a glamorous
happening that needs a rarified, spiritual atmosphere in which to
take place, an "ivory tower" in which to take a monk's vow in some
ethereal way, but refining which is the very warp and woof of
everyday life—right down to the grass-roots level of taking half of
your apple pie to an invalid neighbor, making a batch of rolls for the
family whose mother is in the hospital having a new baby, or sharing your garden produce with an apartment dweller. Malachi talks
about a sharing of money, needful if God is to bless even in this life,
but there is far more; and a portion consists of a concrete sharing of
things that are not just "extra," but an actual part of your own
Sunday-dinner preparation or your Saturday picnic fare. All this is
not to be just when everything is going well for us, and the neighbor
is in the hospital, but when we have a twisted knee or have just had
sad news on the phone or a crushing telegram. Is there no time for
pushing aside others for our private sorrow? No, there is always a
mixture. There is never a time when it is "convenient" to care for
someone else. There is always what could be considered a "conflict," and sensitivity as to what to do first is part of the polishing
process.

We will go into more detail later, when we discuss our finiteness and limitations in relationship to the sufferings in the world. However, as we consider that afflictions bring about a special work inside of us and thus have something to do with our growth, we need to relate this passage in Second Corinthians to our own individual settings. It is when we are having "the most severe trials" that suddenly someone in the bed next to us in the hospital needs our attention in some practical way. We may need to hurry with a pan for that patient to vomit into, or go for a nurse who never answers the bell, or get a face cloth to wash his face—not in our *strength,* but in our *weakness.* (Naturally, someone with a leg in traction cannot get out of bed.) Of course, there are limitations. But there is always *something* that we can do when we are in the midst of our own severe trial or affliction. And it is recognizing this *something* and asking for help from the Lord to do it that accomplishes something inside us which has importance in the whole refining of the "silver" which is you and which is me. *We are being prepared for something that the Lord is preparing for us.* The reality of our growth has meaning in the time ahead. Sanctification is a slow process, but it is meant to be taking place, no matter how slowly. We are not meant to be born again—and then never grow afterwards.

In the parable of the sower, as Jesus told of the various kinds of soil, it was the seed that fell on rocky ground which did not put down enough roots to grow: "And these are they likewise which are sown on stony ground; who, when they have heard the word, immediately receive it with gladness; And have no root in themselves, and so endure but for a time: afterward, when affliction or persecution ariseth for the word's sake, immediately they are offended [stumble]" (Mark 4:16, 17). This is a picture of those who have had only a shallow acceptance of the Gospel with some measure of gladness, but who do not grow at all. When trouble comes, the result is a bitterness toward God, a walking away which shows itself in some form. Rather than running *toward* the Rock, the Shelter, the Strong Tower, the Defense, the Everlasting Arms, they run *away* and reject what they claimed to believe. This is a sign of no growth at all. It is interesting, however, that the evidence becomes clear *at the time of affliction* that the "ground" was as shallow as the dirt on top of a rock. Stony ground, indeed!

This parable teaches only one set of principles and is only one theme in the symphony. The seed that falls on the "good ground" grows and produces varying amounts of fruit. This is true growth, and the roots are there, as well as the fruit. However, we know from other portions of the Bible that the good plants are also attacked. Affliction for the sake of the Word (as well as other difficulties and troubles, the deceitfulness of riches and other kinds of choking temptations) also attack the good plants. Once the seed has taken root and the plants are growing, there are many things that en- danger growth. As seen in our other illustration, the true silver can be very good silver, but not yet finished with its purifying process.

First Peter makes it very clear that growing Christians are going to experience a variety of trials and tribulations. In the King James Version, I like the vividness of the word *fiery:* "Beloved, think it not strange concerning the fiery trial which is to try you, as though some strange thing happened unto you" (1 Peter 4:12). I'll give you the same verse and a bit more from the New International Version:

> Dear friends, do not be surprised at the painful trial you are suffering, as though something strange were happening to you. But rejoice that you participate in Christ's sufferings, so that you may be overjoyed when his glory is revealed. If you are insulted because of the name of Christ, you are blessed, for the Spirit of glory and of God rests on you. If you suffer, it should not be as a murderer or thief or any other kind of criminal, or even as a meddler. However, if you suffer as a Christian, do not be ashamed, but praise God that you bear that name. For it is time for judgment to begin with the family of God; and if it begins with us, what will the outcome be for those who do not obey the gospel of God?
>
> 1 Peter 4:12–17 NIV

This hints at some very amazing kind of joy when Jesus comes back, because we have experienced something of sharing in that which is described as "Christ's sufferings." Can we understand to- tally? No, but we should recognize that our reactions and responses *do* matter as we face the things which happen to us when human enemies (who are also enemies of the Lord) revile us and persecute us and try to do all manner of things against us because they hate God. They matter, not only now, but in something we will share in the realm of joy when we see Jesus face-to-face. I am convinced that, as our archenemy is Satan with his host of demons, there are afflictions which come directly because we are God's people and which do not *seem* to be the persecution of human beings. In these we are also "partakers of Christ's sufferings," as Satan tries to destroy Him.

We are not simply "holding our own" as we bear difficulties, nor are we even only having victories in the heavenly battle, marvelous and fantastic though that thought and truth may be. We are also in some special way sharing in the rejection which Christ suffered, and—marvel of marvels—something is going on within us, so that we are becoming more prepared for what is ahead, little by little, a tiny speck at a time. We are not being hindered in accomplishing something, because we have burned our hands, broken our legs, lost our jobs, fallen into the hands of kidnappers, or even because we are sitting in a prison waiting for the moment of our martyrdom. Something is taking place in us *right now* which is as astonishing as the refining of silver, the purifying of gold, the finishing of the final touches on a work of art! We are His workmanship in a very real way, and only He can know what is in store for us and when the final moment will arrive. We have in His Word the assurance that there is something important taking place which will continue to be important in the future.

Let me stop to say right here that we have absolutely no right to say to someone in the midst of a tragedy, "Oh, you are being tried," as though we could know that God was doing something directly to that person or to that person's children. A little boy drowned because of thin ice on a canal in Holland. Could you have said to the sorrowing parents who were frantic with grief, "God is trying you"? No. How awful. The whole abnormal, fallen world—abnormality of death, the separation from the body because of the Fall, the cause and effect of history, the actions of human beings and the effects of choice, the carelessness and cruelty of human beings, as well as Satan's sphere of power—*all* these things are involved.

God neither pushes little boys under the ice, nor knocks them off a mountain. As the crashing music continues, we hear the drums roll and the strings increase their volume along with the wind instruments—and history is unfolded to us in a crescendo of increasing speed and sound. We are then to realize that a battle is going on and that we have no right to try to analyze for other people just what has taken place in the whole complicated series of events. We do know that our God who is sovereign does not have "chance" to contend with. He has told us that He is able to take whatever has taken place and to work together all things for the good of those

who are His children. We grow in our understanding through difficulties, as God opens to us that which we could not have understood with any other background or in any other set of circumstances. However, that does not eliminate the fact that we simply do not know what flow of factors brought about the accident,
the illness, the fire, the earthquakes, the storm, and the combination
of events in the middle of it all. Our assurance as children of the
Living God is that He is able to bring beauty from ashes and to give
the "oil of joy" for the spirit of mourning (see Isaiah 61:3). And, in
addition, He refines, purifies, proves, and causes to grow in us
something very precious and lasting in our attitudes toward Him
and in our actions to other human beings. As we turn to Him in our
affliction and ask for help, He does not allow our affliction to be
"wasted." As He removed the hedge protecting Job (or any one of
us whom Satan accuses of not loving God, but rather the possessions or health or other things which God has given us), He is also
able to give us the grace to come through the onslaught that follows.
However, there is much more than just "coming through," still
hanging on to our trust and love of God. There is a "coming
through," with a shinier, more gleaming sheen on our surface. We
have the possibility during the hard time to have skimmed off more
of the specks and scum which are hindering the more beautiful
reality of love, joy, peace, long-suffering, and meekness.

In the Book of James, we have been told to consider the lives of
the leaders, the prophets of old: "Take, my brethren, the prophets,
who have spoken in the name of the Lord, for an example of
suffering affliction, and of patience. Behold, we count them happy
which endure. Ye have heard of the patience of Job, and have seen
the end of the Lord; that the Lord is very pitiful, and of tender mercy
[The Lord is full of compassion and mercy(NIV)]" (James 5:10, 11).
In this context of growing, becoming closer to what the Lord would
have us to be, being prepared inwardly for something ahead, and
becoming sanctified, tiny bit by tiny bit, it seems important to look
first at some examples among those who bore afflictions in biblical
times, as we have been told to do.

Think of Joseph, for example. Of course, you know the story, but
think of it again. Here is a beautiful young lad, beloved by his father,
comfortable in his home and his way of life, suddenly kidnaped by
his own brothers who then discuss his fate: "Shall we kill him, or sell
him?" As you know, Reuben won out with his plea to save Joseph's

life, but it was no easy experience to be thrown with rough hands into a pit and then sold as a slave to traders who took him off to Egypt. People in our moment of history in various parts of the world know what it is to be torn away from home, family, and normal life and plunged into a time of terror. They have even experienced it in the American capital, let alone other principal cities of the world. We need not lack understanding of terrorism such as Joseph experienced. Then, when he seemed to be having not too bad a life in Potiphar's household, there comes the attempt by his master's wife to entice the handsome lad and her anger when he flees from her. In her fury at being rejected by a morality she could not understand nor accept, Joseph is falsely accused and thrown into prison for forcing the wife of Potiphar! Could any affliction be more devastating? Of course, people today are being just as unfairly treated and falsely accused and violently dealt with, but Joseph lived through affliction which has many portions that people through the years could relate to.

What happened? The story is one of the most exciting and satisfying in the whole Bible, as we see Joseph given by God clear explanations for the dreams of the butler and the baker who were in prison with him. It makes a thrilling account to read of the exciting moment when Joseph is given by God the opportunity of going before Pharaoh and explaining the meaning of his dream to him. The coming seven years of enormous crops, followed by seven years of famine, is interpreted through the wisdom which God gives to Joseph. Thereby he proposes a plan to organize and prepare for those fourteen years, so that the food will be distributed without waste.

However, what I want us to dwell on, in the "theme" we are listening to right now, is what we are told to give us some understanding of what took place *inside* Joseph during the entire experience. He went through the affliction of having violence done to him and of suffering the kind of deprivation which could be described as "being abased," in Paul's terminology. Then Joseph experienced almost too much in the area of temptation in an opposite direction. Although people do not often enough consider affluence or power an "affliction," there is so much temptation connected with wealth and influence that the prayer to "give me neither poverty nor riches" is a prayer for more than just a balance in "things." It is a cry for a balance of life which makes the inward growth come more easily or continue without an abrupt halt. Joseph experienced the kind of power which was secondary only to Pharaoh's and the kind of wealth provided by this position, creating a situation which was in danger of ruining his spiritual growth. I would choose Joseph as someone with extremes of affliction to whom we can look back, asking the God of Joseph to help us to stay as close to Him as Joseph must have done, hour by hour and day by day. *Oh, God, we need to pray, help me in my suffering from pain and the frustration of being placed in a bed [or a wheelchair]. Help me to not waste this time I have for some special understanding or growth.* But some of us need also to pray:

Oh, God, it isn't just the screeching headache, the sharp pain in my joints, and unbearable increase of pain in my back as I sit here with people not knowing. But I know that I am in an even worse danger of temptation to waste this period of my life. You have thrust me into a place of some degree of prominence, and You have given me what seems like an affluence that could be dangerous to my utter dependence upon You, moment by moment. Help me, my dear God and Father, not to be blinded by such a "switch" of afflictions or such a strange combination of afflictions.

Joseph was maintained and given strength to go on by the same God who is *our* God. Joseph demonstrated what had been going on inside him—the refining and trying, as silver is refined and tried. The "furnace" of both extremes of affliction did not destroy Joseph as both Satan and his brothers hoped he would be destroyed. Come to this most tender portrayal of the growth of a true believer—so long ago that it is in the first book of the Bible. Our God is Joseph's God, and He can "bring us through," with the silver—which He has purified in His own way—gleaming through. Individuals who are His children, through faith in all that He has made clear in His Word, are saved and justified in only one way—on the basis of the Blood of the Lamb. Sanctification is also on the basis of the Blood of the Lamb, but it is a gradual growth, a stream of victories, never to be perfect until the Messiah, the Lamb, Jesus Himself returns and changes us in the twinkling of an eye. However, until then or until we die, we are meant to be growing, to be getting more "pure," as silver or gold. Something is meant to be going on in the area of change in us. During the heat, some very real, observable results are to take place in us, observable at least to God.

Come to Genesis and find Joseph, who has been feeding his family without their ever knowing just who is this great man from whom they are carting away sacks of grain to their father in the midst of famine. Read in chapter 45 the beauty that comes out in the speech of Joseph, who has not become bitter and revengeful against his brothers—nor has he blamed God for all the difficulties he has gone through. There is no "It wasn't fair!" in Joseph's speech, nor any hint of "Why couldn't God have accomplished all this in another way?" Let's read it from the view of discovering Joseph's inner growth in the area of love, joy, peace, long-suffering, meekness, gentleness, kindness:

Then Joseph could not refrain himself before all them that stood by him; and he cried, Cause every man to go out from me. And there stood no man with him, while Joseph made himself known unto his brethren. And he wept aloud: and the Egyptians and the house of Pharaoh heard. And Joseph said unto his brethren, I am Joseph; doth my father yet live? And his brethren could not answer him; for they were troubled at his presence. And Joseph said unto his brethren, Come near to me, I pray you. And they came near. And he said, I am Joseph your brother, whom ye sold unto Egypt. Now therefore be not grieved, nor angry with yourselves, that ye sold me hither: for God did send me before you to preserve life . . . . And God sent me before you to preserve you a posterity in the earth, and to save your lives by a great deliverance.

Genesis 45:1–7

Then move to chapter 50 where Joseph puts it so clearly that his heart is full of love and forgiveness and certainty that God has "worked all things together for good," although what his brothers had done was evil. "But as for you, ye thought evil against me; but God meant it unto good, to bring to pass, as it is this day, to save much people alive. Now therefore fear ye not: I will nourish you, and your little ones. And he comforted them, and spake kindly unto them" (vv. 20, 21).

What a fantastic work, of "trying" as one tries silver by heat, had been going on in Joseph, and how beautifully he came through all the trials! The tribulation or affliction of affluence and power in the land of Egypt had made him neither arrogant and proud nor domineering and cruel. He did not take his opportunity to pay back or give the same measure of "evil for evil" to his brothers. Joseph had come through the two extremes of affliction by the grace of God in a way which brought much glory to God. Many years later, in the Book of Psalms, praise to the Lord is sung as the history of God's people is retold. Among other things we find:

Seek the Lord, and his strength: seek his face evermore. Remember his marvellous works that he hath done; his wonders, and the judgments of his mouth . . . . He sent a man before them, even Joseph, who was sold for a servant: Whose feet they hurt with fetters: he was laid in iron: Until the time that his word came; the word of the Lord tried him. The king sent and loosed him; even the ruler of the people, and let him go free. He made him lord of his house, and ruler of all his substance: To bind his princes at his pleasure; and teach his senators wisdom.

Psalms 105:4, 5, 17–23

We should be encouraged by the remembrance of Joseph and his victories—so evident in the inward struggles that must have been his, as he faced not only the agonies of separation from his family, prison life, and the terrible falseness of accusations, but also the temptations of extraordinary power and riches. His story should strengthen us in our own lives, as a variety of things come to us—one thing tumbling after another in quick succession—in the midst of which we are meant to be growing, being sanctified, being purified as silver or gold in the work we are building, as described in 1 Corinthians 3. This passage gives us some understanding that there is a believer's judgment. We are all saved on the basis of the perfect work of Christ, but evidently there will be a difference as to what has truly taken place during our lives after we have become Christians. Here the description speaks of fire in a different way. This is the picture of a moment when the life we have lived is behind us. Only the results—the realities of what went on inside us during that time and the things accomplished—are counted through the Lord's perspective as having done His will. The "works," the things we have done inwardly and outwardly, are pictured as a building, and the evaluation or judgment of these buildings is pictured as fire. The building materials differ tremendously. Our being in the Lord's will—having the reactions He means us to have, having the victories He can enable us to have, loving Him and trusting Him, being what

He would have us be, and doing what He would have us do—comprise lasting materials which will come unscathed through the fire. "Worthless building material" consists of wrong motives and all the things He warns us against: rebellion against His will, murmuring against Him, desiring things for our own fulfillment of pride and comfort rather than for His glory, wasting the opportunities we have had to do what perhaps no one else has had the combination of opportunities to do. All these things comprise the perishable sort of buildings which turn into ashes when the fire sweeps through them. The day will come, we are told, when we will find out what this means, but we are to understand sufficiently now and to call out for help while there is yet time, so that we may build with the precious and available materials. He who gives us the strength when we ask Him will supply us with the right materials when we ask Him.

For no one can lay any foundation other than the one already laid, which is Jesus Christ. If any man builds on this foundation using gold, silver, costly stones, wood, hay or straw, his work will be shown for what it is, because the Day will bring it to light. It will be revealed with fire, and the fire will test the quality of each man's work. If what he has built survives, he will receive his reward. If it is burned up, he will suffer loss; he himself will be saved, but only as one escaping through the flames.

1 Corinthians 3:11–15 NIV

Clearly this is speaking to believers, children of the Lord who have been born into His family, who will always be His, and who have eternal life. However, it is just as clear that there is to be a difference which can be described as "suffering loss." Salvation is not of works, but we are warned that it will matter to us in some very real way as to whether or not we have taken the whole Word of God seriously. We have been told, with the clarity of a scene seen through freshly washed glass windows, that not only are there treasures in heaven, but that we are slowly, hour by hour and day by day, building with *some* kind of material, and that it is going to matter to us, as well as mattering to God. The next chapter warns us not to judge each other. God knows how prone we are to apply everything to *someone else!* So He gives us: "Therefore judge nothing before the time, until the Lord come, who both will bring to light the hidden things of darkness, and will make manifest the counsels of the hearts: and then shall every man have praise of God" (1 Corinthians 4:5). We are told not to be puffed up with pride. We are told to remember that only God gives us anything that differs from anyone else's "things," and therefore we have nothing to be proud of.

With all that ringing in our ears, played by the oboes, the bassoons, as well as the piano, we should then turn our minds to what area can be real for us *today*. Right now we have our own particular or peculiar piece of affliction, our own "impossibility," our own "last straw." Perhaps today you are in the hospital, and the lab is so slow getting your tests done that the doctor has to wait until after the weekend to even have a good idea of what to start to do for you. Perhaps today your car broke down just as you started off with all the children for a day-off picnic, and the whole family looked at you to see what idea you would come up with. Perhaps today you started out by asking the Lord for more reality, and what took place was a new attack of searing pain in your knees and elbows—and your preparations for Sunday dinner were interrupted by the arrival of four people who needed help, one after another. Today is the day, not tomorrow but always today, to discover what it means to find a practical area in which to ask that the "melting heat" will not be wasted.

"But I can't stand him. I can't even stand the sight of him. It makes me feel like vomiting to be in the same room with him." This wail came from a girl whose prettiness was hidden by a sullen look. As she described how she felt about the boy she had married some period of time before, the outstanding words were: "I . . . me . . . mine . . . my right . . . my fulfillment . . . my life . . . my happiness . . . ."

"Dear ————," I said, "will you try one thing for me: Take one day and use it in a completely different way than you have ever used a day? Will you think back over the years you have known him from the time he was a little boy? Try to remember what he likes to eat, to drink, to talk about, to do. Plan a picnic, fill a thermos with whatever hot or cold you can think of that would please him the most. Get the kind of fruit, filling for sandwiches, and cookies that he likes best. Think of a place in the mountains or by the lake, the kind of place you think he would enjoy most. Ask him to go with you for a day; take a book along to read that you think he would enjoy; start conversations about subjects you know he is interested in. Try to make an effort to see whether you could accomplish in one whole day an elimination of thinking of yourself at all. Take it as a challenge, as a work of art, as a project, as a complete production—accomplishing in one whole day the work of concentrating on someone else's pleasure, on his enjoyment."

She did it. Joy of joys, she did it. The report came from her: "I was amazed. It was such an amazing experience. I never thought it could be like that. It was actually a fantastic day."

Everything perfect from then on? No. But tiny step by tiny step, there was a coming back together. Then came the day when I gave a talk on affliction, and among other things I spoke of the need for thanking the Lord in the midst of making a request, but thanking Him with honesty, not as a parrot repeating empty phrases. "You can't lie on the street in agony after an auto accident and just say, 'ThankYouLord . . . thankYouLord . . . praisetheLord . . . praisetheLord . . . thankYouLord,' and have any reality of being prepared to make your request known. You aren't supposed to be thankful for the accident, but you can think back over things you really are thankful for, and the very memory of them and of thanking the Lord for them will help you in your time of need as you get ready to make your special request."

It was Thursday morning at my Bible class that this came into my talk, and that evening dear ——— was using an ironing machine, one of those things with a roller, ironing sheets and tablecloths for the hotel next door where she and husband were working. It was late; she was tired; and the accident came so easily. One minute the sheet was going through and the next minute her hand! Before the machine could be stopped and her hand extricated, she had a terribly mashed and burned hand with excruciating pain. When I called her at the hospital sometime later, her first tones were full of really awed thankfulness instead of wails of complaint. "Oh, Mrs. Schaeffer, what you taught this morning worked. It really did. All the way on that long drive to the hospital with my hand paining so much, I thought back over how much I had to thank the Lord for in these last few months, and I named them and thought about them, and it helped so much to keep my mind off the pain, even before I prayed about my hand at all. I'm so glad I was in your class this morning." Could this be the same self-centered person talking? But I hadn't yet heard all there was to come. "And, Mrs. Schaeffer, I have to have an operation tomorrow on my hand, and . . . and . . . could you have ——— over for a cup of coffee and talk to him during his break from work? You see, I am so worried for him, because I know he is so sad and worried about my hand. He really needs help."

I wept at my end of the phone. I couldn't help it. I was listening to a miracle. Not the flash of lightning and crash of thunder in answer to prayer, not the sun standing still, not even the healing of an excruciatingly painful burned hand. It was a greater miracle than anything—a changed heart. Sins forgiven? Ah, yes, but also visible growth, a polishing of the surface so that a glimpse of His face was being seen in this particular reality of selflessness. Perfect? No. Always to go on in a steady, unbroken, uphill line? No. But something real, tangible, true, the taking place of a process that shows up in the stuff of everyday, unglamorous affliction that is "trying" hearts. "The fining pot is for silver, and the furnace for gold: but the Lord trieth the hearts." Proverbs in action!

Don't let's miss the moments; don't let's waste the brief time when the Master Silversmith bends over us to skim something off that is hindering us. *Do thou for me, Lord, whatever You see needs doing in me, right now, before this moment becomes past history.*

Once again consider the illustration of an orchestra's full scope, playing your favorite symphony and needing every instrument and every note, as a call to being more balanced in studying and absorbing and living by the whole Bible. Then turn and think of ourselves as both musicians needing constant practice and work and as instruments needing mellowing and refining through years of being made and used. See ourselves as being prepared for some magnificent "symphony" under the Conductor's direction, facing what is ahead of us in His plan for eternity. We are to be handmade instruments and also diligent music students, preparing and being prepared for a concert ahead, in which the preparation time has significance—*really matters.* Our today has a reality of meaning beyond the present. The refining and the preparation have a day of fulfillment ahead.

9
School for Comforters

All schools should have a required course called "Comforting People." That should apply to schools for nurses, pastors, farmers, teachers, artists, homemakers, mothers, fathers, bankers, businessmen, public-relations workers, and friends—as well as to police academies, medical and law schools, and engineering colleges. In fact, this goes for every human being. Each person needs comfort at times, and each one of us also needs to give comfort at some time. Perhaps some people have never given anyone comfort, and perhaps some people have never received comfort. But that does not change the fact that everyone needs comfort. Unhappily, even if there were courses of study on how to give comfort, that in itself would not ensure that comfort would be properly given in time of need. Human beings are so spoiled because of the Fall that it takes far more than a course of study to call forth the compassion for others which results in a fertile imagination about how to give comfort.

We have looked at some of the facets of how "tribulation worketh patience." There is a need to go on to discover that God has made it very clear that He Himself will teach us in the area of comfort. A beginning point is that suffering or affliction or trouble of some kind needs to precede the giving or receiving of comfort. First, we cannot ever experience what it is like to be comforted if *we* have never had any sadness, sorrow, affliction, or trouble in which comfort is needed. Second, we have to recognize our need for comfort before we will let ourselves be comforted. Have you ever had a little child come running to you with a bleeding knee or finger, or a big bump on his or her head, and find the child suddenly fighting off your loving arms—or kicking you in the shins? He may roll on the floor in pain, not accepting your antiseptic-soaked cotton and the bandage you have quickly prepared, nor even the cup of hot chocolate, your welcoming lap, and the open storybook. The anger and rebellion and fury at being hurt push away the comfort entirely at first, until there is a change, a sudden softening of the little heart, and a different kind of weeping which sends into your arms a limp little body, instead of the tangled, fighting mass of resisting arms or legs.

Finally, we cannot know how to comfort anyone if we have never been comforted ourselves in some way. The really effective "school for comforters" is life itself. Life consists of a great variety of difficult times, as well as joyous times. Although no two lives are exactly alike, the similarity is that we all experience what it is to be kicking against the affliction, at some points in our past histories. We also know what it is like to run crying to the Lord, asking and accepting His "lap," His Band-Aids, His cup of hot chocolate, His comfort in all its variety.

David describes our lives very vividly: "The righteous cry, and the Lord heareth, and delivereth them out of all their troubles. The Lord is nigh unto them that are of a broken heart; and saveth such as be of a contrite spirit. Many are the afflictions of the righteous: but the Lord delivereth him out of them all . . . . The Lord redeemeth the soul of his servants: and none of them that trust in him shall be desolate" (Psalms 34:17–19, 22). The afflictions of the Lord's people have always been many. Job was not alone in his sufferings. The troubles are plural and follow one another through life, but there is a vast difference when we have someone to cry to and run to, someone to listen when we need to pour forth our broken-heartedness. There is a great difference between being comforted and being desolate. There is a difference as wide and deep as an ocean between our recognizing someone else's need for comfort—because we have been comforted ourselves and can recognize the utter desolation of another's moment of need—and our being cold and hard because *we* have never been comforted.

The school for comforters, however, cannot be found in just any life which has been lived with some understanding of being comforted. Paul makes it very clear that we are taught, time after time and instance after instance, what comfort is all about, and that we are meant to be learning more completely day after day how to comfort other people who are going through similar difficulties:

> Praise be to the God and Father of our Lord Jesus Christ, the Father of compassion and the God of all comfort, who comforts us in all our troubles, so that we can comfort those in any

trouble with the comfort we ourselves have received from God. For just as the sufferings of Christ flow over into our lives, so also through Christ our comfort overflows. If we are distressed, it is for your comfort and salvation; if we are comforted, it is for your comfort, which produces in you patient endurance of the same sufferings we suffer. And our hope for you is firm, because we know that just as you share in our sufferings, so also you share in our comfort.

We do not want you to be uninformed, brothers, about the hardships we suffered in the province of Asia. We were under great pressure, far beyond our ability to endure, so that we despaired even of life. Indeed, in our hearts we felt the sentence of death. But this happened that we might not rely on ourselves but on God, who raises the dead. He has delivered us from such a deadly peril, and he will deliver us. On him we have set our hope that he will continue to deliver us, as you help us by your prayers. Then many will give thanks on our behalf for the gracious favor granted us in answer to the prayers of the many.

2 Corinthians 1:3–11 NIV

What an excitingly complete course of study in the school for comforters is described in this passage. First, we are reminded that our wonderful Heavenly Father is "the Father of compassion." That is something to exclaim about. Do you feel sick with concern for suffering people in countries you can do nothing about? Do you feel heavy with longing to do more for someone in your family or for a friend? Do your feelings of compassion sometimes keep you awake at night? Then know that God has infinitely more compassion than any of us and that He is called, among many other names that describe Him to us, "the Father of compassion." There would be no compassion if He had not made us able to have compassion. We are made in His image, and He is the Father of compassion. Then to go on and add much more to this—so much that it should make us tremble with awe—He is described as "the God of all comfort." *All* comfort! There is no variety of comfort needed that He does not know about. This is the One who, if we are His children through the Lamb, the Saviour, will "comfort us in all our troubles." How? First of all, we need to run to Him, not away from Him. And we need to not kick and fight and *blame* Him for our being hurt. We must come, trusting Him and ready to listen to His Word, as we climb on

His lap and let Him speak to us through His Word. We can talk to Him. He listens to us. We can pour out all our troubles and tell Him our fears and doubts, as well as our love and trust, and ask for help where it is really needed, not in a pious way as if from someone with perfect courage and bravery which is not ours at all. We come exactly where we are and tell Him the truth about our needs. He is patient with us in our trouble *about* the trouble—as well as in the trouble itself! All this gives us no possibility of just repeating phrases we have learned or heard someone else use. There is no magic formula. We are talking to a Person, our Father the Comforter, and we need to be natural and open and honest in our private time with Him.

One of the astonishing reasons for the worthwhile nature of our affliction, trouble, or pain is added to all the other understanding we have been given when we are told: ". . . so that we can comfort those in any trouble with the comfort we ourselves have received from God." We are meant to have learned a precious lesson, a very useful and valuable reality about comfort, when we have been comforted and then enabled to take another step in life as God comforted us. We are meant to be able to comfort someone else— not just one person but *plural* persons—with the comfort we have received from God. We are meant to be able to say, "It is possible to go on. It is possible to dry your tears after a while. He doesn't mind our tears and sorrow, but He does comfort us. He did comfort me. I love you and I'm going to stick by you, too. I'll call you at twelve noon every day and pray for you for five minutes." Or perhaps, "I know just how you feel, and the Lord pulled me out of the same spot so wonderfully. I can go on without my leg and discover a terrific variety of things to do with only one leg. I'll stick with you in these times of adjustment and try to call or write once a week."

Don't stop there. Paul goes on, giving us a couplet that arrests our interest with a need to reread to make sure that we have understood correctly. There is a parallel drawn, indicating that the sufferings of Christ overflow into our lives. (We therefore can expect suffering because of this factor among all the others—we are not always to have easy lives, when Jesus knew such titanic suffering.) Likewise, the comfort we are given through Christ also overflows into other people's lives. In other words, real comfort cannot be silently contained inside a person. There is a spilling over that causes that comfort to help someone else, as an overflowing supply of water would help a thirsty neighbor. Paul goes on making the point that this exchange of comfort and the resulting greater patience and endurance are something to be continued as life goes on—a central portion of the relationship among Christians. This is to be a constantly repeated experience, the need for comfort and the giving of comfort to others. We are meant to be using our imaginations as to how to go about this practically, day by day.

Paul does not hide for the Corinthian church family the hardships which he and the others suffered in Asia. He tells of the terrible pressures that were really beyond human endurance, to the point that they were sure they would die. As he speaks of God's deliverance from these harsh and extreme afflictions, he thanks the Corinthians for their help. What kind of help? This is a key to our own giving of help. Paul thanks them for their *prayers*. He does not just leave it there, so that we might think that the prayers of other Christians were a comfort from the viewpoint of knowing that they cared enough to pray. It is far more practical than that: Paul says there were *results* from their prayers. Something was changed in history: "Then many will give thanks on our behalf for the gracious favor granted us in answer to the prayers of many." Something took place in answer to the combined prayers of many people which is so great a thing that many give thanks for that "favor," a special sort of deliverance. So prayer is one of the most important and continual parts of the variety of things we are to do in comforting each other in times of need. Prayer is not to be the only thing, but it seems to me that it is to be added to any other thing we do. It is something we can do when we are thousands of miles away from each other, which really makes a difference in the immediate situation. In taking prayer seriously as a portion of our giving comfort to those who are in serious affliction or deep suffering, we can be providing comfort and help without the troubled ones knowing about it, perhaps until we "compare notes" at some later time.

Any of you who have read the L'Abri story, which I wrote about the way the Lord began the work at L'Abri, will remember the deep period of affliction we went through in those weeks when Franky became ill with polio, Susan with rheumatic fever, and floods and avalanches hit our village and threatened our chalet. Then came the climax when we received papers which informed us that we were being given six weeks to get out of our home, that village, the canton of Valais, and all of Switzerland. The reason given was:

"You have had a religious influence in the village of Champéry." To have the full story you have to read the book, but there is something I never told in the book, something which fits into this need to pray for each other, when the Lord puts "each other" into our minds in some especially definite way.

With the six-hour time difference between Philadelphia and Switzerland, my mother was deeply asleep on that morning when we had the telephone call from the *gendarmes* (police), asking us to come to be told something about our *permis de séjour*. As Priscilla and her father (Prisca went along to translate) went off to the *gendarmerie* I naturally stopped my baking of a heart-shaped chocolate cake and prayed for them. I had no idea that anything dramatic was going to happen, or that our whole lives were going to be changed from that morning on. I had no idea that the hardest blow of affliction was going to descend upon us in a matter of minutes, or that we were going to need both comforting and help.

At three o'clock in the morning, Philadelphia time, my mother awakened from a short but vivid dream. She had dreamt that I had knocked on her door. As she opened it, I tried to speak but could not say a word. She said (when she wrote later to tell me about it) that my face was distressed and my arms were full of heavy packages. She asked, "What is wrong, Edith? Are you in some trouble? You look so burdened." And though my mouth seemed to be forming words, I couldn't make a sound. Then she awakened. Being a woman of prayer, she felt that it was not a chance thing that she had awakened, feeling so certain that something was wrong—and she got out of bed to spend the next few hours in prayer. She prayed for whatever the need might be, read her Bible, and then continued praying for our comfort, strength, wisdom, and guidance in our need. Knowing Mother, she would have been careful to pray for each member of the family individually, each of the four children and Fran and myself. This meant that, while Prisca and Fran were receiving the shock of having that edict handed to them, Mother prayed thousands of miles away, and I was praying with less urgency than hers, just a mile away. It also meant that, as Fran gathered the whole family together to make a decision, Mother was praying for each of us individually.

As Fran said, "We have two possible courses to follow. We can either seek the most important and influential people to write, telephone, or wire for help, or we can decide to *not* ask for human help at all, but use this opportunity to trust God literally to be able to work in space and time and history in this thing, even as He did in times past, and simply pray for His help and guidance in this." Fran put it to a vote as to which path to follow. It meant that, as we were voting as a family, Mother was actually praying for "wisdom in whatever is the need," and that her prayer was being answered. We voted unanimously to choose to live by prayer in those six weeks we had been given to leave. The results of our prayers and Mother's prayers—and gradually those of a great many other people who prayed for us in our time of amazingly unique series of afflictions— are recorded in the L'Abri story. And the results are still continuing.

We don't all awaken in the middle of the night (with or without a dream), suddenly feeling an urgency to pray for someone, but we all have wakeful nights and at times cannot get some person out of our minds. It is important that we not push away that person and read a book or try to get back to sleep without stopping to pray for him, her, or them. However, the middle of the night is not the only time we may suddenly think of someone we haven't thought about for a long time, or of someone else in the same house! We should make it a practice to always stop to pray for that person, even if it is a very brief time of prayer. "Comforting others with the comfort whereby you have been comforted" includes this sensitivity to pray for each other. Stop and consider that each one of us is so terribly limited in our finiteness that we can't pray by name for very many people, nor can we go to the hospital, old-folks' home, prison, or the next-door neighbor's home to comfort a succession of many people in one day. However, if every single true Christian, every child of the Lord, comforted a few people in person, as the Word of God tells us to, and prayed seriously and frequently for those who came into each of our minds, what a fantastic lot of comforting would take place. Enough to go around!

No one can really comfort anyone else unless there has been a measure of the same kind of affliction or some kind of suffering which has brought about an understanding and in which we have ourselves experienced the Lord's comfort. One good thing that can come out of a fresh deluge of trouble can be a fresh flow of understanding, a preparation to be a comfort that will bring about ripples of results which will flow out beyond our wildest imagination. However, the results are often not known in our lifetime, and thus we can't get caught up in giving comfort with an expectation of some exciting immediate result. Our main motive should really be giving comfort to others as it has been given to us by the Lord in our times of trouble, so that His compassion is made known in a very real way in our circle of people. We are meant to make known the wonder of who He is by how we love one another and especially by our vivid expression of love in times of need. *His* compassion and love in giving comfort is to be reflected in *our* giving comfort. How else are people to know that God is all that His Word makes clear that He is?

The Twenty-third Psalm has been a comfort to the Lord's people through many centuries, and it never loses its quietness and reassurance. This is the comfort of a shepherd to his sheep—and in this picture we are the sheep and the Lord is our Shepherd. We then are to comfort others as under-shepherds, with Him as our example, although we can only do this in minor and very fleeting ways.

The Lord is my shepherd; I shall not want. What an assurance of His constant care and sensitivity to our needs.

He maketh me to lie down in green pastures; he leadeth me beside still waters. Dear David, who saw so many wars, so many bloody battles, knew the Lord's power to provide quietness in the midst of it all. In our twentieth-century horrors, the Lord can likewise provide an oasis of quiet moments in the middle of the struggle. We can also use our imaginations to provide some dear person in the midst of deep need with a "day off" in the fields or on a sandy shore, in the woods or by a river or lake—in order that he or she may have a surrounding of peacefulness and a break from the pressures.

He restoreth my soul: he leadeth me in the paths of righteousness for his name's sake. Only He can restore our souls and lead us in His paths, but we can pray with and for someone in need of restoration and refreshment and in need of being led. We can read the Word of God with one in need, or simply talk together over a cup of tea, so that there will be an opportunity to think things over aloud.

Yea, though I walk through the valley of the shadow of death, I will fear no evil: for thou art with me; thy rod and thy staff they comfort me. What fantastic comfort is promised to us, as the Shepherd's rod beats off the wolves that Satan would send against us to destroy us, and as His staff (which has a crook to fasten around our necks) pulls us back when we stray into dangerous spots.

Right here I must digress a moment. Affliction is at times chastening:

Thou shalt also consider in thine heart, that, as a man chasteneth his son, so the Lord thy God chasteneth thee. Therefore thou shalt keep the commandments of the Lord thy God, to walk in his ways, and to fear him. For the Lord thy God bringeth thee into a good land, a land of brooks of water, of fountains and depths that spring out of valleys and hills; A land of wheat, and barley, and vines, and fig trees, and pomegranates; a land of oil olive, and honey; A land wherein thou shalt eat bread without any scarceness, thou shalt not lack any thing in it; a land whose stones are iron, and out of whose hills thou mayest dig brass. When thou hast eaten and art full, then thou shalt bless the Lord thy God for the good land which he hath given thee. Beware that thou forget not the Lord thy God, in not keeping his commandments, and his judgments, and his statutes, which I command thee this day: Lest when thou hast eaten and art full, and hast built goodly houses, and dwelt therein; And when thy herds and thy flocks multiply, and thy silver and thy gold is multiplied, and all that thou hast is multiplied; Then thine heart be lifted up, and thou forget the Lord thy God, which brought thee forth out of the land of Egypt, from the house of bondage.

Deuteronomy 8:5–14

Here in the Old Testament, God makes it very clearly understood that He is saying that He has taken His people out of a terrible bondage and has brought them into a very fruitful land. However, there is a warning to the Israelites and to us. When we have been "saved from bondage," we are not to use our joyous freedom and our enjoyment of His supply of our needs to put other things in the place of God. We are not to turn away from His express commandments to us, made very specific now in the New Testament as it enlarges upon the Old Testament laws. By the power of the indwelling Holy Spirit and on the basis of the victory which Christ died to give us in daily "overcoming by the blood of the Lamb," we are to live a life of resisting the devil's temptations to turn away from the way the Lord is leading us. If, as children of the Lord, as true "sons" (and that includes both *sons* and *daughters* in one word), we turn away from His Word and all that it instructs us to be and to do, then we are told there will be a chastening or discipline.

Look at it in the New Testament, in Hebrews, and you will see that we are warned again, given a very fair explanation, and treated as responsible, intelligent children:

In your struggle against sin, you have not yet resisted to the point of shedding your blood. And you have forgotten that word of encouragement that addresses you as sons: [Then the writer of Hebrews quotes from Proverbs 3:11, 12.] "My son, do not make light of the Lord's discipline, and do not lose heart when he rebukes you, because the Lord disciplines those whom he loves, and punishes everyone he accepts as a son." Endure hardship as discipline; God is treating you as sons. For what son is not disciplined by his father? If you are not disciplined (and everyone undergoes discipline), then you are illegitimate children and not true sons. Moreover, we have all had human fathers who disciplined us and we respected them for it. How much more should we submit to the Father of our spirits and live! Our fathers disciplined us for a little while as they thought best; but God disciplines us for our good, that we may share in his holiness. No discipline seems pleasant at the time, but painful. Later on, however, it produces a harvest of righteousness and peace for those who have been trained by it. Therefore, strengthen your feeble arms and weak knees! Make level paths for your feet, so that the lame may not be disabled, but rather healed.

Hebrews 12:4–13 NIV

This fits in with the picture of a shepherd who finds it necessary to break a little lamb's leg. Why? Because the lamb runs away and climbs on dangerous cliffs where it might fall into a ravine and be destroyed. The story goes that the shepherd puts a splint on the lamb's leg but then carries the lamb in his arms until the leg is strong again. That lamb never strays away again, but grows to love the shepherd so much that it always stays nearby and goes wherever it is led.

The chastening or disciplining of the Lord is needed by each of us at times. How can we tell when an affliction has come from an attack of Satan, thereby trying to put a wedge between the Lord and ourselves? Or when it is something which God has sent to turn us away from a dangerous and sinful thing we are doing, dangerous in its taking us further and further from Him? First of all, we can do what Job did; we can search our lives—our actions and our thoughts—and ask the Lord to help us find anything which needs confession to Him, anything in which we need to ask His forgiveness. We are told that if we confess our sins, He is faithful to forgive us and to cleanse us from all unrighteousness. Then if we, like Job, are convinced that there is nothing specific, we can have the comfort that there are other sources of affliction and other results that can come forth from suffering and troubles. We can remember the battle in the heavenlies and can pray for victory in the area of continued trust and love for the Lord. We can also ask for patience to come as one result, even if Satan is trying to make us have an opposite result, and we can pray for whatever refining can take place during our time of being buffeted by whatever winds blow, or by the heat of whatever furnace is fired. We can always ask for comfort. Comfort is never out of place, as we remember that the only chastening which the Lord gives His children is to bring them back to him, not to punish them. Jesus took the punishment upon Himself, and our penalty for sin has been paid. The chastening things are only to draw our feet out of a path that is taking us away from the Lord's will, from His way for us.

In First Corinthians are verses which speak to us about the need for judging ourselves, so that we won't need to be judged and disciplined by the Lord. We are told that this is a viable alternative to being disciplined. We are not to judge others, but we are to judge ourselves. Listen: "But if we judged ourselves, we would not come under judgment. When we are judged by the Lord, we are being disciplined so that we will not be condemned with the world" (1 Corinthians 11:31, 32 NIV). All this is given in the context of Communion, the Lord's Supper. We are being warned not to partake of the bread and cup of Communion without seriously examining ourselves before the Lord and confessing our sin to Him. It is very interesting that it is each one of us who is responsible for himself or herself in this admonition. We are not to go around judging other people, and certainly not in the guise of coming to "comfort" someone by suggesting that perhaps his or her deep trouble is a result of needing to be chastened by God. Let Job's words sting us into a remembrance of never being in the place of his dubious comforters: "Then Job answered and said, I have heard many such things: miserable comforters are ye all" (Job 16:1, 2). Let us cringe from being described as "miserable comforters." Our searching for hidden sin should be the searching of our own hearts before God. If

we are worried about someone else, the first need is to pray for that
one very seriously, using energy and time as a hidden gift . . . .

But we were in the middle of the Twenty-third Psalm. The next
verse is: *Thou preparest a table before me in the presence of mine
enemies: thou anointest my head with oil; my cup runneth over.*
What comfort—and in such practical form! With the utter safety of
His care, God feeds us openly and cares for our needs in a place
and time when we are surrounded by enemies. We are anointed
and given such variety of care by Him that we can say in life, even at
times in the midst of tribulation and suffering, "My cup runneth
over." However, again we are given an example of *how* to give
comfort. There are so many practical situations we can enter into
and "prepare a table," when confronted with family or friends or
even strangers in trouble. There is an endless variety of ways to
"spread a table in the presence of enemies"—an invitation to a
meal, taking someone on a picnic, carrying some special food into a
hospital or other institution, sending a food package to someone
shut off from pleasant meals, providing food for hungry, desperate
people in flood or famine areas. These are things we can do over
and over again to give practical comfort to others. It is one of the
actual forms of comfort with which the Lord had comforted David,
but so has He comforted each of us.

*Surely goodness and mercy shall follow me all the days of my life:
and I will dwell in the house of the Lord for ever.* This Psalm is so
complete, as we shall see later in this chapter. It really gives a total
scope of the kinds of comfort we are meant to give each other—in
the *present,* reminding each other of the Lord's *past* goodness, and
in looking forward to the *future.*

The Twenty-third Psalm, along with the simple hymn, "Jesus
loves me! this I know, For the Bible tells me so," are so uncomplicated that any very ill person—hot with fever, wracked with pain, or
weak with an illness that is "unto death"—can be comforted with
them. These deep but simple truths, expressing the compassion and
love of the Lord, are digestible, understandable, and available to
weary, tired, feeble, pain-distracted minds. The comfort of the Lord
is given so that it may even be "taken through a straw," so to speak,
when strength to drink from a cup is gone. *Though I walk . . . the
shadow of death . . . thou art with me . . . .*

This is the Lord, our dear Father and Shepherd of the sheep, the
Father of all comfort who says, "Comfort ye, comfort ye my people,

saith your God" (Isaiah 40:1) and who gives us constant assurance of His consistent caring for His people:

Sing, O heavens; and be joyful, O earth; and break forth into singing, O mountains: for the Lord hath comforted his people, and will have mercy upon his afflicted. But Zion said, The Lord hath forsaken me, and my Lord hath forgotten me. Can a mother forget her sucking child, that she should not have compassion on the son of her womb? yea, they may forget, yet will I not forget thee. Behold, I have graven thee upon the palms of my hands; thy walls are continually before me.

Isaiah 49:13–16

"But," you may say, "I am not Jewish; I am not part of Zion." The reply is that this assurance is for all believers, the children of the Lord. Anyone who has become a part of the Lord's family through accepting the Lamb, the Messiah, the Lord Jesus Christ as his or her Saviour—and has believed in this One, the Son of God, and thanked Him for taking our sins upon Him on the cross—has also become a spiritual seed of Abraham. The promise comes to us that God does not forget us, and that nothing will separate us from His love. The Holy Spirit is making intercession for us when we cannot pray or do not know what we should pray for. The Trinity is involved in comforting us in our times of need.

This One who comforts us and tells us to comfort others with the comfort we have been given in our afflictions, is the One who went without comfort Himself in His terrible time of affliction, so that we could be given comfort. We can find in Psalms a description of that lack of comfort which Jesus faced, as God the Father turned His face away from the Son, and the Son cried out: "My God, my God, why hast thou forsaken me?" We come across this in Psalms 69:20, 21: "Reproach hath broken my heart; and I am full of heaviness: and I looked for some to take pity, but there was none; and for comforters, but I found none. They gave me also gall for my meat; and in my thirst they gave me vinegar to drink." Consider again the depth of His suffering and loneliness which Isaiah describes, so long before Jesus came:

He is despised and rejected of men; a man of sorrows, and acquainted with grief: and we hid as it were our faces from him; he was despised, and we esteemed him not. Surely he hath borne our griefs, and carried our sorrows: yet we did esteem him stricken, smitten of God, and afflicted. But he was wounded for our transgressions, he was bruised for our iniquities: the chastisement of our peace was upon him; and with his stripes we are healed. All we like sheep have gone astray; we have turned every one to his own way; and the Lord hath laid on him the iniquity of us all. He was oppressed, and he was afflicted, yet he opened not his mouth: he is brought as a lamb to the slaughter, and as a sheep before her shearers is dumb, so he openeth not his mouth.

Isaiah 53:3–7

The loneliness and the separation from all comfort and comforters were experienced by Jesus, who stands in the middle of all time and history as the most afflicted One, the One most separated from comfort. And—He did it so that we would never be separated from the comfort of God as we come to God through this One who ". . . bare the sin of many, and made intercession for the transgressors" (v. 12). He not only made intercession (the *past* tense), but He *is* constantly interceding for His people today.

No one who has not known loneliness can comfort anyone else who is lonely as well as one who has been lonely himself or herself. No one who has never known the sharp separation which death brings in stark reality—when a loved one has slipped away from communication—can share the feeling of vast loss which sweeps over a mourner for a loved one as closely as another person who has experienced the same shock. Someone who has faced a frightening trip down a hospital corridor on a stretcher is able to comfort with special understanding another who is about to leave for the emergency room or operating room. People who have experienced the Lord's help, as they have sat waiting in the crowded waiting room of a hospital for news from the intensive-care unit, are better prepared to help others in that same tense situation. Someone who has kept vigil by a child's bed, waiting for that precious pair of eyes to open again as he or she comes out of anesthesia, can comfort with greater sensitivity another person who is going through that particular waiting.

People who have had pain can comfort others who are suffering similar pain. One who has gone through bankruptcy—and has seen how the Lord has comforted and opened new doors—is ready to comfort and encourage another who is in the midst of feeling the "impossibility" of starting all over again. Someone who has never felt depression, anxiety, nervousness, or fear cannot have the same depth of sensitivity to these feelings in another as someone who has actually experienced the reality of what would seem "unreasonable" to a constantly cheerful, optimistic person. The strain of living day by day with another human being who irritates and distresses you is best understood by someone who has lived under the same strain, but has been comforted and shown how to go on. The ordeal of going through a trial and sentence and then spending time in prison can prepare someone to help others in the same position with an understanding that is different from someone who can only imagine such an affliction. God can give us the needed comfort and sensitivity with which to help others, but going through the same experience with His comfort can be a special preparation which is costly—but thorough.

We are assured that the Lord can comfort us, and that the comfort He gives us in specific and varied situations will be used, through us, to bring comfort to someone else. It is a fantastic economy. Our present affliction contains a tremendous possibility for lasting results. While we are being refined as silver, we may be directly attacked by Satan. We may also have a time of needed and helpful discipline which will change our lives. We may have an opportunity to understand the Lord's comfort with such vividness that we will be ready for a gigantic task of comforting scores of people in the midst of an earthquake or fire. The combination of events is known only to the Lord, but we have been given sufficient glimpses to give us enough to be occupied with, enough to ask help for, day by day and hour by hour. *May I learn, dear Father, in today's hard thing, that which You want to teach me, so that today's school of comforters may have this pupil ready to put to use all that is being discovered.*

There is someone whose combination of needs will be what is closest to the things you are experiencing and through which you are finding that the Lord is sufficient in His comfort to keep you going. This is the present and immediate fulfillment of your present and immediate preparation. Comforting someone—with the comfort with which you and I have been comforted—speaks of specific situations and an immediate passing-on of the comfort.

There is, however, a very marvelous "lecture" which the Lord gives us in His school for comforters. It is a direct command about the subject matter we are to include somewhere in our "comforting" discussions with another. We are not to quote trite formulas or phrases, but are to include this subject matter: this true hope, this great expectation, this most helpful of all comforts. The King James Version of 1 Thessalonians 4:18 tells us: "Wherefore comfort one another with these words." The New International Version has this translation: "Therefore encourage each other with these words." That is a command, as well as a suggestion. We need comfort, and "each other" needs comfort. We should be comforting each other in the midst of all sorts of tribulations, even among such worries caused by reading the daily newspapers, *Newsweek,* and *Time!* For we are afflicted with fears and discouragement as we think of our children and grandchildren and read the news of violence, injustice, cruelty of people to people, greed—incredible evidence of inhumanity and of pragmatic rulers in high places. We cringe as we read of the increase of twisted, heathen religions and practices, as well as of the twisted use of the Word of God and the abnormal, upside-down ideas being taught. The very air seems full of a blight of gnats, blinding the eyes of everyone. In our afflictions and sudden fears, we have been given something to talk about. How often do we spend time giving this comfort to each other? What is this comfort we are to share?

> Brothers, we do not want you to be ignorant about those who sleep, or to grieve like the rest of men, who have no hope. We believe that Jesus died and rose again and so we believe that God will bring with Jesus those who sleep in him. According to the Lord's own word, we tell you that we who are still alive, who are left till the coming of the Lord, will certainly not precede those who have fallen asleep. For the Lord himself will come down from heaven, with a loud command, with the voice of the archangel and with the trumpet call of God, and the dead in Christ will rise first. After that, we who are still alive and are left will be caught up after them in the clouds to meet the Lord in the air. And so we will be with the Lord forever.
>
> 1 Thessalonians 4:13–17 NIV

What a comfort and what an excitement! Jesus is coming back, and those who have died will again be in their bodies, because they will suddenly be resurrected and have bodies like His after He arose. We will also be changed, if we are alive when He comes, and we will have resurrected bodies, too.

Is it real to you? Is it real to me? Is it like Marry Berg-Meester's "mountain climb with blisters"—the certainty of the lighted house at the top, full of the family? Is it as real as any expectation we have of next week's day off, or the spring vacation, or a family reunion?

Children and adults of all ages can have such an expectation of a reunion—a year away, six months away—that it can be a comfort in a fantastic diversity of levels of drudgery or difficulty. Even children in nursery school can look forward to a family reunion with certainty and vivid imagination of all they want to do with cousins on tricycles or splashing in water. Children who are fretting over multiplication tables and spelling difficulties can be encouraged by the thought that the family reunion is coming closer daily. They might even compare experiences with cousins in school in another country. Teenagers may be faced with struggles—some in boarding schools and others plugging away on a too-full schedule of violin practice, mathematics, language study, and an onslaught of conflicting ideas being thrown at them from books and teachers. They can take comfort in knowing that there will be time to sit under a pine tree or on a rock by the lake, or walk in the fresh spring air and talk over their confusions with beloved cousins who are having similar experiences and thoughts. There is comfort for adults in the family as they look forward to talking to brothers and sisters, parents, and brothers- and sisters-in-law about a great variety of subjects. The immediate moment can be lightened by this amazing quality which God has enabled us to have—called "anticipation." We have been given imaginations which enable us to project ourselves into comforting situations in the future.

Comforting though the thoughts may be of a future concert, fishing or boat trip, skiing vacation, camping time, playing tennis, or planting a garden—whatever you may find comfort in looking forward to—there is always the possibility of disappointment. There are delays and other hindrances which can come up. The most "definite" of our plans can be canceled because of illness, death, loss of money, or varying disasters. We always need to say, "Lord willing . . ." when discussing our plans for the future—including our *earthly* family reunions.

However, when God tells us to "comfort one another with these words," there is no "if," "perhaps," or "maybe" about it. Although we do not know the actual *time* of the return of Jesus, the beginning of the fantastic promised things, we do know that it is in the Lord's will and plan. He has told us so in His Book, the Bible. So we can be assured that it is going to take place. We are not cheating or fooling an adult or a little child when we talk to him or her in a hospital, at an old-folks' home, or in the midst of some special affliction, if we talk about the wonders of what the Bible has hinted at or given glimpses about the return of Jesus. This will be the time of the "new heavens and the new earth," the time of the believers' Judgment, the Lamb's Marriage Supper, and all sorts of other wonderful things. These are comforts to be talked about freely. That a disabled child would think of having a perfect leg when Jesus returns should be as real as the expectation of a new dress next week, or the dessert for tonight's supper. It should be with a feeling of "waiting to see what it will be like," when anyone who has been in a wheelchair all his or her life talks about walking and running as he anticipates the return of the Lord.

"Naomi, don't look directly at the sun. It will spoil your eyes, and you might never see again if you do that too long." Three-year-old Naomi softly corrected her mother with: "Not till Jesus comes back, you mean." That is the naturalness of the certainty that we are meant to be helping each other to have. And we should be excited about it. We should be more excited about the Lord's return than about any expectation which we may look forward to in this earthly life.

"Don't be sad, darling. After your appendix operation, you'll be just a little while in this hospital, and then we're going to have a wonderful time together, camping above the sea in Cornwall. The white cliffs are so beautiful, and maybe we'll even see seals. You can think about it now, and anyway . . . . Look! Here comes a bunch of flowers for you. Somebody is trying to make this room beautiful while you are here." Both these ideas should be present in our comforting. We are to remind each other of the certain future and also provide something concrete for the present need. The expectation is not to be what people often criticize Christians for—a pie-in-the-sky philosophy. It doesn't work that way. The comfort given, as we look ahead, makes us more acutely aware of not wasting the time now. As we look forward, we need to reread a portion of Romans:

> Now if we are children, then we are heirs—heirs of God and co-heirs with Christ, if indeed we share in his sufferings in order

that we may also share in his glory. I consider that our present sufferings are not worth comparing with the glory that will be revealed in us. The creation waits in eager anticipation for the sons of God to be revealed. For the creation was subjected to frustration, not by its own choice, but by the will of the one who subjected it, in hope that the creation itself will be liberated from its bondage to decay and brought into the glorious freedom of the children of God. We know that the whole creation has been groaning as in the pains of childbirth right up to the present time. Not only so, but we ourselves, who have the firstfruits of the Spirit, groan inwardly as we wait eagerly for our adoption as sons, the redemption of our bodies. For in this hope we were saved. But hope that is seen is no hope at all. Who hopes for what he already has? But if we hope for what we do not yet have, we wait for it patiently.

Romans 8:17–25 NIV

What an extraordinary expectation we have been given. What a fabulous description of something beyond our imaginations. What will all "creation" be like when it is "liberated from its bondage"? We hear much about liberation today, but what will it be like to have "the whole creation" liberated? We ourselves will be able to enjoy it with bodies liberated from the hindrances of sin and selfishness, sickness and disablement. This is a liberation which no human beings can possibly imagine, and yet we can think about it with eager excitement.

Any liberation which men or women are screaming for in this life would actually be the worst kind of bondage, compared to the liberation of all nature—with us all in the midst of it, liberated from all hindrances, and with all our talents available for us such as we can't imagine them used now. As my fingers fly rapidly over the keys of this typewriter, I imagine myself in the freedom of all that is ahead, playing a piano to bring forth the music I have always wanted to produce from an instrument! It will not be just lame legs and paralyzed bodies which will be in perfect order. All of our talents as human beings will be freed from the hindrances and abnormalities brought about through the centuries following the Fall. Any kind of human movement for liberation will look like prison bars by comparison. We are to be thrilled at what we are waiting for, in expectation and anticipation, and with thanksgiving voiced right now by faith.

We have a hope that we need not be ashamed of—and this hope is to comfort us, but not with a sitting-in-the-corner-until-it-happens kind of comfort. It is to enable us to "endure to the end," to "get on with the battle," to "run the race." Come to Isaiah: "For the Lord God will help me; therefore shall I not be confounded: therefore have I set my face like a flint, and I know that I shall not be ashamed . . . . For the Lord shall comfort Zion: he will comfort all her waste places; and he will make her wilderness like Eden, and her desert like the garden of the Lord; joy and gladness shall be found therein, thanksgiving, and the voice of melody" (Isaiah 50:7; 51:3). We have a God who knows how to restore beauty, such as no skilled person on earth could equal in restoring spoiled works of art.

It is a breathtaking restoration we contemplate as He hints to us something of its extent.

Therefore the redeemed of the Lord shall return, and come with singing unto Zion; and everlasting joy shall be upon their head: they shall obtain gladness and joy; and sorrow and mourning shall flee away. I, even I, am he that comforteth you: who art thou, that thou shouldest be afraid of a man that shall die, and of the son of man which shall be made as grass; And forgettest the Lord thy maker, that hath stretched forth the heavens, and laid the foundations of the earth . . . . But I am the Lord thy God, that divided the sea, whose waves roared: The Lord of hosts is his name. And I have put my words in thy mouth, and I have covered thee in the shadow of mine hand, that I may plant the heavens, and lay the foundations of the earth, and say unto Zion, Thou art my people.

Isaiah 51:11–13, 15, 16

Comfort? Freedom? Liberty? Let the reality of Isaiah 61 pour over you like fresh spring rain, permeating your whole being with certainty. Can't you feel it as thoroughly as rain in your face? It is true. It is real. He can do what He promises to do:

The Spirit of the Lord God is upon me; because the Lord hath anointed me to preach good tidings unto the meek; he hath sent me to bind up the brokenhearted, to proclaim liberty to the captives, and the opening of the prison to them that are bound; To proclaim the acceptable year of the Lord, and the day of vengeance to our God; to comfort all that mourn; To appoint unto them that mourn in Zion, to give unto them beauty for ashes, the oil of joy for mourning, the garment of praise for the spirit of heaviness; that they might be called trees of righteousness, the planting of the Lord, that he might be glorified.

Isaiah 61:1–3

Jesus came the first time to make it an absolute certainty that He would come the second time and fulfill all that is promised for the future. We have a purpose in the present time, in our today, that is important enough—and an expectation for tomorrow that is great enough—to be able to say, "And I will dwell in the house of the Lord for ever."

10
Affliction and Evangelism—
Affliction and Guidance

The "Thanks a lot . . ." was not very enthusiastic as the girl with the resigned look on her unhappy face hung up her coat on a hook in the hall, and came into the warmth of the kitchen.

"I've only come because someone stole my handbag with everything in it—money, passport, traveler's checks, my Eurail pass, everything—while I was asleep on a train coming into Lausanne from Spain. I called my family collect, and my mother told me to come up to L'Abri and wait for word here. They'll send me more money and stuff. I hitchhiked up here, but it is the last place I wanted to come."

With this negative announcement the girl proceeded to "fence her mind" from invasion by ideas she didn't want to consider at all. Yet, before the money arrived and her papers were in order, the fence had broken down, and an eager flow of questions had developed in discussion after discussion, at meal tables and in personal conversations, until a moment arrived when an amazed excitement replaced the dull flatness. A reverse in direction took place, as this girl stopped running away from God. She bowed before Him, accepting His Word as truth and His gift of eternal life through Christ as authentic for her—as she came to understand something of her own guilt and the reality of Jesus' having died in her place. That it was not just a religion but the truth of what *is*, "blew her mind" in the discussions, as she became convinced of true truth. Who could have planned this "method of evangelism"? Is it to be an incentive to go around the world stealing people's handbags? Come back to Acts 7, where Stephen is speaking:

"You stubborn people, with uncircumcised hearts and ears! You are just like your fathers: You always resist the Holy Spirit!

190

Was there ever a prophet your fathers did not persecute? They even killed those who predicted the coming of the Righteous One. And now you have betrayed and murdered him—you who have received the law that was put into effect through angels but have not obeyed it."

When they heard this, they were furious and ground their teeth at him. But Stephen, filled with the Holy Spirit, looked up to heaven and saw the glory of God, and Jesus standing at the right hand of God. "Look," he said, "I see heaven open and the Son of Man standing at the right hand of God."

At this they covered their ears and, yelling at the top of their voices, they all rushed at him, dragged him out of the city and began to stone him. Meanwhile, the witnesses laid their clothes at the feet of a young man named Saul. While they were stoning him, Stephen prayed, "Lord Jesus, receive my spirit." Then he fell on his knees and cried out, "Lord do not hold this sin against them." When he had said this, he fell asleep. And Saul was there, giving approval to his death.

Acts 7:51–8:1 NIV

When we considered this passage before, we were concentrating on the marvel of Stephen's praying for those who were stoning him, the fantastic answer later given in the salvation of Saul, and, of course, all that flowed forth from Saul's changed life. In the context of the evangelism of the early church in the midst of affliction, notice this time that Stephen's preaching was underlined, emphasized, and accompanied, not by organ music but by the sound of stones whistling through the air and slamming into their target. The battle is so obvious here. Satan is trying to stamp out evangelism through killing God's evangelists, even as Satan had tried to stamp out the life of Jesus as a baby by inciting Herod to have all the baby boys killed. Satan's early attempts were to eliminate our way back to God—first by trying to kill Christ too early and later by tempting Him to sin. Then Satan's attempts turned to trying to stamp out the people who were clearly giving God's message, before anyone would believe. The victory has been God's in the midst of the battle through the centuries, and evangelism has gone forward in the midst of persecution. Stephen died, but Paul was born again and transformed and preached and wrote for the thousands who would come to an understanding of the truth. Paul's preaching and writing were in the midst of the long series of afflictions and persecutions we have already listed. We are told that Paul's "thorn in the flesh" was sent by Satan to "buffet" or "torment" him. Yet, despite the continuing affliction of this "thorn in the flesh," Paul kept on through all his difficulties and continued the greatest evangelistic work ever known.

Paul's boast of weakness would today be considered a way of saying, "I want to tell you that I have proof of *reality*—the reality of God's existence in what takes place in my own life." Read again what he says: ". . . Therefore, I will boast all the more gladly about my weaknesses, so that Christ's power may rest on me. That is why, for Christ's sake, I delight in weaknesses, in insults, in hardships, in persecutions, in difficulties. For when I am weak, then am I strong" (2 Corinthians 12:9, 10 NIV). The first half of verse 9 is God's answer to Paul's plea for the thorn to be removed: "My grace is sufficient for you, for my power is made perfect in weakness" (NIV). In effect, Paul is declaring, "I have complete proof of the reality of the power of Christ, because I know how very weak I am, and in what an impossible situation I am for continuing my work. In the middle of physical pain, the onslaught of insulting criticism, the weariness that reduces me to exhaustion, the difficulties in every part of my life, still I find strength to go on, and I *know* it is not *my* strength."

The reality in the life of an evangelist, or a "teller of the truth," is not pointed out as a series of miracles which remove all sickness, hardship, and fatigue from that person, but a series of hard, slogging days of work during which a sufficient amount of the Lord's strength has become evident in the human being's weaknesses.

Can we sit in a committee meeting and plan to prepare men and women for effective evangelism by planning a series of afflictions for them to go through? Can we rely on a "survival program" of training in the wilds to produce another Paul? Would we plan another stoning to produce a Stephen? Of course not. Yet the wave of preaching and telling which washed over the world at the time of the early church did take place because of—as well as in spite of—affliction, hardship, persecution, and difficulties of all kind. To go back to the Book of Acts:

On that day a great persecution broke out against the church at Jerusalem, and all except the apostles were scattered throughout Judea and Samaria. Godly men buried Stephen and mourned deeply for him. But Saul began to destroy the church. Going from house to house, he dragged off men and women and put them in prison. Those who had been scattered preached the word wherever they went. Philip went down to a city in Samaria and proclaimed the Christ there.

Acts 8:1–5 NIV

In and out of prison, the Christians preached or proclaimed or made known the fact that the Messiah had come, and that He was Jesus Christ who had died and had risen again and was now ascending into heaven. The spreading of truth took place in wider and wider areas geographically *because* of persecutions. As Satan tried to stamp out the truth, the victory was God's.

It is true that in many instances God has delivered His children out of impossible situations and that the deliverance has been a means of evangelism. The men who were thrown in the fiery furnace had the courage to say that their God was able to deliver them, but that if He did not, they still would not worship false gods. Their deliverance caused many to believe that their God was the true God indeed. When Daniel refused to stop praying to God three times a day by his open window, he did not know whether or not God would save him from the lions. However, the result of Daniel's being miraculously protected was the king's declaration to all the people and nations and languages: "I make a decree, That in every dominion of my kingdom men tremble and fear before the God of Daniel: for he is the living God, and stedfast for ever, and his kingdom that which shall not be destroyed, and his dominion shall be even unto the end. He delivered and rescueth, and he worketh signs and wonders in heaven and in earth, who hath delivered Daniel from the power of the lions" (Daniel 6:26, 27). If we think of the two rectangles, Daniel's deliverance from the lions belongs in the second rectangle, and Paul's "thorn in the flesh" in the first. Both men had the courage and faith to continue trusting the Living God. The results of evangelism in the deliverance of Daniel and evangelism in the giving of strength in Paul's weakness were equally spiritual, and both were effective in bringing others to a knowledge of truth.

It is important that the place of affliction in evangelism be given proper recognition. The missionaries who fled from China along the Burma Road met people who never would have heard true truth, had not the terrible violence and expulsion taken place. The missionaries who escaped into Thailand or Laos when they were put out of China reached people whom they would never have met if they had stayed in China. On the other hand, the persecution within China has brought forth a reality in the lives of Christians, so that in spite of the slaying of thousands of pastors and lay Christians, the "remnant" has not been cut off. The church in France may never have recovered from the killing of the Huguenots, but each place to which some escaped has been like a garden with seeds blowing in from some distant spot, springing up and bearing fruit. The Gospel as given in the balanced view which the Word of God itself provides has been spread all over the earth *because of* and *in spite of* affliction.

We could sit around a fireplace, exchanging endless stories of people we know (or know of) who have made the truth of the Bible known to an entirely different group of people than they expected to reach—because of affliction, hardship, or persecution. And then we could change the subject and relate to each other stories of people who *listened* for the first time to the true truth of the Word of God because they heard it in the midst of affliction. Then there could be a third division or category connecting affliction with evangelism, as we think of people who came to believe because of the way Christians behaved during or after some terrible loss or affliction.

If Paul and Silas had not been thrown in prison, the jailer and his family would never have been saved. The result for that family was eternal life, and that was in a very real way dependent upon Paul's and Silas's spending a short period in a horrible jail. However, if one could have the information which God has, one could trace the life of each of that jailer's family and come to the amazing results which sprang up through the years from that one period of affliction which took two men to a place different from the one they intended to evangelize. If Chuck Colson had not gone to prison, the men he helped would never have experienced his careful telling them of the Gospel, his praying with them, and the compassionate love he showed them in the midst of his own affliction and theirs. What has sprung forth from this time has been a work which otherwise would never have taken place. As a result, many people in many prisons are being exposed to the truth of the Word of God, but are also indirectly helped in areas where reform is needed. There can flow from this a whole prison-reform movement and a campaign for fairer trials.

Our own work at L'Abri, now twenty-three years old, was not planned and could never have been the result of human design. It has been the result of a variety of affliction and has come forth in the midst of tribulation. The background of this entirely unanticipated work in the Swiss Alps—which is reaching a great cross-section of ages and types of people in many lands—has a beginning that no committee could decide upon as an introduction to a new work. It included our coming back to the chalet where we had lived for over five years—with materials bought in America to cover couches and chairs, with paint for the kitchen walls, with determination to put our little store of money into getting a hot-water heater, a washing machine, and other conveniences—because we expected to live in that chalet in that village for many more years. It includes a series of afflictions which hit in the midst of this refurbishing of the house. Our two-year-old little boy was diagnosed as having polio after a wrong diagnosis had been made the day before, and we faced the dilemma of whether to travel back to America or to stay on. Our middle daughter came down with rheumatic fever a week later, to be eventually bedridden the better part of three years, from age thirteen to sixteen. Scores of disappointments and difficulties came during that time, in the way of letters reducing our salary, among other such shocks. Added to all this was the week of avalanches and floods, during which not only did we physically help to fight the flow of rocks and mud and try to keep it in the stream bed, but we needed to stay dressed day and night for over a week to be ready to evacuate if that need arose. Twice the rushing torrent of mud, tree trunks, and rocks came directly toward our chalet, and twice the flow split in two, leaving our chalet an island in the midst of a cascade. The blow which seemed most "impossible" following all this was that edict handed to my husband and Prisca on Valentine's Day—giving us six weeks to get out of our chalet and all of Switzerland.

If we had not been put out of our home, thereby losing all the material things we had put into it; *if* we had not been absolutely penniless and without a place to go; *if* we had not been so "at the bottom" due to the succession of blows, the vividness of Fran's "vote" which I told you about would not have been so potent. L'Abri would never have been born without affliction! Then, did God send the affliction? I don't think so. I do think it was part of the battle, and the victory with its flow of answered prayer was real. It

brought forth and is still bringing forth results for God's glory which
would not have taken place otherwise. Satan oversteps himself in
his attacks, time after time. God takes what has been a strike against
His people or His work and, by blending together people, events,
and geographic places, brings forth a fantastic victory again and
again—as His people throw themselves on Him in prayer.

As Paul speaks to Timothy (when the young man comes to the
time of taking over from the older man), Paul very carefully weaves
together and binds in one bundle the affliction or hardship in the
work of an evangelist as a part of the expectation of his future. Any
"evangelist" needs to listen carefully, as it is not Timothy alone who
is being addressed:

> In the presence of God and of Christ Jesus, who will judge
> the living and the dead, and in view of his appearing and his
> kingdom, I give you this charge: Preach the Word; be prepared
> in season and out of season; correct, rebuke and
> encourage—with great patience and careful instruction. For the
> time will come when men will not put up with sound doctrine.
> Instead, to suit their own desires, they will gather around them
> a great number of teachers to say what their itching ears want
> to hear. They will turn their ears away from the truth and turn
> aside to myths. But you, keep your head in all situations, en-
> dure hardship [afflictions], do the work of an evangelist, dis-
> charge all the duties of your ministry.
>
> For I am already being poured out as a drink offering, and
> the time has come for my departure. I have fought the good
> fight, I have finished the race, I have kept the faith. Now there is
> in store for me the crown of righteousness, which the Lord, the
> righteous Judge, will award to me on that day—and not only to
> me, but also to all who have longed for his appearing.
>
> 2 Timothy 4:1–8 NIV

Dear Paul has summed it up so marvelously. He makes it clear
that among all the expected afflictions which he endured (and which
he warns may be expected by any who make the truth known) is
the hardship or affliction of people who turn away and do not listen
to the truth, but rather listen to anyone who will say what they want
to hear, preferring myths to truth. One of the hardest of afflictions is
to have people oppose the truth and in essence cover their ears,
when it has cost a great price physically, psychologically, materially,

and spiritually to speak to them. Paul goes on to speak of this as he tells of Alexander the coppersmith who did much harm to him, and whom he warns Timothy about:

> You too should be on your guard against him, because he strongly opposed our message. At my first defense, no one came to my support, but everyone deserted me. May it not be held against them. But the Lord stood at my side and gave me strength, so that through me the message might be fully proclaimed and all the Gentiles might hear it. And I was delivered from the lion's mouth. The Lord will rescue me from every evil attack and will bring me safely to his heavenly kingdom. To him be glory for ever and ever Amen.
>
> 2 Timothy 4:15–17 NIV

Clearly the persecution and heavy opposition came from "within" as well as from "without," from the time of the earliest days of the church. Heavyhearted loneliness was experienced by Paul as he stood giving a true message, opposed by Alexander the coppersmith in some open way. Evidently no one came to Paul's defense. However, Paul declares to Timothy and to all who have followed him that the Lord is the One who can and will give strength that the message which is His truth may be proclaimed!

The Word of God, the Bible, is constantly fair to us through all ages of history. People have been warned that there will be affliction in all kinds of forms, including opposition to the message of the Word of God itself. Jesus knew what it was to have the crowds follow Him for healing and for free bread—and then to have the same crowds melt away when He proclaimed the truth and stood alone to suffer for the fact that He had said He was the Son of God. His standing alone enabled Paul to say with a surge of joy, "But the Lord stood at my side and gave me strength." Jesus stood alone when He was so terribly opposed and oppressed. In so doing, He paid the price for His standing by our side when we are proclaiming His Word in our moments of history.

"Oh, but . . ." perhaps you are saying, "I'm not an evangelist, or a missionary, or a Christian worker of any kind. I am a hairdresser. [Or a real-estate dealer, a teacher, a mother making a creative home for my children and husband, a secretary, a surgeon, a vet, a scientist, a publisher, a businesswoman, a lawyer, an oil geologist, a horse trainer, a painter, a curator of a museum, a therapist, an inventor, an insurance man, a dress designer, a cattle farmer. I grow and freeze vegetables.] So none of that applies to me." Then we turn to Second Timothy again. The first paragraphs of chapter 3 tell of the kind of people who will be "in the last days . . . having a form of godliness, but denying the power thereof," people who will never acknowledge the truth. (*See* vv. 1–5.) Then Paul speaks of his own life again and his persecutions. He makes it very clear that he is not speaking to just his young understudy or to other Christian workers, but to all who are serious about being believers:

> In fact, everyone who wants to live a godly life in Christ Jesus will be persecuted, while evil men and impostors will go from bad to worse, deceiving and being deceived. [We are all included in that "everyone" when we become believers, part of the Lord's family, as we seriously ask the Lord to lead us in the life He would have us live. We are all being told that we will suffer some kind of persecution, affliction, or hardship. Then we, along with Timothy, are urged not to give up, but to continue to live on the basis of the Bible's direction and teaching.] But as for you, continue in what you have learned and have become convinced of, because you know those from whom you learned it, and how from infancy you have known the holy Scriptures, which are able to make you wise for salvation through faith in Christ Jesus. All Scripture is God-breathed and is useful for teaching, rebuking, correcting and training in righteousness, so that the man of God may be thoroughly equipped for every good work.
>
> 2 Timothy 3:12–17 NIV

The warning is to each of us. We are not to be surprised when persecution comes in the form of nasty remarks by neighbors. We are to be forewarned that persecution might come in the form of our Ph.D. thesis being turned down. We are not to be flattened by the announcement that our expected promotion fell through. We are to be prepared for the possible scorn of unbelievers, the withdrawal of family members who are not Christian, the snubbing of friends, and unfair news reports or criticisms. We are not to forget that Satan can and will also attack us directly in areas of our health, a deluge of disasters, car accidents, our house burning down, higher-than-expected taxes, a baby born with a handicap, loss of a job, or a crippling disease. Satan will persecute us directly, as will *people* persecute us because they hate what we stand for and despise what we believe. Yes, all who will live a "godly life" (that is, a life belonging to God and lived as He guides and by the strength He gives in our weakness to do what He leads us to do) will suffer persecution.

Someone may ask, "But why be a Christian at all? Wouldn't it be easier to just live outside of the battle altogether?" The factor that is important is that Christianity is not supposed to be something just to give us "things," whether it be healing, bread, or happiness. Christianity—the teaching of the Bible, the whole Word of God, the Judeo-Christian teaching—is *true*. That means that the promises for the present comfort and the promises for the future return of Jesus and all that will follow are *true*. We are not being given a painkiller, a bit of occupational therapy, a club to join in which we can have a lot more friends, an insurance policy in case of some sort of disaster. We are being given the *true truth* of what life is all about, of what has happened since God created the world, of how the Fall came about and where all the misery stems from, of how we can be forgiven and brought into a "forever" relationship with God, and of the future marvels of which we can be certain.

We have used Chuck Colson's prison work and our work at L'Abri as two examples of how affliction has been used by God to bring about evangelism in entirely new places and new ways. There could be many other examples given. Think, however, of all who are *not* in any kind of organized Christian work, whose afflictions have opened the way for them to reach people who would never have otherwise heard the truth. The hatred of Satan so often is transformed into an opening for God's snatching another person from Satan's kingdom. In such a way God rescues escaping refugees such as a dear boy who was recently at L'Abri. He had heard the truth after he came out of Cambodia in a dangerous flight into Thailand by tiny boat and later found himself cared for by a Korean man who was a Christian. This boy then became caretaker for fifty small children who had escaped; he was able to teach them the little he had already learned about Christianity. Stories of this sort will be repeated thousands of times over as we ask people (when we have the time in eternity) where they heard the message of Good News, the Gospel which the Bible explained.

We will find many doctors who heard the Good News from a patient in their hospital—or nurses who discovered the truth about the Creator's existence from some accident case that was wheeled in, in the middle of the night. There will be many who will be in heaven because they heard the wonder of what Christ came to do in the middle of the affliction of war; in a submarine, sitting cooped up in an army transport plane, lying in a barracks hospital, slogging through mud in some bush area of the world.

It is true that evangelists—tellers of the truth—go through much affliction, but also that people often come to believe *in the middle of an affliction*. It is hard to untangle the threads of difficulty which seem to weave together to bring about marvelous results. Let me quote from a letter that my young friend Marcia wrote to give me a glimpse of something of all this in her family:

Actually there's more on my mind that I want to thank you for. For a long time it has been on my mind to write you, but my thoughts go back so far, and my thanks so deep, that finding all the words I need seemed impossible. But it all has to do with an incredibly beautiful design that has been woven into my family, and how a L'Abri thread keeps appearing and reappearing. I have such a large family. When I wandered into L'Abri, seven years ago now, I was typical of so many of them—hardheaded, rebellious, and hurt. And when I found the Lord, I prayed for all of them too. But with families it's funny—I thought God worked in other people's families, but mine was too tough (and certainly too big) for Him to handle.

When Roger and I were married, a whole flock of L'Abri friends joyfully descended on the wedding. They all stayed with my brother Maynard, a Marxist, mad at the world and out to change it. You can imagine there were some lively discussions. Well, Maynard was impressed. Shortly after that he dropped out of grad school and ended up at L'Abri. It wasn't until the day before he left that he "bowed his rebellious self," as he put it, and submitted to the Lord. All along he was being prayed for by these L'Abri friends. What excitement when he wrote us of his finding the Lord. But then last October [1975], all of a sudden he went home to be with the Lord. When I heard of it, the significance of my going to L'Abri, then his going, took on an eternal significance. This is where the depth of feeling can no longer find words. This is where I stop—and stand still in awe.

But the story goes on. Remember, it was a very large family. The story of his funeral I am sure will be told and retold—how his twin brother accepted the Lord, when we were all together the night before the funeral, and was so excited he phoned the minister and asked if he could sing and tell of his faith at the funeral. What a testimony. And then my older brother came to believe, right during the funeral, and afterwards wanted to pray with Roger. The whole thing was turned around into a time of triumph. Was it easy? No, Richard sang at the funeral but had to stop to cry at one point. And for anyone who accepts the Lord, the way ahead is tough, even without sudden death to face. Brother James had just left for Europe on sort of a personal quest. The week before Maynard's death, Jim had been with Gini in London where he had met Os and Jenny and several other L'Abri friends. He'd spent much time trying to support his feeble position on the good of humanity. That weekend in October he had gone hiking in Wales with dear friend Donald Drew. How good of our Father to place him in such loving hands at such a time. Jim too found his way up the hill to Huémoz. Last week he wrote to us, "If there is one thing I want to say to you in this letter it is how much I love the Lord and want to serve Him." Oh, there is more too. The story goes on. Someday I am going to tell it to the angels. They probably know it already. They don't know my side of it though! Yes, they *all* have come under His wing now. God does work in families. And so many of mine came through L'Abri.

What I mostly want to share with you is something of the cosmic significance, the eternal perspective (oh, words cramp me all up) that the spreading of the Word has taken on for me, having looked at death. And I want this story to be an encouragement to you . . . .

The letter goes on with more news and is signed, "With love from Marcia." It is one of many encouraging letters, so many of them weaving together afflictions which have brought forth growth or decisions, as if the affliction were the preparation and fertilizer for the good ground which received the seed. Put together these letters with the facts that follow the word *if.* If we had not gone through all our troubles and *if* we had not been put out of our home and village, there would never have been a L'Abri for anyone to stumble into, to decide to visit or to hear about in an *ashram* or a *kibbutz* or on a train or bus or at a funeral—or at which to wait for money from home after the bag was stolen! *If* the L'Abri Workers (whose afflictions could take up many pages of a book and whose difficulties are at times multiplied by living in a "goldfish bowl" of a home shared with many others) had not been willing to "endure hardships," there wouldn't be such reports to copy. There haven't been any stonings in our midst, and no one has been martyred, but in some parts of the world the "afflictions" and "hardships" include martyrdom, even today. Yet in the midst of it all, you may be sure that some are coming to understand and believe.

We have looked at some tiny examples of the mixture of evangelism and affliction. First, the message of God is taken to people who would otherwise never have been touched, because certain afflictions thrust out the evangelists to unthought-of-places. Second, we have looked at some examples of people who listened, because of *hearing* in the midst of some trouble or affliction.

Now for the third category. It was 3:00 A.M. in the Swiss Alps the morning of March 28 (when it was still 9:00 P.M. in Dallas, Texas, the night of March 27). A man driving down the winding mountain road from Villars noticed an orange glow in the village of Huémoz, a glow which lit the sky, and seemed to have a few flames licking up into it. He kept his hand on the horn as he slowed down and drove through the village. Betty got up on one elbow and looked out of her window across the field. "Jane," she cried, "the chapel is burning." "No . . ." and Jane leaped out of bed to begin calling people on the phone. Soon L'Abri Workers, Helpers, and Students were dragging the fire extinguishers from their chalets down to the chapel and, under Barry's directions, began spraying the center beam which was the most important support. Later the village fire squad dragged down their equipment and continued the firefighting efforts with the L'Abri family. By 5:30 A.M. Swiss time, the fire was out, and a call had been put in to Texas to inform those of us who had been present at the final seminar for *How Should We Then Live?* about what had been going on in Switzerland at the exact time that a concluding lecture by Fran had been given in Dallas. It did not seem like a coincidence to any of us that, at exactly the same time that an answer to prayer had been going on in Texas, the L'Abri chapel was going up in flames in Switzerland. The prayer had been: *Give tongues of fire to preach Thy Word*—and those who heard that message that night felt that there had been a special power and forcefulness that could only have come as a work of the Holy Spirit. The "fire" that only the Holy Spirit could give had been counter-attacked with physical fire by Satan, so it seemed. It would seem that it was no coincidence that the news came to us in our hotel: "The chapel has been burning and the organ seems to have been destroyed!"—and another phone message: "There are no flights on the commercial airlines for Philadelphia tomorrow." (The flights were needed for six of us in our family to go to my father's funeral in Wilmington, Delaware.) The news seemed designed to cancel joy in answered prayer and to plunge us into some sort of despair. In this trouble, which seemed to us such a vivid example of the battle in the heavenlies, there was also observable victory for the Lord.

First, the flight to Wilmington was made possible by someone's hearing our need and finding in an amazingly short time a private plane which the owner made available as a gift flight—with just room for the six of us and a baby. The marvel was that no private planes were flying out of Dallas that next morning, as there were storms in every direction, except the one "air passage" going where we needed to go! Second, we later heard both the details of the night of the fire and the immediate results. Barry had done a great job in caring for all the things that needed to be done, and Veronica had made muffins and hot chocolate for all the firefighters. Hence, at 5:00 A.M., people were gathered at Bourdenette, sipping hot chocolate, eating muffins, and starting to have a prayer meeting. Two girls at different stages of approach to Christianity, having asked many questions and having reacted to the answers with many negative statements and more questions, were observing something that night which no other set of circumstances could have enabled them to observe. They had been at L'Abri for different lengths of time, but each of them celebrated that night as their "birthday" into the family of the Lord. They came to their decisions separately from each other. With some differences as to what "hit" each of them, it was the combination of things observed and the reactions watched that startled them into thinking that Christianity must be true.

One of the girls said to me, "It was amazing to listen to L'Abri Workers and Helpers during the time of the fire and right afterwards. No one started blaming anyone, and everyone joined together without complaining at all. Though wakened in the middle of the night with things to carry, in danger, dirty, facing terrible heat, wet and uncomfortable, what they wanted to do was to spend time praying as soon as the fire was out and the danger over. There they sat, having hot chocolate and praying. It was something else, all right!" The prayer that the Lord would bring something good out of all that destruction was answered as two people came "out of the darkness of unbelief, into the light of the truth" that night. There have been many other answers to prayer, and even at this moment the chapel is being rebuilt. The village council gave permission for it to be a little larger, and we pray that the verse in Haggai 2:9 will be true of the new building: "The glory of this latter house shall be greater than of the former, saith the Lord of hosts: and in this place will I give peace, saith the Lord of hosts."

Does one then *plan* disasters, famines, wars, fires, accidents, deaths, or martyrdoms in order to build evangelism? Is it possible for human beings to stage a scene that will shake people into having the right perspective of time and eternity? Of course, the answer is *no, a thousand times no.* However, the Word of God has told us that affliction very often accompanies the actual time of salvation: "They preached the good news in that city and won a large number of disciples. Then they returned to Lystra, Iconium and Antioch, strengthening the disciples and encouraging them to remain true to the faith. 'We must go through many hardships to enter the kingdom of God' they said" (Acts 14:21, 22 NIV). It is not much wonder that they spoke this way, as Paul had just shortly before been stoned for preaching in Lystra. Yes, all who live godly lives will suffer persecution in one form or another.

Now turn to Isaiah 30 and find that God leads His children and gives them guidance in the midst of affliction. There is often a definite connection in our lives between affliction and guidance. We pray that we might be shown what to do, and the guidance often comes in the midst of a sudden knee operation which may have stopped us short in a certain city and kept us there long enough to be shown something we would not otherwise have realized we needed to do! This actually happened when Fran and I were traveling and speaking in America. I was suddenly given this diagnosis: "Your cartilage is torn. I want you in the hospital tomorrow for an operation. You'll need several days in the hospital and then ten days' rest in someone's home before you can go on back to Switzerland."

"Oh, but I can't! I have to . . . and my husband has to . . . ." But my wail was to no avail. Off I went to an operating room. Leaving out all the other interesting side portions of the story, the next two weeks were very important ones for my husband. He realized that he had to work on his manuscript for *How Should We Then Live?* and then go over it carefully with his editor, Jim Sire. There would have been *no other way* of doing it together, face-to-face in discussion, had we kept our original flight plans. My knee operation was a *necessity*, in order to get that manuscript cared for in time. And, as we stayed at the home of Mr. and Mrs. Jack Todd in Pittsburgh, the next two weeks unfolded many things in their lives and ours, as well as being the place for the work on the book. Guidance? The Lord so often gives it in the midst of what looks like a hindering affliction. I found myself praying, *Oh, thank You, Lord, for that operation. There are so many things that would never have come about if we hadn't been in Pittsburgh during that period of time. And thank You for making it so clear that this was the time when Fran was to finish up the work on his book.*

Only God can work things together in that way. The details are incredibly complicated, but the "if things had been different . . ." stagger us even in our time in this life of seeing "through a glass, darkly." What will it be like when we really see how the pieces of the jigsaw puzzle of our lives and others' fit together?

In Isaiah 30, verses 20 and 21 should be first read as a unit: "And though the Lord give you the bread of adversity, and the water of affliction, yet shall not thy teachers be removed into a corner any more, but thine eyes see thy teachers: And thine ears shall hear a word behind thee, saying, This is the way, walk ye in it, when ye turn to the right hand, and when ye turn to the left." Verse 18 has said that the Lord will wait, that He "may be gracious" unto us, and that all those that wait for Him are blessed. This speaks of looking to the Lord *in prayer*, asking Him, crying unto Him, waiting for Him to say, "This is the way, walk ye in it," in one way or another. The picture is one of adversity, difficulties, affliction. Here the child of God is being told that His leading will be given in the midst of difficulties. It is not a blueprint being shown in the bright sunlight, with a road map leading to the place and sufficient luggage provided for a long journey—with everything there at once for the whole time. It is quite different. God's promises are that His provisions will be made *in time.*

When Jesus speaks of care which God gives for the birds and flowers, He pleads with us to seek the Kingdom of God *first*, knowing that *all* the things we need will be "added" to us. Then He says, "Therefore do not worry about tomorrow, for tomorrow will worry about itself. Each day has enough troubles of its own" (Matthew 6:34 NIV). It is clearly a day-by-day provision that God promises to give, not a huge store for the future in this life. (The huge store is being made in heaven: treasures, mansions, and marvelously adequate provisions.) God promises daily provision in this life, and it seems to me that His guidance follows along this same kind of pattern. Why? Certainly not because God cannot plan for an adequate length of time ahead, but rather that He wants us to depend on Him. He wants us to walk along with our hand in His, waiting for Him to give our hand a little tug when we are to go a bit to the left on a path hidden by leaves, or a bit to the right and past that big fern-covered rock. We are not given a map and then left to run ahead on our own. We are meant to stay close and wait for His tug on our hand or His push away from a pitfall.

Now read Isaiah 30:1–3:

> Woe to the rebellious children, saith the Lord, that take counsel, but not of me; that cover with a covering, but not of my spirit, that they may add sin to sin: That walk to go down into Egypt, and have not asked at my mouth; to strengthen themselves in the strength of Pharaoh, and to trust in the shadow of Egypt! Therefore shall the strength of Pharaoh be your shame, and the trust in the shadow of Egypt your confusion.

Here is the warning, the clear, negative promise that trouble will result if we rush for help *away* from God. There is an impatience pictured here, a specific walking in the opposite direction, going somewhere for help and advice from a source that is neither the Bible nor the Lord's guidance in answer to prayer. God is saying, "Woe!" to those who—in the midst of stress and strain, troubles with human relationships and pressures at work, nervousness and tenseness—decide to try Transcendental Meditation to find calm and a new way to put up with life. Woe to those who say, "I just can't stand it another minute, and I'm going to do something about it in my own way. I'll try those fortune-tellers." Or, "I'll go to that Zen class where you can learn to believe that no-thing exists. You are no-thing and everything is no-thing—that kind of emptiness ought to relieve me." Woe to those who say, "I'll go get the help that Mrs. Jones [or Mr. White] got from that new Eastern religion." Woe to those who say, "I'm going to forget God, and throw myself into having the best time I can have and take the path that gives *me* what I want. I'm sick of all this. I'll get advice, all right, advice from some smart person who's 'made it,' and I'll take that advice *right now.*" The rushing-to-Egypt for help is a pushing aside of God, a decision that prayer is too slow a way to go about anything, a disregarding of the truth that God is able to give guidance, and an unbelief that God can communicate His plan or that He can lead in any practical way.

Isaiah 50:10, 11 puts it in another way. Again the picture is one of affliction. Here we are in "darkness," a place where we have no light on our path, no idea what to do next, brought up short by a huge disappointment, an illness, a cancellation of some sort, a death, or a whole series of things which have come upon us like a cloud or a fog settling down around us. Isaiah describes it: "Who is among you that feareth the Lord, that obeyeth the voice of his servant, that walketh in darkness, and hath no light? let him trust in the name of the Lord, and stay upon his God" (50:10). Here we are in our deep trouble and great need, without a clue as to what to do next. The command is to take this opportunity to *trust* the Lord. The command is to *stay,* to wait, to not move until He leads us through all the fog, cloud, darkness. This is where the leading *during* a time of affliction fits in. The picture is not one of ease and sunshine, but darkness and hardship.

The contrast is in verse 11: "Behold, all ye that kindle a fire, that compass yourselves about with sparks: walk in the light of your fire, and in the sparks that ye have kindled. This shall ye have of mine hand; ye shall lie down in sorrow." God is talking to His people, to you and me individually, not just to masses of people. He is telling us that He will not treat us as computers; He will not direct us with cards inserted in a slot and with no choice on our parts. He will not treat us as puppets on strings which He holds. God is saying that we have choice and that our choice is the contrast between verses 10 and 11. We may choose to wait for His direction and leading, His plan to be unfolded. We may choose to have patience, to "stay"— to take a day of prayer and fasting as we wait upon Him, to spend half a night praying alone in the quiet hours, to set aside a special week of so many hours of prayer each day, or to do some other form of really specific "waiting *upon* Him," as well as "waiting *for* Him," in order to emphasize or underline our seriousness in wanting His will. We may do this waiting—or we may "go to Egypt" in the sense of kindling sparks to light our own way. God does not say here that He will stop us if we take our lives in our own hands and rush into a path lighted by our own sparks. He does, however, make a negative promise: "Ye shall lie down in sorrow." At some point this rushing away from the Lord, this taking of our lives in our own hands, will specifically bring sorrow. God keeps His promises.

At the beginning of L'Abri, Fran and I took these two verses as the focus for our first day of fasting and prayer in July 1955. Ever since then we have continued to read and reread these words as we have days of prayer at L'Abri. It is all too easy to "light our own sparks" in one kind of situation or another, and we need to ask God to help us to be sensitive to the subtle dangers of our own rationalizations and alert to the perils of Satan's temptations, which God tells us sometimes come as "prophets." Jesus says, "Beware," or: "Watch out for false prophets. They come to you in sheep's clothing, but inwardly they are ferocious wolves. By their fruit you will recognize them. Do people pick grapes from thornbushes, or figs from thistles?" (Matthew 7:15, 16 NIV). Jesus is here warning against following false prophets and teachers. This warning is repeated in Second Peter: "Many will follow their shameful ways and will bring the truth into disrepute. In their greed these teachers will exploit you with stories they have made up. Their condemnation has long been hanging over them, and their destruction has not been sleeping" (2 Peter 2:2, 3 NIV).

"What kind of a mélange is this?" you may be asking. "Why are you mixing 'guidance' with 'the following of false prophets'?" It seems to me that, when we are crushed with afflictions of one kind or another, the low point emotionally or psychologically is just the point at which Satan or one of his false prophets is able or likely to strike at us. This can happen when money is not available and bills are coming in, when someone is ill and our worry about the illness is increased by dismaying hospital or doctor bills, when an important contract has been cancelled, or when a child, wife, or husband has just died and it seems impossible to go on at all.

As we seek guidance during or immediately after a time of great affliction, these two verses from Isaiah should be pinned on our bulletin board or stuck in a mirror or wherever we would see them frequently. Be warned! The lighting of our own sparks may not come from within our own ideas, our own imaginations or desires.

The temptation may be planted in us from an outside source: "And no marvel; for Satan himself is transformed [fashioneth himself] into an angel of light. Therefore it is no great thing if his ministers also be transformed [fashioned themselves] as the ministers of righteousness . . ." (2 Corinthians 11:14, 15—American Standard Version in brackets). That Satan and his false ministers have succeeded in a frightening way is evident in the tidal wave of false religions which are capturing people in the "post-Christian" countries of the West, with persuasive smiling lads and lassies handing out flowers and false pamphlets in every airport.

As we seek guidance by spending time in prayer, reading the Word of God, and coming directly to Him, we don't need to fear a "tapped line." We have a protected line to our Heavenly Father. However, we are warned:

In addition to all this, take up the shield of faith, with which you can extinguish all the flaming arrows of the evil one. Take the helmet of salvation and the sword of the Spirit, which is the word of God. And pray in the Spirit on all occasions with all kinds of prayers and requests. With this in mind, be alert and always keep on praying for all the saints. Pray also for me, that whenever I open my mouth, words may be given me so that I will fearlessly make known the mystery of the gospel, for which I am an ambassador in chains. Pray that I may declare it fearlessly, as I should.

Ephesians 6:16–20 NIV

Guidance in the midst of affliction is important, necessary, and basic. When affliction brings emotions of crushing disappointment, fear, and sadness, it is easy to be fooled by false comfort, false guidance, and false "light." Paul himself not only gives us all a warning here in Ephesians, but asks for prayers during his own lifetime, so that he would fearlessly keep on doing what God was giving him to do and declaring what God was giving him to declare.

Paul tells us to pray for each other, and if Paul needed prayer, surely you and I do. When we are most "down," we need to cry out for ourselves and for each other, too. However, we can pray with great comfort, along with Paul: "I thank my God every time I remember you. In all my prayers for all of you, I always pray with joy because of your partnership in the gospel from the first day unto now, being confident of this, that he who began a good work in you will carry it on to completion until the day of Christ Jesus" (Philippians 1:3–6 NIV).

Think back to the Bible as a symphony with every note perfectly blended and balanced. We are comforted by this balance. As we long for His guidance in the midst of affliction, we can remember that we are His children and that He has begun a work in us which He will carry on to completion! In our finiteness, we must continually drop to our faces before God in worship, saying, *I bow before You as one of Your creatures. Thank You that, while I cannot understand everything, my hand is held by the eternal, all-wise, Infinite God, the Creator.*

11

Aborting Affliction

"Oh, I wish I hadn't, I wish I hadn't." The girl was sobbing and the words were muffled in my shoulder as I had my arms around her. "Why didn't someone tell me I'd feel like this? Why didn't someone talk to me, just *talk* to me? The doctor just said, 'You're pregnant. When do you want the abortion?' Just like that. He didn't even act like there was anything else to do. Ooohh!" Her sobs grew heavier and her voice went up in a wail of agony. "Now I don't know whether I can ever have a baby. They say there is something wrong. Something went wrong because of the abortion. I was all alone and in a foreign country. I didn't know . . . ."

There is a twentieth-century smog, as formerly "unthinkable" ideas are exchanged for a new set of thinkable ones. In many areas, the former acceptable ideas are like fresh, sweet, spring air, compared with the heavily polluted, foggy, smoggy air of the new ones. People are being affected with "breathing problems" in their minds! Their thinking is simply all fogged up and unclear, and a new set of choices is thrust upon human beings who aren't equipped to argue or set forth an alternative set. We need to do some pretty serious and concentrated sifting of ideas, and we need an absolute standard with which to compare them. Our little ships are going to crash on the rocks if we don't construct some lighthouses where the old ones have been torn down! It's as if some giant hand had gone through all the dangerous waters and removed all the buoys and lighthouses, so that new ships with young captains would surely be wrecked.

"Is it safe, doctor, to have babies as you get older? Is there more chance of a retarded baby?"—"Oh, Madam, we can give a test that will reveal the presence of a mongoloid and then abort it in time." His face had a look of dismay as his patient told him that she did not believe in abortion, but considered it murder of one's own child. Yet that dismayed face belonged to a young assistant to an older doctor still practicing in Switzerland—who would agree wholeheartedly with the mother who was speaking. One generation apart! And the changes are coming more rapidly all the time.

The philosophy of living with an underlying motive of doing everything for one's own personal peace and comfort rapidly colors everything that might formerly have come under the headings of "right" and "wrong." This new way of thinking adds entirely new shades, often in blurring brushstrokes of paint that wipe out their existence of standards or cast them into a shadow that pushes them out of sight. If one's peace, comfort, way of life, convenience, reputation, opportunities, job, happiness, or even ease is threatened, "Just abort it." Abort what? Abort another life that is not yet born? Yes, but also abort the afflictions connected with having a handicapped child, and abort the burdens connected with caring for the old or invalid. Added swiftly are the now supposedly thinkable attitudes of aborting a child's early security in his or her rights to have two parents and a family life; aborting a wife's need for having her husband be someone to trust and lean upon; aborting the husband's need for having a companion and friend as well as a feminine mate; aborting any responsibility to carry through a job started.

The casual attitude toward aborting a fetus has been expanded into the area of commonly accepting the aborting of anything that is a bother, a burden, a heavy work, or a hindrance to whatever kind of freedom an individual wants to pursue by "starting a new life" in some other direction. Affliction—with the various purposes that can be fulfilled through affliction and what it can mean in our lives—is then also to be aborted. If affliction and tribulation are to be aborted, then also are aborted patience, steadfastness, experience, and hope. If these things follow tribulation, then they will also be cancelled out. Do you begin to see where this direction is leading? Like the girl with whom we began this chapter, the end is not freedom but tears.

I had the sadness of a miscarriage at three and a half months. Far from a hospital, in a chalet in the Alps, I had to lie for some hours with that tiny baby beside me—with its threadlike fingers and toes, the ears beginning to form, the arms and legs, curved body, and curled-over head—still connected with me, as the doctor waited for his instruments to come up on the late-afternoon train. I wept for the cut-off life, and I had an incredible desire to push it back into me, to give it a chance to grow . . . . A senseless idea, an impossible desire. It was a death to me. The feeling was the same kind of desperate feeling one has when a person stops breathing, and one longs to give mouth-to-mouth resuscitation. However, when the body dies, there is a sudden desire to do something to make the person *be* there again, breathing, eating, growing. It is the same kind of feeling to be the mother of a much-wanted baby who has died at that moment of growth.

But without further discussion as to the time when the personality is established, the eye color set, the genes all there, it is a fascinating thing to read (in Luke 1:39–45) the story of Mary running to see her cousin Elizabeth right after the angel had talked with her, and Mary had finally replied, "May it be to me as you have said," to indicate her willingness to bear the baby Jesus. Mary had just become pregnant, and Elizabeth had miraculously become pregnant in her old age, with John the Baptist now six months in her womb. The wonder to me is that the baby John jumped in Elizabeth's womb because of Mary's carrying of the Lord Jesus in her womb. Elizabeth greeted her as the mother of her Lord—and Mary had just conceived! The reality of the "person," it seems to me, is a pretty *immediate* reality. Of course, we'll have to wait until we get to heaven to find out how young were the youngest babies who entered heaven. The actual moment that one becomes a person is certainly not something that judges can decide as they sit in a stuffy courtroom, looking as wise and as knowledgeable as they can muster! Handing down decisions by *human* wisdom as to when and when not to kill a life entrusted to a human being's care is astonishingly and frighteningly egotistic.

Let me tell you two stories from families very close to me. A fifth baby was born to a couple in Pennsylvania, and there immediately seemed to be something wrong. Two top specialists came to this conclusion: "Punk kid. Deficient, never will be mentally normal." That was in the days when no medical doctor would suggest such a thing as making a choice about whether a child should live or die. The Christian parents took this baby home to be fed, cuddled, changed, bathed, loved, and prayed for by big brothers and sisters as well as a wide family of Christian friends. Imagination and love brought very wise care, stimulation, and careful teaching at every stage. Was prayer answered and the baby healed? Were the doctors mistaken as to the extent of the seeming defectiveness? Was the care so constant and excellent that other cells in the brain took over for some that had been destroyed? Who but God can know? The facts are that this child grew and developed, went through high school with medium standing, took part in sports, and had gone on to excel in certain areas—with no one ever classifying him as someone with a mental or physical problem. There simply is no omniscient doctor to make a diagnosis that is always perfect.

The other is the story of a child who was not suspected to have any difficulty until very much later, as a slow-to-walk and slow-to-talk little one. The sad, slow development brought about a growing certainty that something was terribly wrong, that up to a point there could be some help, but that the problem would not lift and be cured until Jesus comes back. However, this child has a valuable life to be lived and a purpose to be fulfilled within the framework of who she is. It is a hindering framework during these few years of life on earth, as if born and raised and living a whole life until death in some sort of prison compound or other fenced-in situation. But to say that such a hindrance, handicap, or defect is reason to condemn one to death—with no opportunity to grow and live in this world at all—is to cancel far more than one life. The parents of this particular handicapped child have grown deep and sweet spiritually. It has been a joy (the kind of joy that hurts) to watch them become "polished" like silver and gold and to glimpse the reality of love, long-suffering, gentleness, meekness, and kindness which become more and more visible, as the sheen of molten silver on top of a crucible. Perfect people? No, for no one becomes perfect until Jesus comes back. But the patience worked through tribulation is valuable beyond our comprehension, here in this life but also into the future. Others can observe that it is a reality and not just a sentence in the Bible. The geographic places in which these parents have been used by God have been many different spots on earth, as they looked for proper schools or additional help. The doctors, teachers, and parents of similar children with whom they have been in contact are people they would not have been able to influence, teach, help, and talk to about Christianity, had their child been like their other extremely brilliant child. No one but God can know the blend, the mélange, and the mix of eternally important events that take place "because of" *not* "in spite of" such a child being allowed to live.

There are people who have no hands and paint with their toes, and who have a quality of life that is filled with far more appreciation and creativity than many who are in so-called perfect condition. A young man who has been at L'Abri (a nephew of our friend Rosie, who years ago became a Christian at Chalet les Mélèzes) was born with arms nipped off just below the elbow, one leg shorter than normal and the other a partial limb requiring a prosthesis. This happened to many other women during a particular period of history. As this baby became a young boy, his progress was followed by us all, as we had reports of his strong will and determination to "get on with it" at every stage of life. I remember Rosie telling us of how he was able to relieve the frustration of teething by her fixing a carrot in the prosthesis she had designed so that it could be brought to his mouth naturally. He was also able to go on and learn to feed himself as early as other babies. Then came the time when he did not want anything artificial fastened to his handless arms, since he had discovered how to use what he had in amazingly deft ways. He has since graduated from the University of California and is in seminary, and will tell you himself that "I want to live; thank you." The doctor who had assisted at his birth had informed his mother at the time: "A monstrosity." In today's scene, he might not have had a chance to grow up and tell you that he is glad to be alive and that he has a certainty that God has a very specific purpose for him.

All nature is groaning for the redemption, the restoration—and so are we. Until then, the Fall, the decision of Adam and Eve to believe Satan rather than God, and the effects of sin that continued from that time on have given us an abnormal world to live in for our years on earth before Jesus comes back to give a different so-called quality of life. Do you think that the quality of life of a "defective baby" when compared to that of a "perfect baby" has as great a discrepancy as the quality of life here in this abnormal world when compared to the quality of life ahead of us in all eternity? Our abnormal world reflects the spoiled physical, mental, emotional, psychological, and spiritual condition. Contrast that with the eternity in which we will find complete healing, restoration, and possession of all the faculties which God meant us to have. The quality of life that awaits us is so completely different from the quality of life we can now have in our spoiled condition that there would be no words to describe the contrast. Then does it follow that we should be killed the moment we accept Christ as Saviour, so that we won't be afflicted any longer with the hardships and struggles of continuing to live with our

weaknesses? Is our quality of life worth prolonging? Let me quote
two doctors briefly:

Dr. R. T. F. Schmidt, of Cincinnati, Ohio, and president-elect
of the American College of Obstetricians and Gynecologists,
said that in his personal opinion, which is not necessarily that of
the College, the fact that 17 of the 20 panel members believe
that some severely defective infants should be killed under
certain conditions is "deeply disturbing." This position is not
only disturbing to the traditional concept of the inherent value
of human life but is potentially shattering to the foundation of
Western Civilization, he said ["Physicians Respond to Issue:
When Is It Right to Kill Infant?" *Pediatric News,* April 1977].

One question that has been raised is whether the legal system should be involved in the solution. Another is that if the
legal system is involved, how should the laws be changed and
what would be the costs of such changes, said Dr. Robertson,
of the University of Wisconsin Law School, and Medical
School. Can the law decide whether there is a class of people
who, because of their supposed low quality of life, can be
denied the rights everyone else has? "If there is, how should
these people be identified?" he asked [" 'Quality of Life' as a
Factor in Treating Defective Child." *International Medical
News Service.* Washington].

I would simply remark, "Bravo, Dr. Schmidt and Dr. Robertson,
for defining the extreme seriousness of these considerations!"

Recently in Sweden a prominent man in government seriously
suggested that, since there were 2,000 suicides in the previous year
in that small country, it should be recognized that perhaps the government should provide a building, a comfortable place in which to
commit suicide, so that the discomfort and difficulty of finding a
suitable method and place would not inflict the suffering it does.
This has not been provided; it was only an idea. But don't you see
how the sharp change in thinkable ideas is like an all-enveloping
smog?

Add to this all the current discussion about euthanasia or mercy
killing. Naturally, there is a difference between unnatural living on a
machine for a long period of time and actually giving a pill or
injection which would bring about death. But the whole idea of

some human being's choosing exactly at what point he or she will die, or having someone in the family make that choice, is putting into existence a temptation which is too heavy for human beings to face. Whether they are family, friends, or doctors of the person in question, most humans have such great weakness in the area of honest motives that they could not be trusted with such a decision. Who of us can trust all our motives, moment by moment, day in and day out, week by week, month by month? Who of us can completely trust our motives for the "now," let alone the "tomorrow," for ourselves and all those whom we are in some way responsible for? Who does not go up and down in some measure in wisdom and sensitivity and unselfishness, if not in other basic qualities involved with such decisions?

It seems to me that what we are talking about is this chapter's title, "Aborting Affliction." What do I mean? Just that we face a danger that is creeping in like a tide, rising with each passing moment, making the spot we are standing on in danger of becoming an island. It is a tide of temptation to put "self" first, to rate personal happiness before all else, to claim our "rights" as our basic platform and "search for fulfillment" as our purpose in life. It is hard not to become infected with some sort of breathing trouble, when surrounded by terribly polluted air. Likewise, I feel it is hard not to become infected with some sort of thinking problem, when surrounded by terribly polluted ideas. Just as extreme pollution of air can cause difficult breathing and even lung disease, so we can become twisted by a diseased perspective, a cancerous growth, causing our minds to be malfunctioning in relationship to true truth. We can, in that other picture, suddenly be floating on the tide of the "new thinkables," so that our feet are no longer on the solid ground of our island after all.

The problem is this: *One thing swiftly leads to another.* There is no stopping place when a person cuts loose from an absolute base. "Having a baby would interfere with what I want to do. Having a baby would spoil my rights. I'll abort it." But so quickly might follow: "This baby isn't perfect. Why not kill it?" And who defines that "not perfect"? And who makes the decision? And for what reasons? Abort the difficulty by killing the child? But then what is the difference when it comes to this: "I can't stand life anymore. I want to die. I'll just abort the rest of my life." And then: "How can we care for Grandmother any longer? It's such a burden to us. So much extra work." And the reasons go on, until there is no stopping place. Once it becomes acceptable to decide that the quality of life is no longer worthwhile—just abort it. Abort the rest of Grandmother's life. But then you see we come to a marriage where an accident or illness has hit one of the two on the day after the wedding. An invalid is to be cared for—"for better or for worse." But does it really mean anything? What about divorce? For one reason and another, the selfish human being can find reasons thick and fast. Marriage is an "affliction," old people become an "affliction," children before or after birth become an "affliction." Everything that "gets in my way" becomes an "affliction," and the swiftly growing "thinkable" is to simply abort *all* affliction.

"I just wouldn't stand for it, if I were you. After all, you have yourself to think of. Are you fulfilled? Have you found out yet who you are? Have you found happiness? Are your talents being developed? Are you being squashed? Hurry, hurry! Get rid of everything that is in your way. Abort your afflictions, think about yourself. Erase the word *responsibility* from your vocabulary and think of the 'rights' concept on every level of your personal life. Fight for your own rights; no one else will. Abort all opportunities to serve anyone else; you might become a slave; someone might use you."

Satan has succeeded in selling a bill of goods to the twentieth-century people. Wandering around is a poor generation which has been robbed of the reality of real life, and has been sold sleazy plastic substitutes in exchange for solid mahogany, real oak, solid brass, sterling silver, and handmade pottery. They have been given plastic flowers and ferns in place of gardens and woods and have been handed synthetic substitutes for the produce of vegetable gardens, fruit orchards and berry bushes. The smog is so thick that they haven't been able to discern the difference, and anyway no one has tried to show them. Then comes the wail: "Why didn't someone just *talk* to me? I didn't know." And it has happened in so-called Christian countries where most of the grandparents did *know*.

What people need to be told, as the rapid destruction multiplies, is that when everything is aborted in order to protect an individual's so-called rights, the destruction of everything in the way is not half as devastating as the destruction of that person himself. This applies to human life, human relationships in marriage and family, or a constant shifting of locations and jobs—with no responsibility which could give continuity, apart from what the individual thinks he or she *wants*. The one being most deeply and drastically harmed and destroyed is the one who is constantly *aborting affliction*. The constant search for personal happiness and personal fulfillment is like following a will-o'-the-wisp, an attempt to run through fields and woods to catch a tiny fairy light which is always just out of reach ahead. Meanwhile, we stumble through bogs and bruise our feet on stones, stepping on tiny animals and crushing nests of baby ducks as we go. The light will never be caught. It is like some of the wise old fairy tales of fruitless search for treasure and riches when the real joy was there all the time, right by the fisherman's humble fireside. How can the word *trust* have any meaning, and how can anyone learn enough to know what it means when it is applied to God—if a family of people, all ignoring each other in their stampede for personal rights and pleasures, is multiplied by a community of such individuals? How more serious it is if states and nations are ruled by individuals who have literally pushed their way to the top, and especially if the judges who hand down edicts are made up of such people!

We need to realize that our upstream swim as Christians—our uphill climb, our going against the traffic or in the opposite direction from the pressing crowd—is becoming a more realistic, hour-by-hour concept all the time. We need to resist the small beginnings within ourselves to conform to the whispered suggestion of "Why bother?"

Why bother? We "bother" because if we conform to the thinkability of aborting affliction, in one form or another, rather than sticking to the idea of enduring hardship as good soldiers of Jesus Christ, what we will be doing is helping Satan in his constant drive to abort all who *might* be born again—*before* they can be born. It is not a fanciful thought. It is not stretching a point. He is resistant to letting go of those who are of his kingdom, and he would do anything to try to keep them in this kingdom of darkness, rather than have them step out into God's Kingdom of light. The further we live from what the Word of God teaches, the closer we are to being useful to Satan in muddling people up and keeping them from seeing any contrast or difference at all. The contrast between the Christian's way of life and the unbeliever's way of life is not just as regards personal growth in the areas of sanctification. There is also meant to be a seeable, noticeable, striking difference which the world is supposed to be touched by or to remark upon. The remarks may be sarcasm, but there should be a difference that could give rise to *some* remark! Conforming in the area of ideas is a prelude to conforming in the area of actions—attitudes and reactions are so related.

Do Christians not get irritated with each other? Don't Christian children sometimes get sick of their parents' traits and annoying habits? Don't Christian parents at times get fed up with their children's whining and complaining? Don't Christian husbands get annoyed with their wives and let them know it in no uncertain terms? And don't Christian wives feel that their husbands are entirely unreasonable and thoughtless at times? Aren't there times when children or parents and husbands or wives feel like running away and aborting the whole reality of family life to seek some "peace and quiet," where everything from smells to music, from interior decor to books being read, is a pleasure? Isn't living with other people of a variety of ages—whether in marriage and family or in friends' sharing of a house or apartment, or a dorm situation in college, or a camp or conference grounds, missionary compounds or the local church—simply too frustrating at times to feel like putting up with it any longer?

"What's the use of putting up with it when no one seems happy?"—"Let's quit and go our separate ways!" Or maybe it should be this way: "Let's abort the togetherness and the continuity of life." Continuity is the precious thing that is lost when one starts following the will-o'-the-wisp of fairy light through moors and hills, looking for "perfection" in whatever terms one might define it. And life is so very, very short, that there is scarcely time to build up that continuity in one lifetime. Continuity needs to be protected and worked upon, and a terrific variety of things take place in the doing of that.

"But," you say, "I want love. I need love. This isn't love. I must have the happiness that love brings." And you and I at times lose ourselves in romantic ideas of the perfect understanding and fulfillment that a "perfect love" would bring with that idealized, illusive, nebulous person we conjure up in our minds. And then we come back to 1 Corinthians 13, and you say, "But I know that 'love chapter.' I've read it all my life, and I'm sick of it. Leave me alone." But the thing is that, in our deep smog of acrid pollution, we have lost the definition and the reality of what love is all about. So, read again verses 4 through 8 (NIV).

"Love is patient . . . ." (The King James Version says, "suffereth long.") But don't you see that "tribulation *worketh* patience"? And the very first thing about love is that it is willing to suffer some kind of affliction, some kind of tribulation. Everything can't be "perfect." There have to be real incidents, real moments, where one's own desires are put aside for another person, whether it is the menu for supper, the place for a vacation, having a fire or not, choosing green or orange as a basic color, or letting the children put on their bathing suits and play in the rain. Little things, big things—going to the hospital every day to be greeted with a depressed flow of complaints, bringing home the meat and being told it is the wrong kind. When *can* love be patient or suffer long, if there aren't any concrete opportunities? When can you ever put the other person before yourself—if all your desires are exactly alike all the time? When can love be exercised or practiced as a patient, long-suffering quality—if there is never a time when you need to bite your tongue to stop an angry retort?

". . . love is kind. It does not envy, it does not boast, it is not proud. It is not rude, it is not self-seeking, it is not easily angered [I like the King James' "provoked."], it keeps no record of wrongs. Love does not delight in evil but rejoices in the truth. It always protects, always trusts, always hopes, always perseveres. Love never fails . . . ." *Always . . . always . . . always . . . always . . . never!* Strong words these. But please notice something: they are words of *continuity*. Love is a thing of continuity. It is *work*. It is not a nebulous something that hits you like a bolt of lightning. It is something to be worked at—and at times we get lazy and at times that twentieth-century smog hits us and we ask, "Why bother?"

Whether or not you are married, the reality that love is defined as something that takes years of work and self-*less*-ness, putting other people before yourself, comes clearly across in this passage. The abortion of affliction, the refusing to face hard things, the constant murmuring against the blows and complaining, "I can't see why God could do that to me!" means we miss the reality of the battle and see that we are falling into Satan's trap in that way. But it is also the surest way of missing all the things which God tells us will flow out of the times of difficulty.

Are afflictions only to be considered in the areas of human relationships? No, there are real personal depressions to be dealt with. Can Christians become depressed? Yes, just as Christians can have measles, mumps, chicken pox, and cancer. There are physical reasons which bring on depression and times of worries and fears. These need to be dealt with in the area of nutrition, a time of vacation, the supply of missing vitamins, or the discovery of a hidden infection or trouble somewhere. People can become depressed because of too much work and a drive to be more than finite—or because of too little work and a feeling of wasting life. People can be frail psychologically, just as others are frail in resisting germs, and the spiritual state of a person is not to be judged because one gets "down" or depressed more easily than another. This is exactly what is meant when we are urged to be careful of the "weaker brother." We need to be sensitive to other people's needs for encouragement in the area of comfort or a "lift" in the middle of something which is getting them down, when we are not feeling *down* ourselves. The idea of "two are better than one"—in which we are told that if one falls, the other can pick him or her up—should not just be applied to husband and wife, but parent and child, or friends in our church or Bible class. This is what Christian love and community are all about. The child can be the one to help the parent in the middle of a blinding headache or an injury which has cut off a favorite occupation, as well as the parent can help the child.

Autumn is coming as I write this, and I awakened the other morning to see the beauty of a white icing all over the grass and garden. But the beauty was false, as it meant that beans, squash, and tomato plants had turned black and wilted into an ugly, destroyed mess. "The frost came too soon . . ." I wailed. I wrote an article about it, because I realized that if we had found burlap bags the night before and had covered those plants, they could have been saved. The fog and frost lasted only two days, and the cold would not have penetrated the burlap bags. Nothing could substitute for the sunshine, but the plants could have basked in the warmth of the Indian summer which followed those cold days. My article compared each of us to plants. We are indeed plants in the Lord's garden, once we have supplied the good ground and the seed has sprung up. We aren't all beans. Some of us are broccoli and can resist the frost and go right on growing. However, in my article, I went on to point out that the beauty of illustrations is that they do not need to be carried out to the nth degree. We can switch. You see, we are meant to be the "burlap bags" to each other, although we are also "plants." Sometimes we can supply help which others need; at other times *we* need the help.

We are meant to show real love in *practical* ways, such as the admonition, to "use hospitality one to another without grudging" in 1 Peter 4:9. And being a burlap bag in time, before the frost curls someone up and leaves him wilted, is a very important thing for us to be. "Hospitality" is not just preparing a reception for people you want to do something nice for, nor is it just having a birthday party for a lonely person. It is not just visiting the hospital and stopping to see someone without a visitor, as well as visiting your own daughter; it is also stopping to talk and pray a few minutes on the phone, when you don't really have time to do that. Or getting up and caring for the patient in the next bed, when the nurse doesn't answer the bell (and you are in a condition where you can do it). It is an endless variety of practical real-life things which you could describe as being a burlap bag before the frost comes to someone who is a weaker, frailer plant than you are in some respect.

But isn't the Lord the only true Sunshine? And isn't it in the Sunshine of His presence that people who are His children grow? True, but He has told us to "bear one another's burdens, and so fulfil the law of Christ," and being a burlap bag before the frost comes is just that kind of thing. The tender plant will have the sun again, at this time of the year, and the plant in the Lord's garden will always have available the opportunity to call out to Him. This is where no illustration carries through, but although both the burlap bags and the plants can cry out to the Lord, their needed Sunshine, there is the moment when we can be both burlap bag *and* plant. In so doing, we can fulfill some measure of "By this shall all men know that ye are my disciples, if ye have love one to another."

Are there Christians who haven't had the help they need in time, and who have committed suicide? Yes. And no one who is close to such an afflicted one should blame himself or herself for not being right there, saying or doing the needed thing at that moment. Although we do need to examine ourselves as to what the Lord would have us do, moment by moment and day by day, we *are* finite and limited and our knowledge is also very meager. We cannot always know when frost is coming—we cannot *know* when someone needs us in that drastic moment of violent depression when life itself is suddenly aborted. Yes, suicide is wrong. But listen to Jesus in Matthew 5, as He tells us that when we have been angry with our brother it is comparable to one who has murdered, and that looking

224

Affllictionand lusting is comparable to adultery. He goes on to say that it would be better to lose a part of one's body than to be caused to sin by that part of the body.

As we go over the things we are told *are* sin, we discover that we have sinned. He has forgiven us on the basis of the Blood of Christ and washed us clean. When we sin again, He is faithful to forgive us and to cleanse us from all unrighteousness (see 1 John 1:9). If we get a desperate feeling and wish we could die, when we feel violently like doing some drastic thing, who but God can know whether we have had the same degree of desperation as the person who threw himself from a window or swallowed a bottle of pills? We may drop to our knees and cry, *Oh, forgive me, God. Dear Heavenly Father, I am so sorry. Please forgive me for such wrong desires, such a desire to abort the life You have given me in which to do something for You. I really do want to serve You and please You and defeat Satan, so that my trust and love of You in the midst of this struggle can bring You glory.* The person who swallowed the pills might have come to a place of being sorry, too, but the act was final—even as an abortion is final. One can wail, "Oh, I wish I hadn't . . ." and it can still be heard in the land of the living, but the aborted life which has cut itself off cannot speak those words here. What happens to the Christian who commits suicide? I believe that *every* Christian goes straight to the Lord. Then what regrets will hit the person? Something of the same regrets that might hit us if we have unconfessed sin we haven't talked to the Lord about and told Him we were sorry for.

What about the life he or she was supposed to have lived? The unfinished work and the aborted tasks are similar to the broken-to-pieces work that other Christians have walked away from—when they have rebelliously gone their own way and declared that they were going to live for their own happiness, "no matter what." Many times, people abort the work which God has led them to do, as definitely as though they had aborted life itself. They have aborted the affliction of doing something they felt was too hard, too dull, too exacting, too demanding, tied them down too much, or was too dangerous, as they turned to life that was entirely of their own will or desire. The only real difference between that and suicide is that there is still time to repent and to tell the Lord so, and then have another section of life to give to Him. He can take us right where we are and unfold a path that is His will, from that place on, if we turn back, let go of the determination to have what we are demanding, and ask, "Show me Thy way, Lord," with an intent to *do* His will. I have a letter on my desk from a mother whose child committed suicide. Because there are others who have borne this extreme affliction and who will be reading this book, I'd like to say a bit more. Not only are there sudden bursts of anger or despair, but there are sudden moments of imbalance which so hit a person that one's judgment is all gone, perhaps momentarily, but gone. When our minds and our reasonableness suddenly break, it is similar to another kind of accident, such as a moving blood clot which causes a stroke. We simply are not equipped to make a judgment as to what has happened. Have you ever heard the story "From the Saddle to the Soil"? It is a true story of a man who had been a strong atheist, opposing the Gospel and continually arguing against the Word of God. One day as he was riding horseback, he was thrown violently from the saddle, to lie broken and unconscious on the ground. He entered a coma in which he was to lie for months. No one thought he would recover, but one day he awakened to tell his story with a radiant light in his eyes. He wanted everyone to know that he was a Christian. "But when did this change take place? When did you make that decision?" His answer was that between leaving that saddle and hitting the ground, he had turned to the Lord and cried out for forgiveness in true belief, accepting Christ as his Saviour. How long did that take? A few seconds was all that he had. Had he died, people would not have known (until they got to heaven) that he had become a believer. This man lived to demonstrate a changed life and give evidence of what had happened. The thief on the cross beside Jesus did not have that opportunity, but Jesus told him that he would be in Paradise that day. Just as it is possible to cry out to the Lord in such a brief moment, with sufficient honesty and great enough reality to be born again, it is also possible to cry out for forgiveness in the midst of doing a drastic thing which cannot be reversed.

Do we then shrug our shoulders and rely on last-moment decisions to make up for our not fulfilling our responsibilities? Do we conclude that the affliction which surrounds evangelism is something we can count on? No, that would be as wrong and unthinkable as going around stealing people's traveling bags so that they would be brought to L'Abri! Our personal need is to stand directly before the Lord, asking Him to point out to *us* any place where *we* are in danger of (or in the middle of) *aborting affliction* in one way or another—rather than asking for His grace to go on in the midst of it to do *our* next thing, whether it is being a burlap bag or growing!

We are sometimes given such wrong ideas that it is no wonder we are mixed up. Are Christians meant to be happy all the time? Are we meant to be feeling fulfilled all the time? Are we to be looking inward and examining ourselves to see whether we know who we are? Is life to be a self-centered journey? The ideas that turn us in these directions are like false shortcuts which lead nowhere but into a blind alley, making it necessary to retrace steps and waste a lot of valuable time getting there—wherever "there" is. *If* Christians are meant to be always happy (*if* all their ailments are to be healed if they have enough faith, *if* all their troubles are to disappear as soon as they pray, *if* they are meant to be completely fulfilled all the time), and we are unhappy at the moment (upset by something, sick, have a fierce headache or back pain, are troubled about several people we love very much or about decisions that need to be made today or tomorrow—and would hate to even define what "fulfilled" is supposed to mean) then our conclusion must be that we are not Christians. Or we must quickly smile and say words that will make all these things appear to be okay, in case the smile and the words are what count and will make up for all those inner things that perhaps just *seem* to be opposite. Instead of becoming sensitive to other people's needs because we have been honest and run to the Lord for help in our own needs, we can either become harder and harder all the time and tend to live on the surface in fear—or we walk away from it all and seek some other kind of base for our lives. There is a danger of not being real. *Make me solid wood, Lord, not veneer!*

The Bible gives an opposite way of life to be followed by Christians. This directive turns us away from the constant fight for rights for "self" all the time. The path leads to final fulfillment, however, and to joy unspeakable! It leads not to a dead end, but to what we are looking for. First go back to Proverbs 8: "For whoso findeth *me* findeth *life,* and shall obtain favour of the Lord" (v. 35). "Blessed is the man that heareth me, watching daily at my gates, waiting at the posts of my doors" (v. 34). What a vivid picture of the daily starting place, waiting at the gates of our Heavenly Father, waiting at the posts of His doors. How? In going to a building, a church, a temple, a tabernacle? No, no; happily, His gates and doors are accessible to us in the deepest jungle, whether our "jungle" is in the tropics or in a modern city, in the wildest of woods or northern pine-covered mountains or in a city park. We can find Him as we read His Word from a tiny book we can carry in our pockets or briefcase. We can talk to Him without an appointment, asking for direction and help in the immediate, tearing, searing need.

Balance is what we are asking for, day by day. We will never have a perfect balance, but we need to realize that in the midst of our afflictions we need to turn our thoughts away from ourselves— whether in the modern emphasis on self, or in the circle of trying to be acceptable as a "successful Christian" in the eyes of a certain group of Christians about us. Put together a few verses from the Lord's teaching, forgetting that we have heard them all before. This is the "opposite way of life" expressed strongly and clearly:

[Jesus is speaking:] "Therefore I tell you, do not worry about your life, what you will eat or drink; or about your body, what you will wear. Is not *life* more important than food, and the *body* more important than clothes? . . . . But seek first his kingdom and his righteousness, and all these things will be given to you as well."

Matthew 6:25, 33 NIV (italics added)

Read the whole passage, but note that "life" is important, not negated. Note that the "body" is important, not negated. The Heavenly Father—who knows we need clothing, food, and so on—also knows our other needs in the whole of life on this earth, as He prepares for us an eternity that will be completely fulfilling. He is telling us to put Him and His Kingdom—His glory, His Person, and His will for us—first in our lives, and the other areas of need will be supplied by Him. The opposite way is to seek fulfillment in all the "things" we are certain we deserve and are afraid of losing.

Read on: "And anyone who does not take his cross and follow me is not worthy of me. Whoever finds his life will lose it, and whoever loses his life for my sake will find it" (Matthew 10:38, 39 NIV). "Oh," you may say, "that is an old-fashioned pietistic, ascetic idea." It is God's clearly spoken idea, coming from the lips of Jesus. What exactly is He saying? Here is a clear indication that if we refuse the affliction (if we "abort the affliction," in my terminology), if we refuse hardship and insist on bypassing the difficult thing we are really meant to do, then we may expect *failure* in the end. Failure in business, failure on the farm, financial failure, failure to gain a place in the public eye politically or in some other way? No! no! The failure that the Lord is pointing out is that modern word *fulfillment* which, after all, is a synonym for "a satisfying, fulfilling life." If a person turns away from God and His direction to "find life," there will be an actual losing of life, a dead emptiness. On the other hand, the opposite is promised—if one loses his life for the Lord's sake, he or she will *find it.* Simple? Not so simple, but true. It can be discovered to be true in very simple moment-by-moment experiments.

> Remember Lot's wife! Whoever tries to keep his life will lose it, and whoever loses his life will preserve it. I tell you, on that night two people will be in one bed; one will be taken and the other left. Two women will be grinding grain together; one will be taken and the other left.
>
> Luke 17:32–35 NIV

This is speaking of the Second Coming of Christ and its sudden occurrence. There is the same warning concerning the constant search for personal peace and comfort, personal fulfillment and happiness, rather than having a willingness to put the Lord and then other people before ourselves. In this context, we are shown that it isn't what one is doing that matters when Jesus returns. People aren't meant to be sitting and waiting out on a hill or in a church. But the reality of belief, the actuality of being born again, and the inward blessing of salvation are what matters. It is, however, tied in with these realities making themselves evident through an inner attitude of willingness to "lose one's life," instead of putting *self* first. It is there in the context of preparedness for the Lord's Second Coming. Fit in this portion of John with those other two references:

> Jesus replied, "The hour has come for the Son of Man to be glorified. I tell you the truth, unless a kernel of wheat falls to the ground and dies, it remains only a single seed. But if it dies, it produces many seeds. The man who loves his life will lose it, while the man who hates his life in this world will keep it for eternal life. Whoever serves me must follow me; and where I am, my servant also will be. My Father will honor the one who serves me."
>
> John 12:23–26 NIV

A few days ago, Fran and I ate corn we had planted ourselves. One grain of corn grew into a plant seven feet high. We had a small patch of such plants and marveled day after day that the small grains we had pushed into the ground could produce such enormous plants. This was to be an increased wonder as we looked at the even rows of yellow grain on two ears, both from one plant. What was the "increase"? How many seeds can one seed produce? Fantastic! Yet Jesus was not only telling us of His own need to die—that we might be born, thousands upon thousands of us—but He was making it very imperative that we remember, harvest after harvest and each time we eat wheat or corn or another multiplied seed, that we need to "die to self" and selfish motives. Once in a lifetime? No! Oh, no! Time after time after time, we need to "die" in a tremendous diversity of situations. Do we need to try to copy the affliction of Hudson Taylor by finding a sailing ship to China and traveling afterwards in oxcarts? Do we need to try to adopt the afflictions of Amy Carmichael by going to India, wearing a sari and sandals, darkening our skin, seeking babies in dangerous marketplaces, hoping to save them from temple life? Do we need to get ourselves put into prison like Chuck Colson, in order to become one with men who need help so desperately? Do we need to go through a war, plunge into the heart of modern scenes of violence, or place our lives purposely in jeopardy? Do we need to try to find another tribe like the Auca Indians and repeat the lives and deaths of those missionaries who so courageously gave their lives there?

Of course, the answer is obvious. But so often we have the "dangerous" idea of formulating in our imaginations what "dying to self" means, and then we try to put this pattern on our own lives or use it to criticize others. Some affliction may look like luxury to you from the outside—and other affliction may look like an adventure. Each person's own willingness to put the Lord first and follow Him in the midst of hardship takes on a different pattern, not only from person to person but from day to day and month to month. We need continually to "die all over again" and be willing to not refuse to go on in "this," whatever "this" is. Abortion of life, whether the life be that of an unborn baby, a handicapped infant, a very old person, or the life we are meant to be living for the Lord, is not something that belongs to human decision. Life has a purpose, eternal in importance.

Praise be to the God and Father of our Lord Jesus Christ! In his great mercy he has given us new birth into a living hope through the resurrection of Jesus Christ from the dead, and into an inheritance that can never perish, spoil or fade—kept in heaven for you. Through faith you are shielded by God's power until the coming of the salvation that is ready to be revealed in the last time. In this you greatly rejoice, though now for a little while you may have suffered grief *in all kinds of trials.*

1 Peter 1:3–6 NIV (italics added)

12

Practicing Contentment
or
What Comes Next?

This is going to be a very practical chapter, in which you and I will be considering possibilities in a variety of situations. Both of us being finite and limited, the amount of time we can spend together and the extent of what can be crammed into that amount of time will be only a fraction of the possible ideas about how one might get started in the next step of life after a particularly crushing blow, or how to take the first step out of the bog of dullness and disinterest, or what might be possible in the midst of an "impossible" situation. Since I can't know your background and present set of afflictions or troubles, how can I meet your need? I may not hit upon it at all. True, but even if you were with me, sitting right there on the couch with a teacup in your hand (or a glass of orange juice if you would rather) it would be very important to establish in our short amount of time together that you are not alone in feeling that you can't face the present or the future. You are not alone in feeling overwhelmed by your own strange combination of events and your own inward or outward inadequacies to continue in the midst of them. It isn't just that the old saying "Misery loves company!" is true. It is of basic, *titanic* importance to recognize that you are surrounded by an enormous company of others (whether already in heaven, in other parts of the world, or closer to you in your own county or neighborhood) who have faced or now face difficulties as discouraging as yours—or greater. Different difficulties? Undoubtedly—but the fact that the word *all* is used to describe those Christians who face some form of persecution, affliction, hardship, or trouble makes it so wide

231

that the very first thing we need to think of together is the company in which we are included! For that reason, the very fact that this chapter needs to cover a diversity of possibilities and a variety of needs can in itself be an encouragement. One day, when we walk through that "museum" together, or sit in one of the perfect surroundings ahead of us to compare notes, we will feel the "togetherness" of the entire company which is described in the Book of Revelation:

> After this I beheld, and lo, a great multitude, which no man could number, of all nations, and kindreds, and people, and tongues, stood before the throne, and before the Lamb, clothed with white robes, and palms in their hands. [We are to be among that multitude, and we are being spoken of when, in a later verse, a bit more of that future is opened up to us.] They shall hunger no more, neither thirst any more; neither shall the sun light on them, nor any heat. For the Lamb which is in the midst of the throne shall feed them, and shall lead them unto living fountains of waters: and God shall wipe away all tears from their eyes.
>
> Revelation 7:9, 16, 17

We are being talked about. We are going to taste and eat that food which He will be feeding the great multitude; we are going to let the marvelous waters flow down our throats, refreshing us with a thirst-quenching satisfaction that no liquid on earth has ever provided for us. We are going to have all our tears wiped away and never have to weep again. God's Word speaks about *us,* as well as all those people, some from every tribe and nation and kindred and tongue. Former divisions among people will be wiped away, and the togetherness will be beyond anything anyone has ever dreamed of here. *And all will have their tears wiped away!* Think of that for a moment. We are "together" in having gone through our own peculiar moments of history, not just the world's history but our own personal histories. Our victories and our failures will be comparable because they are real, not myth. We have lived real lives and will fit in among all the others. There will be a unity that will be truly flabbergasting, as well as a diversity that will take an eternity to discover, as we learn about all human beings and about all the rest that lies before us.

The tears have not yet been wiped away. We are expected to be weeping at times. The agonies of sorrow and the terrible physical pains we are feeling are a present reality. We are not meant to deny their existence. The dismay associated with a paralyzed leg or half of one's body after an accident or stroke is so easily recognized as "a part of life" for others, but never expected for ourselves, and it is a deep and real dismay.

The doctor's voice saying, "I am sorry, but it is malignant," or "You need an amputation tomorrow, before it is too late," or any similar shocking set of words sounds far off. Could it be a radio announcement, or someone reading lines from a play? "It can't be *me* he is talking about!" . . . Your wife has died ten minutes after your fourth baby was born: "But it couldn't happen. It is impossible!" . . . Your husband's plane crashed, and years later you still feel the shock of the first announcement . . . . The ambulance comes up to the crashed cars, and this time you are lying among the twisted metal parts—and your child or your wife or your husband is pinned underneath, in a condition you aren't sure of yet. Weeks of pain follow. How to go on? How to go on after a major change in the basic possibilities of day-by-day life?

What comes next when you enter an old-folks' home or nursing home, or find yourself in a wheelchair? What comes next when you lose your job and feel you are a failure, with nothing to contribute day by day? What comes next when you find you are going to be alone, maybe for years ahead, and you want to be surrounded by people? What comes next when you are surrounded by so many people that you long to have a total release from them all and be alone with a tree or a rock, a rowboat or a pair of skis under you, swishing silently along trails? What do you do about having too much—or too little? Too much to do, too many demands on your time and energy, too many ideas to carry out, too many phone calls, too many letters, too much responsibility, too big a house filled with too many children of your own (or orphans), too many patients in a mission outpatient hospital with too few beds and too few doctors and nurses. "Too much" can be a great diversity of excess of any kind. "Too little" to do, no demands on your time, a vacuum of ideas, no phone calls or letters, no responsibilities, no space to live in—only one room, or a bed, or a corner in one room in Hong Kong with twelve others in the same room—no child in your arms when you long for one of your own or one to adopt. There is a great variety of kinds of "too little"—and one of these is emptiness.

"I've flown halfway around the world to come and talk to you here at L'Abri. Udo has already been such a great help to me as we talked together yesterday. Now I want to talk to you. My brother's sudden death was such a crushing blow to me; the grief and sorrow are more than I can bear. Christian friends have been so condemning of my tears and have spoken so lightly of how 'wonderful' death is, that it has upset me even more. Now Udo has helped so much in talking in this area [of death as an enemy, and the separation of soul and body as the unnatural result of the Fall]. But I want to ask you, 'Why couldn't I have been the one to die?' I know my brother was a Christian, but I felt he needed to grow more. Why couldn't it have been me? What comes next? How can I go on?"

This was a brilliant anthropologist speaking, a Ph.D., a university professor, mature and with many "open doors." What kind of an answer could be given? What sort of practical suggestions could be made? First of all, after any death there is a need for looking at things from a different perspective. Yes, death is an enemy, and the world is full of struggle and agony, and we look with hope (as "the world" cannot hope) for the Second Coming of Christ. However, we need to imagine, if possible, that *we* have been the one to die, and that in our imagination we have been able to glimpse something of heaven, with its totally different perspective of "time" and use of time from that viewpoint. After this glimpse, we need to imagine that we have been told, "You are to go back and, remembering this perspective, live the next section of time—before you finally come to stay here—in the light of this new perspective. You are being given a limited time to do what only *you* can do." It is true that each one of us is able to do something that no one else can do. Each one of us has an opportunity to "be" or to "do," to create or to be the audience for someone else's creative work, that no one else has. We have a unique and individual opportunity, task, work, or path to follow.

"You ask, 'Why couldn't I have been the one to die? If he had grown more, he could have done more than I.' But stop to think! You are equipped *now* to do something for other members of your family who need what you have, what you know is true, what you can *now* present. Your hope of what another might do is born of imagination; what you can do is a present reality.

"Right now you may have a discussion group for university students in your big living room. Think of that as a setting for renting a film and inviting your family, one at a time or several together. (That is a decision to be made as time goes on.) The attractiveness of the food, the vividness of the young students' interest, the reality of their honest struggles as they ask their questions, and the introduction to the film's discussion can take away the uncomfortable and seemingly impossible directness of tackling one person after another in private conversation. Think of this as an immediate possibility of using the 'now' as a substitute for what you had hoped one day might take place through your brother."

As for grief and sorrow, naturally they will come back in floods or waves at times—the wave may come in, and there is a lull. Two things cannot occupy the same place at the same moment. Even if you can carry on several streams of thoughts and emotions at one time, there is a kind of "uppermost takeover" of positive ideas, creative ways of doing things, and a putting of other people first in importance in recognizing that time is very limited. There is nothing like seeing things from the perspective of the limited nature of time. This view frees us from wasting time and gets us moving on with something we want to get done before "time" is over. A good comparison is a shipboard period, an ocean crossing. In one way, floating between two continents gives an unrealistic feeling to time. But there are *only* those five or six days in which to read those books, exercise each day, take a plunge in the pool, talk to people at your table with the realization that they may never again meet anyone who will introduce them to truth, or mingle with a person who understands something of your own appreciation of nature, art, family, literature, or the dairy business. The hours go by so rapidly, and you want them to be filled with a balanced program of all you hoped for in this long-awaited trip. In reducing life to periods of jumps—ten-year jumps, one-year jumps, one-month jumps, one-day jumps, one-hour jumps—how many of these blocks of time are there anyway? Obtaining this type of perspective helps us to throw ourselves into the immediate "now."

The Bible class was over, and a young mother pulled me aside into the garden where she could ask a question that was keeping her awake nights after her baby's recent death: "People have said that God took the baby because the world is so wicked. If that is true, how can I possibly have another one? People have convinced me that I must not. What do you think?" My next hour was spent in going back over the whole concept of death, and then pointing out that the whole problem of "being" is amazing . . . .

If I had not had that miscarriage, probably Franky would never have been born . . . . If my mother had not lost her first baby and then her first husband with tuberculosis at the end of her first year of marriage, she would not have gone to Bible school in Toronto in the 1890s, nor gone off to China alone before the end of the century, and then gone through all the dangers of the Boxer Rebellion. If she had not finally broken down in her resolution to never marry again, and said yes, after my father (with the pigtail which men missionaries wore in those days) asked her the tenth time, none of us in the family would have been born . . . . And if my older brother had not died at nine months with dysentery, probably I would not have been born nine months after that . . . .

There is a very precious mystery concerning the exact person who comes into existence at an exact time, as the child of two people who, in another year or month, would have had a different child. You cannot know how very important this child, who may be born when you feel free to have one, will be. The thing to remember is that you are not replacing one with another. No one takes another person's place—he or she is a different person, born in a different place and time. You are not being disloyal to one child by having another; nor is a widow or widower disloyal to the loved one by marrying again.

How do we know? The Bible tells us so. It is that simple. And as you count your children, always number among them the one who is in heaven. It is not "I *had* three," but "I *have* three, one in heaven, two here." There is a dear, yellow-haired, blue-eyed, very contented baby in that mother's arms now, not *replacing* his brother, but coming along to take his own place in the family and in the world.

"I can't stand my marriage any longer. My husband drinks, but it isn't just that. He is always bringing someone home for dinner and getting angry about my forgetting to get the laundry out of the living room. And he complains about my cooking all the time."

A long series of woe poured forth from this wife, who seemed not to have learned to cook or have any orderliness in many areas, yet who really wanted to find a way to keep things together. First I stuck out my five fingers and suggested taking stock under five headings. What may come next? What are the possibilities for *any* of us?

1. Jesus may come back tomorrow.
2. I may die tomorrow.
3. The "other person" may die tomorrow (the husband, wife, employer, or whoever is making day-by-day life a nightmare).
4. The situation may change entirely, through some wonderful change taking place in me, in the other person, or in the circumstances. For example, the job may take the family or the individual (if one is alone) to another city, another country, another set of circumstances for everyday life.
5. Nothing may change.

"Now," I said, "think of each item in the list, one by one."

What would I want to do today if Jesus were coming back tomorrow? Think carefully. Don't answer glibly, "I'd hurry to call the people to whom I want to talk about the truth." And don't answer equally glibly, "I'd plant a tree," as Luther said he would. For me, the carefully thought-over answer is that I would continue in a straight line, trying in the most creative way to care for my home, meals, and children today. I might make new curtains, clean out a few drawers, weed the vegetable patch, read a story to the children, plan an interesting menu and cook it for supper. With what sort of motive? Perhaps with the recognition that doing better what needs to be done right now, where I am in my present set of circumstances, should be my "last day" motive. This includes recognizing that, unless I have rebelled against the Lord's will, I *am* where He wants me to be today—in my home. What motive is there to do it all with more imagination and vim than yesterday's work? Since it is my last day, I want to do it the way I picture myself as being able to do it "someday"—and it has to be today. What other motive? If the Bible is true, there will be people left around after Jesus returns. They might walk into my house, and these signs of creativity and some measure of beauty would be important to leave behind, along with the Bibles they'd find! Substitute for "home" almost any set of circumstances—office, artist's studio, farm, factory, shipyards, airports, oil fields, university dorm or classroom, shared apartment, hospital, old-folks' home, wheelchair. Those five possibilities on the list are ahead of us all.

Then, if I die tomorrow? Wouldn't there be the same motives for doing something today, to the best of my ability and imagination in creative areas, for the benefit of "today's person" who will be eating at my table, sitting next to me and reading what I have written, following me around newly painted walls, or seeing my freshly covered pillows?

And if the "other person" is going to die tomorrow—the one I am striving to please or find out how to go on with as a friend, business partner, secretary, fellow worker, patient occupying the bed next to mine in a hospital, or whatever—isn't that same list of thoughtfully produced and created things important today? Is there any difference in the list?

And if the situation is going to change suddenly? What if there is a geographical change and I am going to move halfway around the world—leaving the city for the country or the seaside for a city apartment, being transferred from the hospital to a recuperation home in some parklike area, moving from America to Arabia or from Hong Kong to Switzerland, or exchanging a tiny hut for a palace or a huge home for a fisherman's cottage? Maybe there will be a huge change in your husband's personality, or yours or your boss's or your partner's. Whatever material, psychological, emotional, or physical changes are ahead tomorrow, this points up the fact that one needs to be as ready as possible by using one's imagination, creative abilities, energy, and willingness to work harder to finish today's events—so that the huge push of work for tomorrow's change may be done without having to regret the waste of what will be "yesterday."

And if nothing changes? Then *you* are the one to enjoy the new curtains, the freshly covered cushions, the flavor of the meal and the pleasure of others who are eating it. You are the one to enjoy the results of your creative work today, as you are able to go on to a better idea tomorrow. You are the one to benefit from the growth, both inside yourself as a personality and in gaining courage, incentive, and confidence to try something a bit more complicated tomorrow. You have done something in your situation which you couldn't have done in any other combination of circumstances, and it has surprised you—and possibly someone else. On top of that, it has been a day lived with the possibility of doing what you have done with love for the Lord, who accepts even a cup of cold water which is given with love for Him. He has appreciated whatever it was, even if another human being didn't seem to notice or say, "Thank you."

We return to the little woebegone wife of the rather important executive, who told me she can't think of anything to have for dinner when he pops in with a business guest. (She once just opened a can of tuna on a plate, served it in the shape of the can, unadorned except for some not-quite-cooked rice!) This may seem far from where you are, but there are many parallels in a variety of situations in our human relationships. The following suggestion could be used either literally, as it was with her, or applied with individual changes to fit other weaknesses or circumstances.

Whether you are living with other people in a family, in some other "shared" situation, or whether you live alone, it seems to me that my suggestion to her fits the needs of all of us. At least, I couldn't get along without this "encouragement" myself.

"Go home," I told her, "and buy pads of art paper, at least two different sizes. I like white, but you could use colored paper if this would please you more. Get felt-tipped pens. I prefer black, but get five colors, at least at first, and try to make yourself pay attention to what you write by using a variety of colors. Every day sit down first thing and make a list. A list of what? First, your ABSOLUTELY NECESSARY WORK—in one column, or in a circle you've drawn, or in a box of a different color. Then plan MENUS, not just for the shared evening meal but for your own lunch, if you eat alone. Decorate your menus, whether or not you can draw. At least make a few daisies or curlicues, but if you like to draw, give yourself a few minutes as a treat to decorate the list differently each day. After the menus, make a SHOPPING LIST for the food and also for any other needs for that day. If you have a weekly shopping day, make at least a rough list of menus for the week on another sheet of paper, so that you can have all the things on hand.

"Add another list for things that are not absolutely necessary to be done that day, but that are creative projects. Head that PROJECTS.

Painting? Dressmaking? Knitting? Gardening? Writing? Exercising carefully for your back, or to get two inches off your waistline? Always have some projects in progress, even if you have to neglect them. It is quite a different thing to feel that you have neglected cutting out your new dress, or the leather animal you are designing, or the wooden tray you are decorating with an electric needle, than to have nothing concrete to have 'neglected.' It is psychologically very different. Always put down items like INTERRUPTIONS, so you can check off the interruptions as they come, and feel that you haven't done just 'nothing.' Also put down READING and include a few minutes to read each day, choosing books for your particular need at the time: education, recreational, 'to lift me away from here to another space and time'—as well as remembering to tick off somewhere a time for prayer and Bible reading."

Those were my suggestions to that young wife. There are more . . . . Make a weekly or monthly list of bigger aspirations or projects: "Prepare for Christmas," "Plan Some Sort of Birthday Party," "Fit In a Family Concert," "Vacation—Where?" "Start Regular Swimming," "Design a New Kind of Children's Bedroom," "Make a Sailboat," "Make a Piece of Furniture," "Learn to Play a Musical Instrument," "Take Language Lessons From a Record." Print it out in fancy letters (or if you haven't that much use of your hands, do it all on a typewriter). The big lists can be discarded and new ones made, but the daily lists should be renewed each day whenever possible. That young woman went home and faithfully bought colored pencils and art paper and started. Perfection followed? No, of course not, but there was encouragement and a new start for her. It is not enough to simply say, "The Lord will show you daily how to do what you need to do." We need to give each other practical help at times, ideas for getting started, when we have come to a place of feeling absolutely hopeless about putting out a foot to take even one small step.

"I'm hemmed in by four walls," someone may say. "I'm stuck caring for a disabled husband [sister, mother, friend] and I don't have the freedom to go swimming, much less take a vacation. My horizon is so tiny and I'm depressed." I know individuals whose affliction is this kind of an imprisonment. I would say, "Take stock!" both as to the five possibilities, and also as to what it is possible to do in this particular set of circumstances that could *not* be done if you had what might seem "freedom" from your restrictions. Perhaps there would then be a different set of responsibilities. What can you do right now? The "list idea" is for you, too. And the more colorful and interesting the better. Make one for the absolutely essential things that you have to do daily for the person or persons for whom you are caring. As you look at these essentials, think what kinds of changes could be made, even if it is only in giving a sponge bath with a new kind of bubble-bath fragrance or soap-filled sponge—for your own pleasure in the smells, as well as for the other person. Think what kinds of food combinations you could make for the person who can scarcely swallow. For instance, you could grind chicken or veal and put it into a broth with gelatin to make a mousse that will slide down easily. Someday you might put together a little specialized cookbook of these recipes. In all the "necessities," think of whatever variety you could possibly introduce. Then list the possibilities during the hours your "patient" is asleep or watching TV, and start projects that you would never have the freedom to do in a more normally active life—rag rugs, old-fashioned patchwork, and so on.

"But my energy is all gone after I've done the essentials." True, so often true. But energy also diminishes when there is not enough incentive, and beginning a creative work, some sort of project you can watch take shape, can often carry with it a fresh supply of energy. I have had a short two-month period of being hemmed in by two rooms, caring for Grandmother Schaeffer after her stroke. This was before we brought her to Switzerland to care for her for seven years there. I didn't leave the two rooms except to run—and I do mean run—to the corner store and back. All the tempting, easily swallowed food was made in my "test kitchen" and resulted in her being nourished "back to life" when the doctor had said that she was dying.

At first I had my own affliction, in the longing to be with my own children and husband back at L'Abri, where I had been accustomed to having such a variety of people to care for and things to do. Then I suddenly realized that I was being given time to do some of the things I could never do any other time without feeling guilty. So I set out to make doll clothes. When Grandmother was better, she insisted on all the lights being out, with me sitting beside her. But I found it possible to sit on the floor and see enough by the bluish light from the TV to make the tiny clothes with wee buttonholes and lacy ruffles which I couldn't have otherwise made for my grandchildren. It gave me a feeling of being with the grandchildren, as well as enjoying the welcome variety of creativity. I also faithfully did twenty minutes of exercises in a small floor space each morning and thus kept in shape in spite of not getting out. It was also possible to write endless letters when Grandmother was asleep and I could have the light on at the kitchen table.

"Necessity is the mother of invention" may be a trite old quote which I think of too often, but it is so very true and ought to become more real for you right now. Life is far too short for all the possibilities, anyway. Therefore, the possibilities of the "now" and the reality of being able to answer the question of "What comes next?" after some tragic or tremendously hindering occurrence, give us a small enough range to recognize what we have open to us. Look around you, but don't neglect to pray for guidance and for the Lord's ideas to come to you. Ask for "open eyes" to see what you can do now, what you would never have done if things had not come to such an abrupt disruption.

There are not two classes of things—"spiritual" and then a lesser class on the creative level, in all the areas that word covers in the arts or daily living. As we are "scattered" into hospitals, old-folks' homes, other countries, different jobs, wheelchairs, and small hemmed-in places where we care for other people in need, we are always in contact with a different set of people. This great variety of human contact can include the people running the grocery store, the newspaper boy, the doctor who comes to see the patient, a few neighbors who might drop in, the people in our prison cell, the nurses in a hospital, the other old folks in the home, or fellow refugees on an island or boat. We always have available some sort of contact, even in solitary confinement—where we can still have contact with God.

Mrs. Byram, a missionary doctor who with her doctor husband was in a solitary cell (he in another) in a concentration camp in Manchuria, had her Bible with her. She did a fantastic study of God's Word, writing in the margins of her Bible with "ink" made of saliva and the dust of the dirt floor and using a hairpin for a pen. It made legible writing. I saw it when she visited us in Chester,

Pennsylvania, after their release. It was this background of study and prayer during that time which prepared her to later give an hour and a half to prayer—each day for the rest of her life—for whatever the Lord would lead her to pray. After spending a certain amount of time for guidance, she became convinced that forty-five minutes a day should be devoted to prayer for L'Abri. For the rest of her life she spent that time with a loose-leaf notebook open. There was one page for John Sandri, one for Udo Middlemann, and one each for Ranald Macauley, Jane Stuart Smith, Betty Carlson, Hurvey Woodson, Dorothy Jamison, and, of course, for our own children and Fran and myself. She even included a page for each person who was ever mentioned in the family letters during our first ten years at L'Abri. She had been "scattered"—and although she was physically in California, she was as thoroughly a part of L'Abri as any of the Workers. She was "scattered" from her medical work in Manchuria for a variety of new and different things.

Does that mean that *only* prayer and *only* the actual time of telling the truth to others are important to God? I would say not. The God who made us in His image made us to be creative, as He is the Creator, and the things which might seem unimportant by certain worldly standards are important to Him, I am certain. Making doll clothes has value, not just for the pleasure it will give the children, not just because it is a therapeutic act for the person designing and doing the sewing, but because it is a creative work, fulfilling the creativity which God has made us able to do. Because we are meant to be creative, such activity is a help to us when we are in the midst of sorrow, trouble, affliction, persecution, pain, difficulty. It is a real help, not just a made-up occupation to keep us busy. Our "being scattered" through affliction of one kind or another is not just being dispersed into a place where we will be in touch with different people, but is a scattering into some form of creative activity that we would otherwise never have been able to do. Yes, my Rectangle A in the museum of heaven—where there is victory over Satan's attacks by simply loving and trusting God and not complaining against Him—gives us sufficient purpose in the midst of trouble. But God's opportunities or possibilities are so rich, so varied, and so multiplied. Several things *can* be happening at the same time in the same space—and in this sense we have a multiplied use of time.

Amy Carmichael fell into a cesspool when a plank broke during her inspection of a building on their compound in India. As one who was used by God to found that important work for rescuing girls and boys from the evil practices of temple worship, she was tirelessly occupied, day in and day out, with the children themselves and all other aspects of the work. A broken leg and all the terrible complications which followed were not to result in the "six weeks in bed" which the doctor originally pronounced, and to which she replied, "Oh, I can't!" as she wondered how the work could go on for even one week without her active participation. No, she was not in bed for six weeks, but for twenty-one years. Out of her "furnace" of ghastly pain and constantly recurring times of disappointment when complications multiplied, came the books which have been such a help to so many thousands of people.

People were to write letters to Amah (her name to her own people), telling her that if she had enough faith she would be healed. It would be hard to find anyone who has lived so completely by prayer, and who has such strong and consistent faith as Amy Carmichael. Being shut away from her "normal" work scattered her, not just into seclusion when her pain no longer permitted her to be very often with her people, but into writing. She wrote daily to her children and workers, as her "thought for the day." She wrote *Rose From Brier* and *Gold by Moonlight*—for the sick, from the sick! She wrote the story of the work, several books about the lives of individual Indian people, and others which told of how the Lord met their needs for food and material things in answer to prayer through the years. Twenty-one years! *Scattered* not far from her work of all the previous years. But what a walk of affliction—and what a lasting result in the lives of others, as well as in the area of creativity. Amah wrote not only prose but poetry. Such important creativity and important content were brought forth in spite of the four walls which limited her in her former work. Such beauty was brought forth *because of* the limiting walls. And the pain? The sharing of the comfort which she felt the Lord was giving her has spilled over in her books as a source of comfort to those who won't see her until they get to heaven.

"I can't read *The God Who Is There*. I can't read the *L'Abri* story. I can't even read the Bible. You have to understand that I can't concentrate at all . . . . The words don't stick together . . . . My mind goes into a fuzz."

The girl who spoke those words had been at L'Abri for quite a time, although she herself couldn't understand how she ever got here. She was once often drunk, deep into drugs, and had been living in a kind of stupor for months in a "pad" where others emerged from the fog of smoke as shapes rather than people. Because of drugs found in her possession at the airport, she had landed in jail the first time she started off to L'Abri. Now she had actually come and, strangely enough, had stayed. At times, her struggle to get out of the morass of unreality was pretty feeble, but as she found love and acceptance as a person and discovered that she wasn't kicked out (as she expected), there was a gradual change emerging. This account is not to go into the entire marvel of all that God did in that girl's life, step by step—and the wonder of answered prayer which was interspersed with constant attack and new pitfalls. This brilliant mind was brought back to the point of continuing her studies in medicine and music. I have included her story to add one more tiny but important and practical "What next?" to the other ideas for "getting started."

Ena (not her real name) was a twentieth-century intellectual who had gone the route of mind-blowing drugs. The first books which held her attention at L'Abri—and carried her out of herself into another world, another moment of history, and new attitudes she didn't know existed—were Grace Livingston Hill's novels, L. M. Montgomery's *Anne of Green Gables* and the whole series of "Anne" books and *Emily of New Moon, The Harvester* by Gene Stratton Porter, and Laura Ingalls Wilder's *Little House in the Woods*. Her amazement, as she read them and then came to talk to me, was the same quality of wonder which is shown by a city child or adult first introduced to mountain brooks, fields of flowers, pastures with cows (munching calmly as their bells *bong-bong* in different keys and intensities), or a sunrise over a lake or hill, accompanied by a noisy chorus of birds. Ena was enabled to concentrate and be carried out of her self, her painful moments of history, all she had experienced in the past which had left her without strength and without the interest in going on.

Books are such an important part of being taken out of whatever is your affliction or depression at a particular time. We have found to our own surprise that many sophisticated and jaded young people can step into a brand-new world with some of the books one might expect them to scorn. People with depression often find it difficult to get into serious reading when they are "down," but easy-to-read books, ones that are refreshing in their descriptions of simple pleasures and the rare beauty of nature, have been a tremendous help to many to whom we have offered them. Such a gentle, easy book can be a bridge to the more serious and inspirational reading which will follow—although sometimes the latter may have to be reread. Our reading aloud at Sunday High Teas, where a variety of people sit around comfortably with the children of the family, needs to include such books with which the children can have a rapport and "make new friends." It needs also to draw the most stiff, unbending people into a relaxed pleasure whereby the books' characters become friends to *them*. Books can bring new friends wherever you are—your lonely apartment or cabin, your "alone" vacation room, or a solitary spot on the beach.

Don't scorn the reading of one of these gentler, lighter, nineteenth-century books as a part of the help you need when you are "down" or lonely or just plain sorrowing or suffering. When a person is ill, and fever or pain make concentration difficult, a book can transport him perhaps to Prince Edward Island, that peaceful Canadian province, or to the woods where one can watch a butterfly emerge from its cocoon. Such a journey can be as helpful as a friend coming in with flowers or a cool drink. Traveling through the world of books can be as uncomplicated as reaching a hand toward a library shelf. There are, of course, those who, because of their weight of sorrow and affliction or apathy, lack even the incentive and interest to set off on this journey by themselves. They can be started and guided on their way by any of us who make the effort to suggest a book for their pleasure, or even read aloud to them. In this way, we can provide, through offering the printed words, the new friends, new interests, new world, and new perspectives which can sometimes be the spark to set a troubled one on his or her feet again—or can at least ease the pain in some measure.

Malaysian Mus and his wife, Verena, had a terrible automobile accident last winter, just before New Year's Day. They were actually driving from Germany, expecting to arrive at Franky and Genie's for dinner, when the car hit an unexpected piece of ice on the highway, sailed straight up in the air, flew over a fence, and landed upside down in a field. In retelling the story, Mus says that he felt as if he were landing a plane for just a few seconds before he hit and blacked out. It was Verena who struggled out, despite her broken back, and crossed the field to get help in time. Through her efforts, Mus, who had a punctured lung which was filling with fluid and was losing blood rapidly, was taken to the hospital "just in time." However, there was the agony of an operation on his broken shoulder (without anesthesia, because of the lung) and a fight for life that meant an active struggle on Mus's part. He felt too full of pain and weariness to make the repeated effort to blow up a balloon, yet roused enough to do so. Verena's back was broken, but her recovery was more rapid than Mus's.

Mus had become a Christian at L'Abri many years ago, and he has gone through many difficulties of a great variety. Verena is a Swiss-German schoolteacher, a Christian who also came to her understanding and belief at L'Abri. They are like a part of our family. In addition to this, Mus has completed his preparation for a photography career. Not only did he handle all the still photography when he accompanied the film crew for the *How Should We Then Live?* book and film series, but for much of the time he was the assistant to the film's photographer. An assistant film photographer has a heavy load to carry on his shoulder as filming progresses. There are often many steps, scaffoldings, or mountains to climb! A still photographer also has heavy equipment. Mus has a still painful and weak shoulder with "pins" in it, and his immediate need for work after the months of recovery was important, as you can well imagine. This is where "creativity" and "imagination" came in. Mus is a good cook of Malaysian dishes and has mastered quite a number of very special creations in this field. With much prayer for guidance, certain steps were slowly taken—and at one point a trial run was undertaken for a Malaysian take-out food stall. The opening was held at a three-day fair in Basel, and Mus's Malaysian stall was a great success. "I only haven't enough hands," he said to me on the phone! Now a little place has turned up to be rented and turned into a food store where people in Basel can come to carry out food for a Malaysian dinner at home. Mus and Verena have been "scattered." What will come of it? Not "nothing" but "something" very important.

There are many things in the circle of our own possibilities, even if the hemming-in is very restrictive, giving us little apparent scope for variety. There is so much we can do of value, things which will give us a new start and fresh incentive, and which can lead to so many results which are beyond our imagination. Only God can know the full range. The constant, never-changing marvel is that God cares about leading each one of us—not just the David Livingstones of history, or the Calvins and Luthers, but every one of us. We are all important to Him. We are important in the total victory pictured in my imaginary museum, important in His plan of history. There is always an answer to "What comes next?"

Mus's dismayed remark about his success—"I only haven't enough hands"—is echoed by all of us in many different circumstances, but perhaps never more often than by doctors who are trying to care for so many patients that some always have to be turned away. This is an affliction if one has a deep compassion combined with the limitations of finiteness, if one has the skill to help which cannot be spread around to each one needing that help. This is a heavy affliction indeed, whether for medical men or those dealing with people who are bruised and broken emotionally, psychologically, and spiritually. Being finite is painful at times. I have a letter from a doctor who spent some months at L'Abri. He tells of the discouraging situation in the clinic where he helped—its crowded condition with people waiting to be treated who simply couldn't be included. He asks:

How does one show compassion for the multitude, when this must mean showing compassion for the individual as well? How is one seen to be compassionate if people are away from home for two or three nights to be seen and treated, waiting in a compound, when people who are so sick are turned away? And yet to spend less time for the individual to care for the multitude, there is not time to hear the people's problems, to explain and show concern, and people become just numbers. At that point we deny in practice what we say we believe and try to show, i.e., that "I love and am concerned about you, dear little withered beetel-nut-chewing granny from the sticks, because you are of value as a person to the God you as yet do not know." Christ had compassion for the multitude and yet people were still people; and by His grace we can, we must, do the same . . . . But how?

I have no answer that would satisfy the hurt, except to say that we need to bow constantly before the Lord and tell him:

I know I am finite. You made me to be finite, and I cannot do everything; I cannot take care of everybody. Please bring to me the people of Your choice for me to help, and send others to someone else for help. Please send me to the places of Your choice and take others to other places to help. Please give me the wisdom in choice and the strength for what You want me to do. And then let me accept what You give me with thanksgiving and the grace to really receive Your gifts, as well as to be compassionate and ready to help others.

This is a constant need we have: to tell each other and remind ourselves that we are limited. We need to live within the circle of the strength we have, the possibilities we have, as well as within the circle of whatever other "wall" hems us in. Wheelchairs, hospital walls, prison bars, spoiled parts of our bodies, lack of energy, disintegrating cells, virus diseases, accidents, kidnapings, terrorist reign—all kinds of walls can change our lives and set up new limitations within which to live. But we all have the limitation of finiteness, and we need to recognize that this is the circle within which we must live. This can apply even when we are in Bombay with one million needy people sleeping on the sidewalks, or in Thailand or other crowded parts of the world—with too many people our eyes can see, yet with the constant problem of not having enough hands.

How can we go on and enjoy anything in this life with so many who have nothing? Is this your worry, the danger of bringing guilt feelings into any moment of joy? A balance is so very much needed here, and the Word of God gives us this balance over and over again. The places where we are told to "rejoice, and again I say rejoice" are meant to have times of fulfillment here, as well as in the future. The total equalizing of fulfillment is coming, but we are not to turn away from the joys which the Lord gives us here, any more than we are to spend our whole lives on self-centered pursuits. Putting the Lord first and the sensitivity for being ready to meet other people's needs are all bound up with learning something of the richness of capacity for enjoyment which the Lord has given us.

The fact that we can taste, smell, hear, feel, touch, think, love, have ideas, make things we can think of making, communicate in a variety of ways that God has made the world with a variety of things to satisfy these capacities. There is sufficient evidence that He means us to enjoy a variety of pleasures and fulfillments. The "endure hardship" admonitions do not cancel the rounded-out need to accept the beauty He has made possible and also to provide beauty in every possible way for other people.

Some may feel guilty about having suddenly come into a new kind of "affliction," the burden of having too much of this world's material goods. This can be a heavy burden as we seek clear guidance as to how to use our affluence and how much is to be enjoyed with other people and in what way. In 1 Timothy 6:17 is a clear word to the rich which makes it plain that it is not necessary to give it all away immediately. It is also clear that there is no suspicion about how the richness came about. The words are very straightforward: "Command those who are rich in this present world not to be arrogant nor to put their hope in wealth, which is so uncertain, but to put their hope in God, who richly provides us with everything for our enjoyment" (NIV). The next verses say that the rich should be generous and willing to share, and that in this way they may lay up treasures in heaven. The exciting thing to notice is that God has said that He richly provides us with everything for our enjoyment. We are meant to enjoy things. Paul has added to this in Philippians 4:11, 12 by telling us that he has learned to be abased (to have little), or to abound (to have much). He has learned to be content in all kinds of circumstances.

What did Paul mean—that he had learned "to be content"? Could it have any relationship to this couplet: "Two men looked through the prison bars. The one saw mud, the other stars"? It came to me sharply the other day that it isn't just a question of seeing mud—or stars—but the constant danger of wasting the immediate moment (and any appreciation that could be had) by cancelling out the ingredients of contentment through unnecessary "noisy busyness" going on in our heads. My morning had been filled with many things that had to be done—and a variety of interruptions. My head was swimming with both positive ideas about what to do next, and negative groanings about the choices that would have to be made because of human limitations. Big and little necessities and possibilities for work were buzzing around in my head like angry flies caught in a bottle.

My conflicting thoughts about what might be the most important thing to do next in the midst of this needy world—or what would give the preparation to do it—were suddenly penetrated by the soft lap-lap-lapping of small lake waves against nearby rocks, and the almost-silent swish of baby swans hurrying to move closer to their majestically gliding mother. We were having a picnic lunch, sitting on the stone steps by the lake. The immediate setting of that lunch hour was one of sunshine after days of thunderstorms. At that moment there was the warmth of the stone steps to *feel,* pleasant sandwiches and fruit to *taste,* nearby honeysuckle to *smell,* lake life to *see* (as ducks and swans glided against the background movement of boats and swooping gulls), and sounds to *hear* (blended bird songs, boat horns, a passing airplane motor overhead, and the soft swish of water at our feet). It came to me that I was cancelling out the possible contentment of the immediate moment, so filled with the things which God had given me richly to enjoy. I was ignoring these wonders by concentrating on the problems of the present and future.

As I turned my mind and concentration toward actively appreciating and being content with the things I could enjoy during that immediate hour, Paul's Letter to the Philippians came to me in a new light. We should often think of the words of Philippians 4:11 which point us to contentment with God's life plan for us, rather than compare ourselves with some other child of God who seems to have *more* earthly goods, interesting work, health, or strength. We apply it often, it seems to me, in the big sweeping directions of our lives, or at least to a situation covering an appreciable span of time. As I sat there, tasting brown bread with lettuce, tomato, and bacon, and turned my mind to being content—actively content with flavor—I looked at the rocks at my elbow. I examined carefully the wonder of tiny fern and the perfection of minute lavender and pink flowers growing out of the crevices. Then I listened with attention to the bird songs and the sounds of splashing water against the rocks. I took the time to be really aware of the smell of fragrant honeysuckle and I thought of the reality of being actively content as a *command.*

You and I are to really learn to be content. We need to practice this as we would practice the scales on the piano. It came to me that an active contentment is a moment-by-moment practice, not a big sweeping thing. The major ingredient of contentment is not necessarily some overwhelming emotional or spiritual experience, after which one is always content, no matter what. The raw materials which bring about contentment are a varied, diverse number of things, differing from moment to moment, hour to hour, day to day. It is the active *noticing* of what we have been given in any one moment to enjoy which brings the active result of contentment.

We need to *stop* to actively "practice contentment," time after time. Fran was so struck by what I wrote about this that he and I have often stopped recently just to point out not just sunsets and stars and birds, but also the curve of a roof, the changing red of a vine in autumn—the *immediate* seeable, feelable, hearable, smellable things of the moment that we might ignore in the midst of a concentrated conversation. Contentment involves stopping to notice the heavens which "declare the glory of God" and the richness of all that we can enjoy in spite of the immediate hindrances or afflictions or difficulties that threaten our activities—and in spite of the fears and worries that burden our thoughts.

Hebrews 13:5 tells us to be without covetousness and to be content with what we have: ". . . for he hath said, I will never leave thee nor forsake thee." So we are again reminded that He is also at our elbow, moment by moment. Without brushing aside the wonder of prayer and communication with Him, we are to consider the fact that God has given us the possibility of appreciation by tasting, hearing, seeing, smelling, and feeling, and He has created a whole universe full of fantastic things to enjoy through these senses. If Jesus is coming back tomorrow, tonight, or this morning, we are to practice contentment in the realm of what He has given us right now. There is a twofold activity called for in practicing contentment. First, we are to turn off the fears and worries, the busyness and plans, the concern over fatigue, and the buzzing thoughts which are blotting out all that might be enjoyed at the moment. Second, there is a need to look around and concentrate on what we can marvel about, appreciate, and notice—sensations which would otherwise be lost altogether in the history of our experiences. We need to be actively contented for a moment that will never be repeated.

But how does it all fit together when some are suffering so much right now—and cannot even sit up, let alone see anything? How can it be meaningful when I undergo a worse affliction tomorrow? From where is to come the confidence to give me freedom for the moment? Once again, it is the remembrance that we are among a great company of people who are together going to experience perfect contentment forever in our new bodies. In that eleventh chapter of Hebrews, where God is telling of those with much faith, although the faith of some was the faith of martyrs, we find this: "But now they desire a better country, that is, an heavenly: wherefore God is not ashamed to be called their God: for he hath prepared for them a city" (v. 16). How utterly satisfying! God sees the perfection of all He is preparing as He reserves a place for us. What He is preparing is so fantastically marvelous and without comparison that He can say firmly, gently, without hesitation, that He is not ashamed to be called the God of those who have suffered.